HELP YOUR KIDS WITH
Language
Arts

Grammar

Punctuation

Spelling

Communication skills

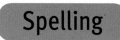

PUNCTUATION

HELP YOUR KIDS WITH
Language
Arts

A STEP-BY-STEP VISUAL GUIDE TO GRAMMAR, PUNCTUATION, AND WRITING

LONDON, NEW YORK, MELBOURNE,
MUNICH, AND DELHI

Senior Project Editor Victoria Pyke
Project Editors Carron Brown, Camilla Gersh,
Matilda Gollon, Ashwin Khurana
US Editor John Searcy

Managing Editor Linda Esposito
Managing Art Editor Diane Peyton Jones
Publishers Laura Buller, Andrew Macintyre

Preproduction Controller Adam Stoneham
Senior Producer Gemma Sharpe

Senior Designer Jim Green
Project Designers Paul Drislane,
Hoa Luc, Mary Sandberg

Publishing Director Jonathan Metcalf
Associate Publishing Director Liz Wheeler
Art Director Phil Ormerod

Jacket Editor Manisha Majithia
Jacket Designer Laura Brim

First American Edition, 2013

Published in the United States by
DK Publishing
375 Hudson Street
New York, New York 10014

13 14 15 16 17 10 9 8 7 6 5 4 3 2 1
001—187017—6/13

Published in Great Britain by Dorling Kindersley Limited.

A catalog record for this book is available from
the Library of Congress.

ISBN 978-1-4654-0849-5

DK books are available at special discounts when
purchased in bulk for sales promotions, premiums,
fund-raising, or educational use. For details, contact: DK
Publishing Special Markets, 375 Hudson Street, New York,
New York 10014 or SpecialSales@dk.com.

Printed and bound by South China Printing Co. Ltd, China

Discover more at
www.dk.com

LINDA B. GAMBRELL is Distinguished Professor of Education at Clemson University. She is past president of the International Reading Association (IRA), Literacy Research Association, and the Association of Literacy Educators and Researchers. In 2004, she was inducted into the Reading Hall of Fame. She is a former classroom teacher and reading specialist. Linda has written books on reading instruction and published articles in major literacy journals, including *Reading Research Quarterly*, the *Reading Teacher*, and the *Journal of Educational Research*.

SUSAN ROWAN is a former Head of English and Leading English and Literacy Adviser for a London borough. She has a Certificate in Education (Bishop Otter College of Education), a BA in English and History (Macquarie University, Australia), and an MBA—Education (University of Nottingham). With more than twenty-five years of teaching experience, Susan now works as an independent English and Literacy consultant supporting schools in London and southeast England.

DR. STEWART SAVARD is an eLibrarian in the Comox Valley of British Columbia. He has written a number of papers on the development of school libraries, the use of online and paper resources, and strategies for working with students to prevent plagiarism. Stewart also has extensive experience as a classroom and Learning Assistance teacher. He has worked on almost twenty books.

Foreword

The ability to speak and write well is essential for good communication in everyday life and in school. Our messages—whether spoken or written—need to be clear and easy for others to understand. While the importance of proper speaking and writing skills is often lost in our world of texting, e-mailing, and instant messaging, these skills are very important. Good speaking and writing skills help get a message across clearly and accurately, and give it credibility. Writing that is riddled with errors of grammar, punctuation, and spelling will reflect poorly on the writer, even if he or she is very knowledgeable about a topic. A good command of the English language and basic communication skills can lead to better grades in school and give a student a clear advantage over someone who is less skilled in language usage.

The rules of grammar, punctuation, and spelling, and the skills needed to communicate effectively can be bewildering. That's why *Help Your Kids with Language Arts* is an essential resource. This book presents examples that help to make the rules of grammar, punctuation, spelling, and communication clear and accessible. Wondering whether to say "you and me" or "you and I"? This book will provide an easy-to-understand explanation.

This book sets out to explain in simple terms the rules of clear and effective speaking and writing. It is divided into four chapters that focus on the key English language arts topics: grammar, punctuation, spelling, and communication skills. The information within each chapter is designed to make these English language arts interesting and enjoyable to learn. Engaging examples supported by step-by-step, simple-to-follow explanations will make even the most confusing concepts easy to grasp. This book will equip parents with the information they need to help students develop the skills required to communicate effectively in both speaking and writing.

As a former teacher, I am very aware of the importance of good communication skills. Success in school and in life is enhanced by these skills. *Help Your Kids with Language Arts* is an essential resource because throughout life we refine our use of the English language—always striving for clear and accurate communication with others.

LINDA B. GAMBRELL

abbreviations, accents, **acronyms**, adjectives, **adverbs**, alliteration, **apostrophes**, Arabic numerals, **articles**, asterisks, **auxiliary verbs**, brackets, **bullet points**, capital letters, **clauses**, collective nouns, **colloquialisms**, colons, **commands**, commas, **common nouns**, compound sentences, **compound words**, conditional sentences, **conjunctions**, consonants, **dangling participles**, dashes, **dialects**, direct speech, **ellipses**, exclamations, **exaggeration**, figures of speech, **first person**, fragments, **gender**, homographs, **homonyms**, homophones, **hyperbole**, hyphens, **idioms**, indefinite pronouns, **indicative mood**, indirect questions, **infinitives**, interjections, **irregular verbs**, italics, **jargon**, linking verbs, **main clauses**, misplaced modifiers, **moods**, morphemes, **negatives**, noun phrases, **nouns**, numbers, **objects**, ordinal numbers, **parentheses**, participles, **personal pronouns**, phonetics, **phrasal verbs**, phrases, **pitch**, plural nouns, **possessive determiners**, prefixes, **prepositional phrases**, present participles, **pronouns**, proper nouns, **puns**, punctuation, **question marks**, questions, **quotations**, relative pronouns, **reported speech**, rhetorical questions, **Roman numerals**, roots, **sentences**, silent letters, **singular**, slang, **subject**, subordinate clauses, **suffixes**, syllables, **tautology**, tenses, **third person**, tone, **verbs**, voices, **vowels**

CONTENTS

4 COMMUNICATION SKILLS

5 REFERENCE

Why learn the rules?

THERE ARE MANY BENEFITS TO LEARNING AND MASTERING
THE RULES OF THE ENGLISH LANGUAGE.

The rules of English are indispensable and will help English speakers of all ages in a variety of situations, from sending a simple e-mail and giving travel directions to writing the next best-selling novel.

English is the primary language of **news** and **information** in the world.

Ways with words

The rules or skills of English can be divided into four major areas. These areas show how words should be organized in a sentence, how they should be spelled and punctuated, and how they should be used in specific situations.

Grammar	**Punctuation**	**Spelling**	**Communication skills**
Grammar rules show how different types of words—such as nouns and adjectives— should be put together in a sentence to create fluent and clear writing.	Punctuation refers to the use of symbols—such as periods, question marks, commas, and apostrophes—to tell the reader how to read a piece of writing.	Spelling rules help English speakers understand and remember the ways in which letters and groups of letters combine to form words.	Communication skills help English speakers interact with others effectively: for instance, when writing a letter, passing on instructions, or delivering a speech.

Access all areas

A solid grasp of English will help students succeed in all subject areas, not just in English lessons. Whether writing a science report, instructing a basketball team as captain, or auditioning for a play, English language skills help students fulfill their potential.

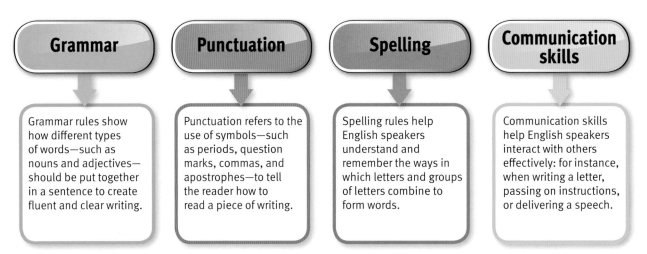

Report Card		
Student: *Paul Drislane*		
Course	**Percentage**	**Grade**
English	97%	A
Math	94%	A
Science	90%	A
History	92%	A
Geography	97%	A
Drama	93%	A
Phys. Ed.	95%	A

English language skills can help students succeed in all subject areas.

Dream job

When applying for jobs, good English language skills can make all the difference. Knowing the rules will help a candidate write a perfect application, and speak clearly and confidently in an interview. All employers, regardless of the industry, look for candidates who can express themselves correctly and assertively because these skills are valuable in most jobs every day.

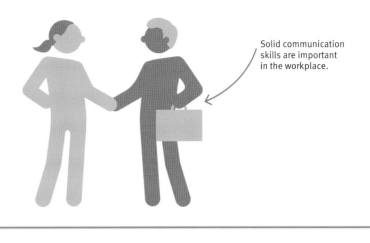

Solid communication skills are important in the workplace.

Time out

Language is used creatively in a variety of social situations, from a rowdy sports game to a sophisticated stage show. At a big game, fans sing rhyming and repetitive chants filled with playful jokes or insults directed at the opposing team. In the theater, actors perform dramatic, evocative lines to express feelings of love, passion, sadness, or anger. Whether watching a funny movie, reading a newspaper, or listening to a pop song, a person who has a good working knowledge of English will get the most out of these experiences.

Is love a tender thing? It is too rough, too rude, too boisterous, and it pricks like thorn.

William Shakespeare's character Romeo compares love to a sharp thorn, suggesting that love hurts. An audience with a good understanding of English will appreciate this subtle, visual use of language.

Travel the world

English is one of the most popular languages spoken across the globe, and it's the main language used in the business world. Fluency in the language makes it easier to travel to English-speaking places for work or vacations. What's more, a knowledge of grammatical terms makes learning other languages easier.

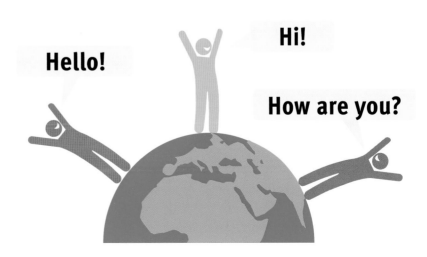

Hello!

Hi!

How are you?

Spoken and written language

BOTH WRITTEN AND SPOKEN ENGLISH HAVE UNIQUE FEATURES.

It's important to understand the differences between written and spoken language—as well as the different uses within each—to improve these two types of communication.

The **earliest known written language** was **Sumerian**, which developed in **Mesopotamia** (modern-day Iraq) in about 2600 BCE.

Written language

Pieces of writing such as novels, letters, and newspaper articles are carefully constructed because writers usually have time to think about the words and sentences they use. This means that written English is organized into complete sentences and uses formal vocabulary and correct grammar.

Dear Jane,

I am having a wonderful time in Thailand. It's a beautiful country with a fascinating culture. The sun shines every day, so we spend most of our time at the stunning beaches, sunbathing and snorkeling. I would love to come back another year.

Love from Nick x

08-01-2013

Jane Palmer

28 Maple Street

Springfield, IL 62704

USA

Written English should be in complete sentences.

Spoken language

In general, spoken language is more spontaneous than written language, so it contains features such as repetition, pauses, and sounds like *er* or *um*. Words are often left out or shortened to speed up a conversation, and the vocabulary and pronunciation varies according to the background of the speaker.

The words *I had an* have been left out.

The words *yeah* and *awesome* are informal words used in speech.

Hey, Jane! Yeah, awesome trip, thanks. Good weather, good beaches...um... we went snorkeling, too. Can't wait to go back another time.

People often repeat words when they are speaking.

It Is more common to shorten or abbreviate words in spoken language. Here, *cannot* has been shortened to *can't* and *I* has been omitted.

People pause and fill silences with sounds when they speak.

Writing spoken language

Some pieces of writing intentionally mimic the features of spoken English. For instance, the dialogue in novels or dramatic scripts is often written to sound spontaneous, and uses words and spellings that suggest the background of the characters, to make them more authentic.

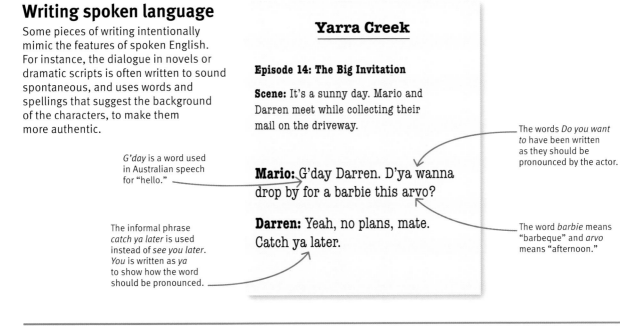

Yarra Creek

Episode 14: The Big Invitation

Scene: It's a sunny day. Mario and Darren meet while collecting their mail on the driveway.

Mario: G'day Darren. D'ya wanna drop by for a barbie this arvo?

Darren: Yeah, no plans, mate. Catch ya later.

G'day is a word used in Australian speech for "hello."

The informal phrase *catch ya later* is used instead of *see you later*. *You* is written as *ya* to show how the word should be pronounced.

The words *Do you want to* have been written as they should be pronounced by the actor.

The word *barbie* means "barbeque" and *arvo* means "afternoon."

Formal or informal

In general, spoken English can be less formal than written English; however, there are important exceptions. For instance, a text message to a friend may be informal, but a work presentation should be delivered in formal language. The level of formality depends on the situation and the audience.

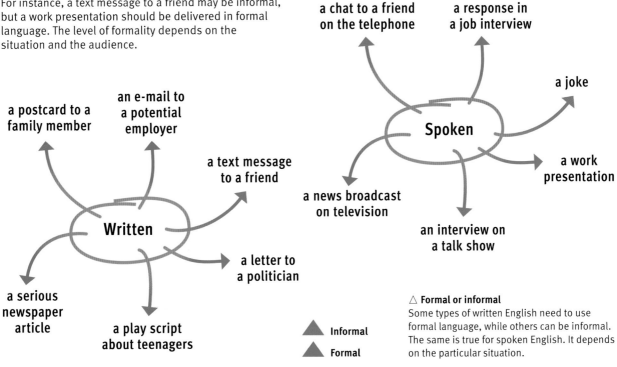

a postcard to a family member

an e-mail to a potential employer

a text message to a friend

Written

a serious newspaper article

a play script about teenagers

a letter to a politician

a chat to a friend on the telephone

a response in a job interview

a joke

Spoken

a news broadcast on television

a work presentation

an interview on a talk show

▲ Informal

▲ Formal

△ **Formal or informal**
Some types of written English need to use formal language, while others can be informal. The same is true for spoken English. It depends on the particular situation.

English around the world

ENGLISH IS USED THROUGHOUT THE WORLD, BUT NOT ALWAYS
IN THE SAME WAY.

Many countries throughout the world use the English language,
but the way it's used—especially spoken—can differ hugely
between regions, even within the same country.

Spread the word

The English language can be traced
back to a combination of Anglo-Saxon
dialects more than 1,500 years old.
It started to spread around the world
from the 1600s onward, when the
British began to explore and colonize,
taking their language with them. Today,
the English language continues to grow
in popularity, especially in Southeast
and eastern Asia, where English is seen
as the preferred language for business
and trade with Western countries.

1. In the Caribbean and Canada,
historical links with the UK compete
with geographical, cultural, and
economic ties with the United States,
so their language reflects both British
and American forms of English.

2. Most of South America speaks
Spanish or Portuguese because Spain
and Portugal once had empires there.
However, in a few countries in Central
and South America—such as Guyana,
which achieved independence from
Great Britain in 1966—the official
language is English.

Spot the differences

After the English language was taken to
North America, the spelling of certain
words started to change. Published in
1828, *An American Dictionary of the
English Language* established spellings
such as *center* and *color* (instead of the
British spellings *centre* and *colour*),
creating a broader acceptance of
American and British English as two
distinct entities. These variations in
spelling still exist today.

▷ **Spelling and punctuation**
British and American English use different
spellings and punctuation. For example,
verbs such as *criticise* are spelled with an
s in British English but a z in American
English. American English often uses
longer dashes and more commas in a
list than British English.

**The new musical *Hello Darling* has been cancelled after
just nine performances – the shortest run in the theatre's
history. The show has been severely criticised after many
jokes caused offence. One critic described the humour
as "crude, dated and unimaginative".**

British version   American version

**The new musical *Hello Darling* has been canceled after
just nine performances—the shortest run in the theater's
history. The show has been severely criticized after many
jokes caused offense. One critic described the humor as
"crude, dated, and unimaginative."**

3. North America was the first English-speaking colony, but it developed a distinct form of English with different spellings.

4. English became the dominant language in Great Britain during the Middle Ages (5th to 15th centuries).

5. A 2010 survey found that around two-thirds of Europeans can speak some English.

6. Today, English is an international language of business, and is taught in schools in many Asian countries, including Japan and China.

7. In India and parts of Africa, English was imposed as the administrative language through centuries of colonial rule, but—in most cases—it was spoken only as a second language by the local populations.

8. The expansion of the British Empire during the 1700s in Australia and New Zealand saw European populations quickly outnumber indigenous populations, and English became the dominant language.

What's that?

English speakers around the world use different words and pronunciation, according to their background, age, and sense of identity. An accent is the way in which the words are pronounced, while a dialect refers to the use of certain vocabulary and grammatical constructions. In the UK alone, there are many distinctive dialects, such as Geordie (Newcastle), Brummie (Birmingham), and Doric (northeast Scotland). Similarly, around the world, English is spoken and written in many different ways, so that some common objects are called by different names in Britain, America, Canada, and Australia.

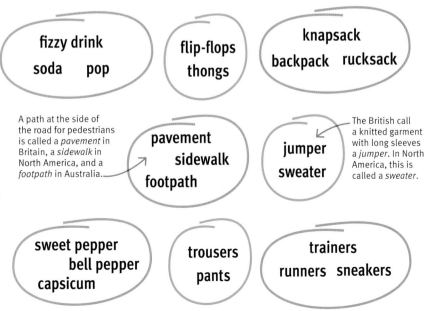

fizzy drink
soda   pop

flip-flops
thongs

knapsack
backpack   rucksack

A path at the side of the road for pedestrians is called a *pavement* in Britain, a *sidewalk* in North America, and a *footpath* in Australia.

pavement
sidewalk
footpath

jumper
sweater

The British call a knitted garment with long sleeves a *jumper*. In North America, this is called a *sweater*.

sweet pepper
bell pepper
capsicum

trousers
pants

trainers
runners   sneakers

Grammar

The purpose of grammar

THE STRUCTURE OF A LANGUAGE IS KNOWN AS ITS GRAMMAR.

Words are the building blocks of language. Grammar is a set of rules that determines how these building blocks can be put together in different combinations to create well-formed phrases, clauses, and sentences, which enable and enrich conversation.

The **first** published **book** about English **grammar**, *Pamphlet for Grammar*, was written by **William Bullokar** in 1586.

Evolving languages

All languages change over time. As a language evolves, its grammar adapts to incorporate new words and ways of organizing them. Different languages have different sets of rules, so sentences are formed in different ways, even if they mean the same thing. Thus, it's often difficult to translate sentences exactly from another language into English.

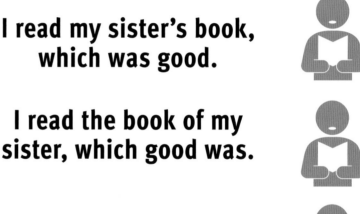

▷ **English word order**
This is a grammatically correct sentence in English. The verb *read* follows the subject, *I*, and the adjective *good* follows the linking verb *was*.

I read my sister's book, which was good.

▷ **Old English word order**
This sentence has been translated into Old English, and then translated directly back into modern English. The first part of the sentence still makes grammatical sense in modern English, but in the second part of the sentence, the verb is now at the end.

I read the book of my sister, which good was.

▷ **German word order**
This sentence has been translated into German, and then translated directly back into English. The word order is the same as that of the Old English sentence, because Old English is a Germanic language.

I read the book of my sister, which good was.

Learning grammar

When a child learns a language, he or she absorbs information about how that language is structured. This knowledge is refined as the child learns to read and write. Although much of this learning is subconscious, some grammatical rules simply have to be learned.

I'm coming with you, aren't I?

Wrong! What you meant to say was, "I'm coming with you, am I not?"

Parts of speech

Words are grouped together according to the functions they perform in a sentence. There are ten parts of speech in English. Nouns (or pronouns) and verbs are essential to the structure of a sentence, but it's the other parts of speech, including adjectives, adverbs, conjunctions, and prepositions, that make a sentence interesting.

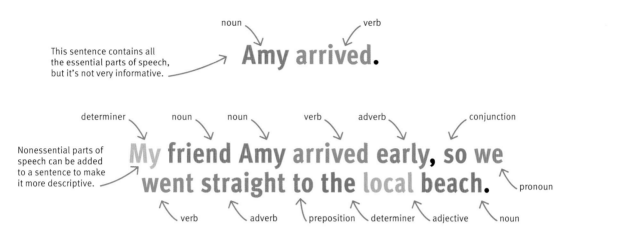

noun verb

Amy arrived.

This sentence contains all the essential parts of speech, but it's not very informative.

determiner noun noun verb adverb conjunction

My friend Amy arrived early, so we went straight to the local beach.

Nonessential parts of speech can be added to a sentence to make it more descriptive.

pronoun

verb adverb preposition determiner adjective noun

Structuring sentences

Without the rules of grammar, words would be placed in a random order, and no one would be able to understand what anyone else was saying. An ability to communicate effectively comes from following these rules. A sentence must also be correctly punctuated for it to make sense. Grammar explains which order to put words in, while punctuation marks such as periods and commas indicate how the sentence should be read.

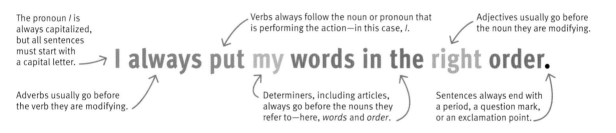

The pronoun *I* is always capitalized, but all sentences must start with a capital letter.

Verbs always follow the noun or pronoun that is performing the action—in this case, *I*.

Adjectives usually go before the noun they are modifying.

I always put my words in the right order.

Adverbs usually go before the verb they are modifying.

Determiners, including articles, always go before the nouns they refer to—here, *words* and *order*.

Sentences always end with a period, a question mark, or an exclamation point.

Everyday grammar

A good grasp of grammar enables people to speak and write clearly and concisely, and to understand all kinds of reading material. These skills are invaluable when it comes to job applications, as employers will always show a preference for candidates who have submitted grammatically correct applications. Similarly, candidates who can express themselves clearly will be more successful in interviews. Good grammar improves creative writing, too, and even the best-known writers—past and present—have followed a few simple rules.

"My suffering left me sad and gloomy."

The opening line from Yann Martel's *Life of Pi* follows the rules because it starts with a noun, followed by a verb, and includes adjectives that make the sentence memorable.

Parts of speech

WORDS ARE THE BUILDING BLOCKS OF LANGUAGE, BUT
THEY MUST BE ARRANGED IN A RECOGNIZABLE ORDER.

Parts of speech refer to the way in which particular words are used.
Some words can be classified as more than one word type, and they
change type according to the sentence they belong to.

Word types

The main parts of speech are nouns, verbs, adjectives,
pronouns, adverbs, prepositions, and conjunctions.
Interjections are also important, since they are used so
often in everyday speech. Nouns (or pronouns) and verbs
are the only essential components of a sentence.

▽ **Different roles**
Each type of word performs a different
function. Some depend on others for
sense; some exist solely to modify others.

Noun

A word used to name a person, animal, place, or thing.

EXAMPLES
William, mouse, supermarket,
ladder, desk, station, ball, boy

ball

Adjective

A word used to describe a noun or pronoun.

EXAMPLES
shiny, dangerous, new, bouncy,
noisy, colorful, wooden

colorful ball

Verb

**A word that expresses an
action or a state of being.**

EXAMPLES
run, be, kick, go, think, do, play,
stumble, touch

kick the ball

Adverb

**A word that describes and adds
information to a verb or a verb phrase.**

EXAMPLES
quickly, soon, very, rather, too,
almost, only,
quietly   **quickly** kick the ball

Pronoun

A word that takes the place of a noun.

EXAMPLES
he, she, them, him, we, you, us,
mine, yours, theirs

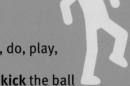

kick the ball to **him**

Preposition

**A word that indicates the relationship between two
people or things, usually in terms of where they are.**

EXAMPLES
with, under, on, behind, into,
over, across

kick the ball **behind** you

Putting words together

For speech to make sense, words must be linked to other words in the right way to form sentences. Imagine a sports team—each player representing one word. A lone player cannot achieve very much, but, teamed with other players and following strict rules, he can achieve a lot. These rules of play are like grammar—they determine both direction and purpose.

When we are joined together, we make a great team.

Conjunction

A word used to link words and clauses.

EXAMPLES
and, but, so, yet, or, neither, nor, because

bat **and** ball

Interjection

A word that usually occurs alone and expresses emotion.

EXAMPLES
oh, hello, ah, ouch, phew, yuck, hooray, help, er, um, oops

ouch!

Article

A word used with a noun to refer to a specific person or thing, or someone or something in general.

EXAMPLES
a, an, the

the ball

Determiner

A word used in front of a noun to denote something specific or something of a particular type. Articles are also determiners.

EXAMPLES
those, many, my, his, few, several, much, many

my ball

Summary sentence

article · noun · adverb · verb · determiner · adjective · noun · preposition · interjection

The boy quickly kicked his bouncy ball past a defender, but in his haste he stumbled. oops!

article · noun · conjunction · preposition · determiner · noun · pronoun · verb

Nouns

NOUNS ARE USED TO NAME PEOPLE, ANIMALS, PLACES, OR THINGS.

Nouns are often known as "naming" words. Every sentence must include at least one noun or pronoun. Most nouns can be either singular or plural, and can be divided into two main groups: common and proper nouns.

Common nouns (concrete)

Common nouns are used all the time to describe everyday objects, animals, places, people, and ideas. They do not have a capital letter unless they appear at the start of a sentence. Every sentence must contain a noun, and this noun is usually a common noun. Common nouns that describe things that can be seen and touched are known as concrete nouns.

book

goat

bread

birds

girl

piece

Common nouns (abstract)

A type of common noun, abstract nouns are more difficult to define. Unlike concrete nouns, which refer to physical things, abstract nouns refer to ideas, feelings, occasions, or time—things that can't be seen or touched.

love

happiness

bravery

trust

afternoon

health

The goat's afternoon was ruined down and snatched the piece of

• With the exception of some abstract nouns, if the word **the** can be put **in front of a word** and the resulting combination **makes sense**, then that word is a **noun**.

• Nouns can often be recognized by their **endings**. Typical endings include **-er, -or, -ist, -tion, -ment**, and **-ism**: *writer, visitor, dentist, competition, argument, criticism*.

GLOSSARY

Abstract noun The name given to something that cannot be touched, such as a concept or a sensation.

Collective noun The name given to a collection of individuals—people or things.

Concrete noun The name given to an ordinary thing, such as an animal or object.

Noun phrase Several words that, when grouped together, perform the same function as a noun.

Proper noun The name given to a particular person, place, or thing, which always starts with a capital letter.

Prepositional phrase A preposition such as *in* or *on* followed by a noun or pronoun that together act as an adjective (describing a noun) or an adverb (describing a verb) in a sentence.

The word *time* is the most **commonly used noun** in the **English** language.

Common nouns (collective)

Another type of common noun, collective nouns refer to a group of things or people. They are usually singular words that represent a number of things. Different collective nouns refer to different concrete nouns, and the collective nouns used to describe groups of animals are especially varied.

a crowd **of people**

a swarm **of bees**

a flight **of stairs**

a bunch **of grapes**

a flock **of birds**

Identifying noun phrases

A noun phrase is made up of a noun and any words that are modifying that noun. These modifying words are usually articles such as *the* or *a*, determiners such as *my*, *this*, or *most*, adjectives such as *happy* or *hungry*, or prepositional phrases such as *in the field*. Noun phrases perform exactly the same role as common nouns in a sentence.

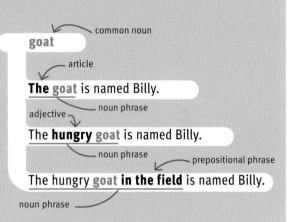

The goat is named Billy.

The **hungry goat** is named Billy.

The hungry **goat** **in the field** is named Billy.

when a **flock** of birds swooped bread from Emily's hand.

Proper nouns

A proper noun is the name given to a particular person or place, or to a religious or historical concept or period. Proper nouns always start with a capital letter. This helps to distinguish them from common nouns. The most common proper nouns are the names of people or places, but titles, institutions, days of the week, and events and festivals are also proper nouns.

Type of proper noun	Examples
Names of people	John, Sally Smith, Queen Elizabeth II
Titles	Mr., Miss, Sir, Dr., Professor, Reverend
Places, buildings, and institutions	Africa, Asia, Canada, New York, Red Cross, Sydney Opera House, United Nations
Religious names	Bible, Koran, Christianity, Hinduism, Islam
Historical names	World War I, Ming Dynasty, Roman Empire
Events and festivals	Olympic Games, New Year's Eve
Days of the week, months	Saturday, December

Plurals

A NOUN'S PLURAL FORM IS USED WHEN THERE IS MORE THAN ONE OF SOMETHING.

The word *plural* refers to the form a noun takes when more than one thing is being mentioned. Most nouns have distinctive singular and plural forms.

Regular plural nouns

The most common way to make a noun plural is to add *s* or *es* to the end of the singular form. Most nouns take the ending -s, except for those ending in -s, -z, -x, -sh, -ch, or -ss, which take the suffix (ending) -es.

**One dragon
Two dragons**

**One wish
Two wishes**

Follow the rules

Some nouns are given different plural endings to make them easier to pronounce. In most cases, it's possible to follow a few simple rules. If a word ends in -y, for example, and it has a vowel before the final -y, the plural is formed in the usual way: An *s* is added. If the final -y is preceded by a consonant, however, the *y* must be changed to *i*, followed by the ending -es.

If a word, such as **cactus**, has been borrowed from **Latin**, the Latin **plural** form (here, *cacti*) is often used.

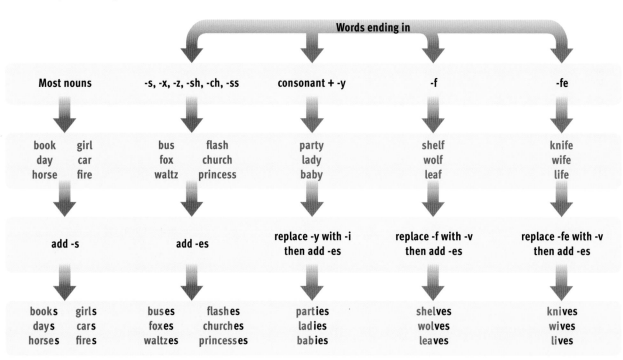

Words ending in				
Most nouns	**-s, -x, -z, -sh, -ch, -ss**	**consonant + -y**	**-f**	**-fe**
book girl day car horse fire	bus flash fox church waltz princess	party lady baby	shelf wolf leaf	knife wife life
add -s	add -es	replace -y with -i then add -es	replace -f with -v then add -es	replace -fe with -v then add -es
books girls days cars horses fires	buses flashes foxes churches waltzes princesses	parties ladies babies	shelves wolves leaves	knives wives lives

Irregular plural nouns

Some words just don't follow the rules. Although many nouns that end in -o are made plural by adding an *s*, others take the ending -es. Some nouns change their spelling completely when they become plural, while others do not change at all. Words that originate from Latin and Greek often have irregular plural endings. These exceptions have to be learned.

• If the plural form of a **noun** is used in a sentence, the **verb** that follows it must also be **plural**.

• Do not confuse **plural** words with the **possessive**. For example, "There are **two Jasons** [plural] in my class, and this is **Jason's car** [possessive]."

Staying singular

Collective nouns such as *flock* or *crowd* have plural forms, but usually appear in the singular. Some nouns do not have a plural form at all, even though they usually represent multiple things. Furniture, for example, is a singular word, but it may encompass a table, a chair, a sofa, and a cabinet.

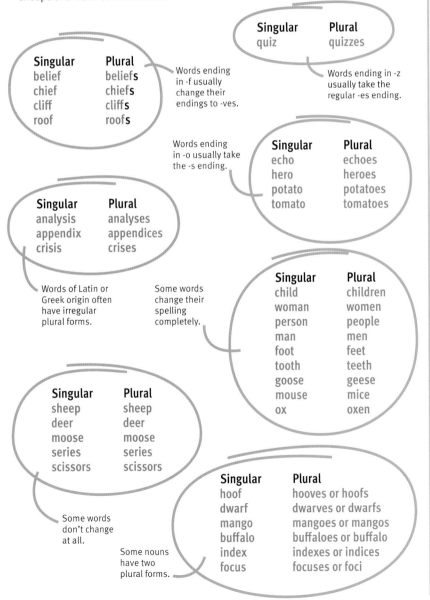

Singular	Plural
quiz	quizzes

Words ending in -z usually take the regular -es ending.

Singular	Plural
belief	belief**s**
chief	chief**s**
cliff	cliff**s**
roof	roof**s**

Words ending in -f usually change their endings to -ves.

Singular	Plural
echo	echoes
hero	heroes
potato	potatoes
tomato	tomatoes

Words ending in -o usually take the -s ending.

Singular	Plural
analysis	analyses
appendix	appendices
crisis	crises

Words of Latin or Greek origin often have irregular plural forms.

Some words change their spelling completely.

Singular	Plural
child	children
woman	women
person	people
man	men
foot	feet
tooth	teeth
goose	geese
mouse	mice
ox	oxen

Singular	Plural
sheep	sheep
deer	deer
moose	moose
series	series
scissors	scissors

Some words don't change at all.

Singular	Plural
hoof	hooves or hoofs
dwarf	dwarves or dwarfs
mango	mangoes or mangos
buffalo	buffaloes or buffalo
index	indexes or indices
focus	focuses or foci

Some nouns have two plural forms.

education
furniture
information
homework
livestock
evidence
weather
knowledge

GLOSSARY

Collective noun The name given to a collection of individuals—people or things.

Plural noun When more than one person or thing is being described.

Suffix An ending made up of one or more letters that is added to a word to change its form—for example, from singular to plural.

Adjectives

ADJECTIVES ARE WORDS OR PHRASES THAT MODIFY OR DESCRIBE NOUNS OR PRONOUNS.

A noun by itself does not offer much information. If a man wanted to buy a shirt in a store, he would need to narrow down what he was looking for by using descriptive words like *thin* or *silky*. These words are known as adjectives.

• If you are unsure whether a word is an adjective or something else, see if it answers questions such as: **What kind? Which one? How much? How many?**

• Adjectives should be used **sparingly**, for effect. Too many adjectives can make a sentence difficult to follow.

Describing words

Most adjectives describe attributes (characteristics) of nouns or pronouns and answer the question *What is it like?* They are used to compare one person or thing to other people or things. Adjectives are usually placed directly in front of the noun—a position known as the attributive position.

the weary painter

adjective in attributive position ⟶

⟵ noun

The weary painter took off his
and ate a day-old Chinese

GLOSSARY

Attributive position When an adjective is placed directly in front of the noun or pronoun that it is modifying.

Clause A group of words that contains a subject and a verb.

Linking verb A verb that joins the subject of a sentence to a word or phrase—often an adjective—that describes the subject.

Predicate position When an adjective follows a linking verb at the end of a sentence.

Proper noun The name given to a particular person, place, or era, which always starts with a capital letter.

Compound adjectives

Compound adjectives are made up of more than one word. When two or more words are used together as an adjective in front of a noun, they are usually hyphenated. This shows that the two words are acting together as a single adjective.

This two-word adjective means "not fresh today."

day-old meal

"Proper" adjectives

Some nouns can be modified and used before other nouns as adjectives. These include proper nouns, such as the names of places. Adjectives formed from proper nouns should always start with a capital letter. They often end in -an, -ian, and -ish.

Chinese

Australian   **English**

Roman

Identifying adjectives

Adverbs such as *very* or *extremely* can be used to exaggerate the state of a subject. These adverbs are sometimes confused with adjectives. A simple way of checking whether a word is an adjective or an adverb is to break down a sentence, pairing each descriptive word in turn with the noun to see if the resulting phrase makes sense.

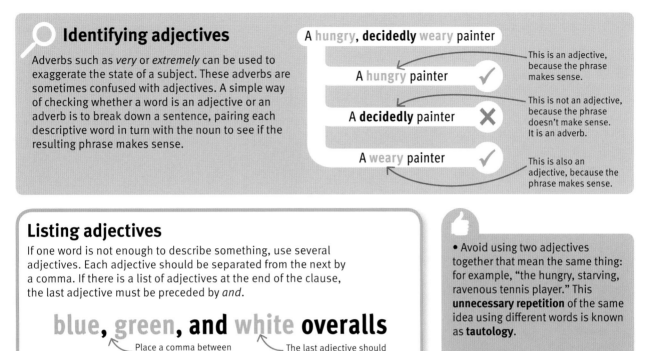

A hungry, **decidedly** weary painter

A hungry painter ✓

This is an adjective, because the phrase makes sense.

A **decidedly** painter ✗

This is not an adjective, because the phrase doesn't make sense. It is an adverb.

A weary painter ✓

This is also an adjective, because the phrase makes sense.

Listing adjectives

If one word is not enough to describe something, use several adjectives. Each adjective should be separated from the next by a comma. If there is a list of adjectives at the end of the clause, the last adjective must be preceded by *and*.

blue, green, and white overalls

Place a comma between adjectives in a list.

The last adjective should follow the word *and*.

• Avoid using two adjectives together that mean the same thing: for example, "the hungry, starving, ravenous tennis player." This **unnecessary repetition** of the same idea using different words is known as **tautology**.

blue, green, and white overalls meal because he felt ravenous.

Predicate adjectives

Many adjectives can also be placed at the end of a sentence, following a verb. This is known as the predicate position. A verb used in this way is called a linking verb, because it connects a subject with a descriptive word. Common linking verbs include *seem, look, feel, become, stay,* and *turn.*

he felt ravenous

linking verb

adjective in predicate position

Adjective endings

Many adjectives can be recognized by their endings. Knowing these endings can help to distinguish adjectives from adverbs and verbs.

Ending	Examples
-able/-ible	comfort**able**, remark**able**, horr**ible**, ed**ible**
-al	fiction**al**, education**al**, logic**al**, nation**al**
-ful	bash**ful**, peace**ful**, help**ful**, beauti**ful**
-ic	energet**ic**, man**ic**, dramat**ic**, fantast**ic**
-ive	attract**ive**, sensit**ive**, impuls**ive**, persuas**ive**
-less	home**less**, care**less**, end**less**, use**less**
-ous	raven**ous**, mischiev**ous**, fam**ous**, nerv**ous**

Comparatives and superlatives

ADJECTIVES CAN BE USED TO COMPARE NOUNS OR PRONOUNS.

SEE ALSO

❬ **22–23** Nouns

❬ **26–27** Adjectives

Prepositions **60–61** ❭

Syllables **134–135** ❭

Comparatives and superlatives are special types of adjectives that are used to compare two or more things. Most comparatives are formed using the ending -er, and most superlatives are formed using the ending -est.

• **Never use double** comparatives or double superlatives—"more prettier" and "most prettiest" are wrong.

• Not every adjective has a comparative or superlative form. **Unique**, **square**, **round**, **excellent**, and **perfect** are all words that can't be graded.

Comparatives

A comparative adjective is used to compare two people or things. It is formed by adding the ending -er to all one-syllable adjectives and some two-syllable adjectives. When two nouns are being compared in a sentence, they are usually linked using the preposition than.

The Ferris wheel is bigger than the carousel.

This word is used to link the two nouns being compared: the Ferris wheel and the carousel.

The Ferris wheel is bigger than the the biggest ride of all. The ghost

Superlatives

Superlative adjectives can be used to compare two or more people or things. They are formed by adding the ending -est to one-syllable adjectives, and using the word the in front of them: "the biggest ride."

big
bigger
biggest

small
smaller
smallest

thin
thinner
thinnest

REAL WORLD

Biggest and best

Multiple superlatives are often used in advertisements to sell things, whether they're books, vacations, or circus attractions. Words like greatest, best, and cheapest enable a seller to exaggerate the quality or value of the product being sold, making it more appealing to potential customers. Superlatives should be used in moderation in formal text, however.

Identifying irregular adjective spellings

Some adjectives do not follow the rules when it comes to forming their comparatives or superlatives. If an adjective already ends in -e (*rude*), only -r needs to be added to make it comparative (*ruder*), and -st, to make it superlative (*rudest*). Words ending in -y or a vowel and a single consonant have to change their endings.

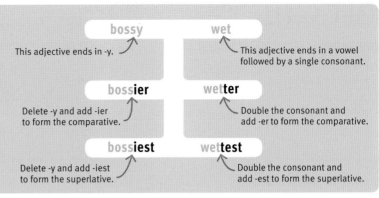

bossy
This adjective ends in -y.

wet
This adjective ends in a vowel followed by a single consonant.

bossier
Delete -y and add -ier to form the comparative.

wetter
Double the consonant and add -er to form the comparative.

bossiest
Delete -y and add -iest to form the superlative.

wettest
Double the consonant and add -est to form the superlative.

Exceptions

Some two-syllable adjectives, such as *lovely*, can take either form of the comparative or superlative (see "Awkward adjectives"). Other adjectives change completely when they are used to compare things. These comparative and superlative forms have to be learned.

Adjective	Comparative	Superlative
good	better	best
bad	worse	worst
much	more	most
many	more	most
little	less	least
quiet	quieter or more quiet	quietest or most quiet
simple	simpler or more simple	simplest or most simple
clever	cleverer or more clever	cleverest or most clever
lovely	lovelier or more lovely	loveliest or most lovely

carousel, but the roller coaster is train is the most frightening.

Awkward adjectives

If adding the ending -er or -est results in an odd-sounding adjective, the comparative and superlative are formed using the words *more* or *most* before the adjective. This applies to most two-syllable adjectives and all adjectives with three or more syllables.

The ghost train is the most frightening.

The superlative *frighteningest* is hard to say, so—because *frightening* has three syllables— the superlative is formed using *most*.

Articles

THERE ARE TWO TYPES OF ARTICLES: DEFINITE AND INDEFINITE.

Articles are a type of adjective and a type of determiner. They are always used with a noun. Similarly, many singular forms of nouns must be used with an article.

The definite article

The definite article is *the*. It always precedes a noun, and refers to a specific person or thing. This person or thing may have been mentioned before, or there may be only one to talk about. Alternatively, it may be clear from the context which noun is being referred to.

the rhinoceros

There is only one rhinoceros on the bus, so the definite article is used.

In **many languages**, including French, German, and Spanish, **the article** tells the reader whether a word is **feminine**, **masculine**, or **neutral**. In **English**, very **few words** have a **gender**.

The rhinoceros and his best a bus to visit the struggling

The indefinite article

The indefinite article, *a* or *an*, is used to refer to any one person or thing. Words that begin with consonants (*bus*) use *a*, while words that start with a vowel (*a, e, i, o,* or *u*) or a silent *h*, such as *hour*, use *an* to make pronunciation easier. The indefinite article also indicates that someone or something belongs to a specific group. For example, "The animal is a giraffe" explains that this particular animal is one of many members of a group of animals known as giraffes.

The indefinite article indicates that this could be one of a number of buses, whereas the definite article *the* would refer to one particular bus.

a bus

The form *an* is used before a vowel to make it easier to say.

an elephant

Articles and adjectives

If a noun is preceded by one or more descriptive adjectives, the article goes before the adjective. The resulting phrase (article + adjective + noun) is known as a noun phrase. If the indefinite article is used in front of an adjective that begins with a vowel, the form *an* is used.

The article precedes the adjective *struggling*, which goes before the noun *ostrich*.

the struggling ostrich

The adjective *anxious* begins with a vowel, so *an* is used.

an anxious rhinoceros

Identifying when to use an article

If a singular noun can be counted, this noun will require an article—definite or indefinite. For example, "I saw elephant today" doesn't make sense. Some nouns, such as *happiness, information,* and *bread*, do not have a plural form, and therefore cannot be counted. These nouns can be used without an article (zero article) or with the definite article. They never take the indefinite article.

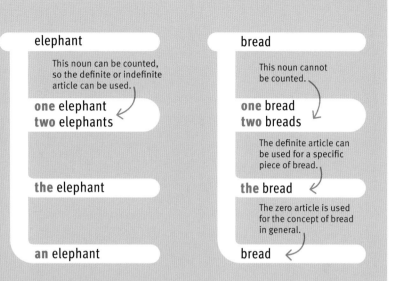

elephant

This noun can be counted, so the definite or indefinite article can be used.

one elephant
two elephants

the elephant

an elephant

bread

This noun cannot be counted.

one bread
two breads

The definite article can be used for a specific piece of bread.

the bread

The zero article is used for the concept of bread in general.

bread

friend, **an** elephant, took
ostrich at flying school.

The zero article

Some words, such as *school, life,* and *home*, take the definite article when a particular one is being referred to, and the indefinite article when one of several is being described. When these words are used to describe a general concept, such as being at school, the article is removed. This absence of an article is known as the zero article.

at flying school

This describes school as a concept—a place where a person goes to learn something—so the zero article (no article) is used.

at the flying school next to the zoo

This describes a particular school—the one next to the zoo—so *the* is required.

• Many **geographical areas** and features, including **rivers, deserts,** and **oceans,** use the **definite article**: for example, the North Pole, the Pacific Ocean, or the Rocky Mountains.

• If an **article** is at the beginning of the **title** of a work, such as *The Secret Garden*, it should start with a **capital letter.**

• **Unique things,** such as **the sun,** always take *the.*

• Watch out for words that begin with a **vowel** that **sounds like a consonant,** such as *university.* These take the indefinite article *a,* rather than *an.*

Determiners

DETERMINERS ARE ALWAYS PLACED BEFORE A NOUN,
AND HELP TO DEFINE IT.

Articles are determiners, and other determiners work in much the
same way: They are used in front of nouns to indicate whether
something specific or something of a particular type is being referred to.

Determiners and adjectives

Determiners are often considered to
be a subclass of adjectives and, like
adjectives, they belong to nouns and
modify nouns. Unlike adjectives,
there is rarely more than one
determiner for each noun, nor can
determiners be compared or
graded. They precede the noun
and include words like *several*,
those, *many*, *my,* and *your*, as
well as articles (*the*, *a,* and *an*)
and numbers.

The determiner
always precedes
any adjectives,
which, in turn,
precede the noun.

several furious members

adjective   plural noun

• **Many sentences do not make
sense without determiners**.
Adjectives, by contrast, are
optional; they color the words
rather than glue them together.

• Most **noun phrases** only use
one determiner, but there are
exceptions: for example, "all the
bats" and "both my cats."

definite article

**Several furious members of the
broomsticks. "That witch has nine**

GLOSSARY

Cardinal number A counting
number such as *one*, *two*,
or *twenty-one*.

Linking verb A verb such
as *be* that joins the subject
of a sentence to a word
or phrase—often an
adjective—that describes the
subject.

Ordinal number The form
of a number that includes
first, *second*, and *twenty-first*.

Demonstrative determiners

Demonstrative determiners give an idea of distance between
the speaker and the person or thing that he or she is referring
to. *This* (singular) and *these* (plural) are used to describe things
that are nearby. *That* (singular) and *those* (plural) are used for
things that are farther away.

This indicates a witch who is
not present at the meeting. → **that witch**

The witches are discussing
a noise they can hear—that
of shrieking bats—so *this*
is used. → **this noise**

Identifying determiners

Sometimes determiners look very similar to adjectives. One way of figuring out whether a word that precedes a noun is a determiner or an adjective is to try placing the word at the end of a sentence, following a linking verb such as *be*. If the sentence makes sense, that word is an adjective; if it does not make sense, it is a determiner.

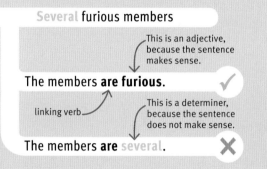

Several furious members

This is an adjective, because the sentence makes sense.

The members **are furious**. ✓

linking verb

This is a determiner, because the sentence does not make sense.

The members **are** several. ✗

• Some words, such as *each* or *all*, are used both as **determiners and pronouns**. The rule to remember is that a **determiner** is **always followed by a noun**, whereas a pronoun replaces a noun.

Possessive determiners

The possessive determiners *my, your, his, her, its, our,* and *their* are used before nouns to show ownership. They should not be confused with possessive pronouns—for example, *mine, yours, ours,* and *theirs*—which replace, rather than precede, the noun.

their **broomsticks**

The broomsticks (plural noun) belong to the witches.

indefinite article

coven held a meeting on their shrieking bats!" they grumbled.

Numbers and quantifiers

Cardinal and ordinal numbers and other words that express quantity are considered to be determiners when they appear before a noun. These include *much, most, little, least, any, enough, half,* and *whole.* Beware of determiners such as *much* (singular) and *many* (plural) that can only modify singular or plural nouns.

nine **shrieking bats**

This cardinal number is being used before a noun phrase (*shrieking bats*) as a determiner.

much **noise**

This determiner can only be used with a singular noun.

many **bats**

This determiner can only be used with a plural noun.

Interrogative determiners

Interrogative determiners include *which* and *what* and are used before a noun to ask a question.

Which **witch?**

What **noise?**

Pronouns

PRONOUN MEANS "FOR A NOUN," AND A PRONOUN IS A WORD THAT TAKES THE PLACE OF A NOUN.

Without pronouns, spoken and written English would be very repetitive. Once a noun has been referred to by its actual name once, another word—a pronoun—can be used to stand for this name.

Using pronouns

If the full name of a noun were used each time it had to be referred to, sentences would be long and confusing. Pronouns are useful because they make sentences shorter and therefore clearer. The noun is still required when someone or something is referred to for the first time.

noun   noun

Rita loves playing the guitar. She finds it relaxing.

This personal pronoun represents *Rita*, the subject.

This personal pronoun represents *playing the guitar*, the object.

Types of pronouns

There are seven types of pronouns, which are used for different purposes. Do not confuse these with determiners or adjectives, which modify rather than replace nouns.

• *I* is the only pronoun that is spelled with a **capital** letter.

Personal pronouns

These **represent people, places, or things**. They vary according to whether the noun being replaced is the subject of a sentence (performing the action) or the object (receiving the action).

I, you, he, she, it, we, you, they (subject)
me, you, him, her, it, us, you, them (object)

This pronoun represents the singular subject.

She gave them a guitar lesson.

This pronoun represents the plural object.

Possessive pronouns

These **show ownership and replace possessive** noun phrases. Don't get these confused with possessive determiners such as *my* and *your*, which precede but do not replace the noun.

mine, yours, his, hers, its, ours, yours, theirs

The guitar is hers.

This pronoun replaces the possessive noun phrase *Rita's guitar*.

Relative pronouns

These **link one part of a sentence to another** by introducing a relative clause that describes an earlier noun or pronoun.

who, whom, whose, which, that, what

Rita is the person who plays the guitar.

This pronoun is describing *Rita*, the subject.

Reflexive pronouns

These **refer back to an earlier noun or pronoun** in a sentence, so the performing and receiving of an action apply to the same person or thing. They cannot be used without the noun or pronoun that they relate to.

myself, yourself, himself, herself, ourselves, themselves

She taught herself.

This pronoun refers back to the earlier pronoun *she*.

Demonstrative pronouns

These **function as subjects or objects** in a sentence, replacing nouns. Don't confuse these with demonstrative determiners, which precede but do not replace the noun.

this, that, these, those

This pronoun is acting as the subject of the sentence.

This is my instrument.

Interrogative pronouns

These are **used to ask questions** and represent an unknown subject or object.

who, whom, what, which, whose

This pronoun represents the subject, an unknown musician.

Who is playing?

Indefinite pronouns

These **do not refer to any specific person or thing**, but take the place of nouns in a sentence.

somebody, someone, something, anybody, anyone, anything, nobody, no one, nothing, all, another, both, each, many, most, other, some, few, none, such

I haven't seen anyone.

This represents an unknown person, the object of the sentence.

• As a rule, **a pronoun cannot be modified** by an **adjective** or **adverb** in the way that a noun can: For example, "the sad I" does not make sense. Some exceptions include "**what** else" and "**somebody** nice."

• *Somebody* and *someone* **mean the same thing**, as do *anybody* and *anyone*, *everybody* and *everyone*, and *nobody* and *no one*.

Talking about myself

Many people wrongly opt for the reflexive form *myself* because they are unsure whether to use *I* or *me*. Reflexive pronouns should only be used to refer back to a specific noun or pronoun that has already been mentioned in the sentence. This noun or pronoun is usually (but not always) the subject.

I imagined myself on the stage.

This reflexive pronoun correctly refers back to the subject, *I*.

Rita performed for Ben and myself.

This wrongly used reflexive pronoun has no noun to refer back to—there is no *I* in the sentence.

Identifying when to use *I* or *me*

People often make mistakes when deciding whether to use the personal pronouns *I* or *me*. To figure out which to use, split the sentence into two short sentences. It should then become clear which one is right. Remember to put others first in a sentence.

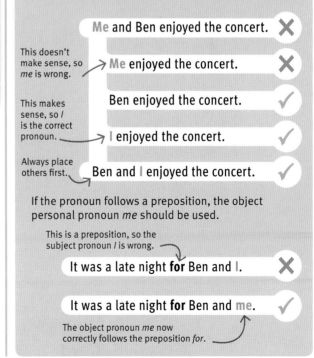

Me and Ben enjoyed the concert. ✗

This doesn't make sense, so *me* is wrong.
Me enjoyed the concert. ✗

This makes sense, so *I* is the correct pronoun.
Ben enjoyed the concert. ✓
I enjoyed the concert. ✓

Always place others first.
Ben and I enjoyed the concert. ✓

If the pronoun follows a preposition, the object personal pronoun *me* should be used.

This is a preposition, so the subject pronoun *I* is wrong.
It was a late night **for** Ben and I. ✗

It was a late night **for** Ben and me. ✓

The object pronoun *me* now correctly follows the preposition *for*.

Number and gender

PRONOUNS AND DETERMINERS MUST AGREE WITH THE NOUNS
TO WHICH THEY RELATE.

In English, there are no personal pronouns or possessive determiners
that can be used to refer to someone without identifying whether
that person is male or female. This often results in mismatched
combinations of singular nouns and plural pronouns or determiners.

SEE ALSO

❮ 24–25 Plurals	
❮ 32–33 Determiners	
❮ 34–35 Pronouns	
Verbs	38–39 ❯
Verb agreement	52–53 ❯

• If a piece of text is likely to become
clumsy with the repetition of **his or
her**, try using certain nouns in the
plural form to add **variety**.

Matching numbers

Pronouns must agree in number
(singular or plural) with the nouns
they represent. Plural nouns or
pronouns must be followed by
plural pronouns or determiners,
and singular nouns or pronouns
must be followed by singular
pronouns or determiners.

Pronoun	Determiner
I	my
you	your
he	his
she	her
it	its
we	our
you	your
they	their

GLOSSARY

Indefinite pronoun A pronoun such
as *everyone* that refers to nobody or
nothing specific.

Number The term used to identify a
noun or pronoun as singular or plural.

Personal pronoun A pronoun that takes
the place of a noun and represents
people, places, or things.

Possessive determiner A word that is
used before a noun to show ownership.

They were preparing for their
told his students that everyone

• When using the word **each**, think
about **"each one,"** as it makes
it easier to remember that **each**
is always followed by a **singular
pronoun** or **determiner**.

• Some words, such as **each** and
all, are used both as **determiners**
and as **pronouns**. Remember that
a determiner is always used in front
of a noun, whereas a pronoun
replaces a noun.

Indefinite pronouns

Indefinite pronouns such as
everyone and *anything* often
cause problems. Although they
appear to refer to more than one
person or thing, these pronouns
are, in fact, singular words.
One way of establishing whether
a pronoun is singular or plural
is to put the verb form *are*
right after it. If the resulting
combination sounds wrong,
then that pronoun is singular.

Singular	Plural
everyone is	both are
somebody is	all are
something is	many are
each is	most are
nothing is	others are
another is	few are

Identifying who's who

If there is more than one person or thing in a sentence, it must be clear which pronoun refers to which person or thing. If it is not clear, the sentence needs to be reworded. Alternatively, the name of the relevant person can be repeated to make it clear who is doing what.

In this case it was Anna's first climb, not Emily's, so the name *Anna* has been repeated to make this clear.

Emily wanted **Anna** to come, although it was **her** first climb. ✗

It is unclear whether it was Emily's first climb or Anna's.

Although it was **her** first climb, **Emily** wanted **Anna** to come. ✓

This sentence has been reordered so that the pronoun is next to the subject it relates to—it was Emily's first climb, not Anna's.

Emily wanted **Anna** to come, although it was **Anna's** first climb. ✓

Misusing *their*

The plural form *they* doesn't have a gender, and people often use this form when speaking or writing to avoid having to distinguish between males and females. In many cases, this results in a singular noun or pronoun being paired with a plural determiner. The only way to avoid this problem is to use *his or her* instead of *their* for the singular, or to make the noun plural and use *their*.

Everyone had to bring his or her own rope.

The indefinite pronoun *everyone* is singular, so the determiners *his* and *her* are used to refer to a group made up of males and females.

The students had to bring their own ropes.

The sentence has been reworded to include a plural subject (*students*), so the plural determiner *their* can be used. The object (*ropes*) has been made plural as well.

climbing expedition. The instructor had to bring his or her own rope.

Male or female?

Sometimes it's hard to know whether to use *he*, *she*, or *they* when referring to both men and women. Historically, writers used the masculine pronouns and determiners *he*, *his*, *him*, and *himself* to represent both sexes, but this approach is now considered outdated. Assumptions about male and female roles should also be avoided.

The instructor told his students to bring ropes.

This sentence refers to a specific instructor, who is known to be male, so the determiner *his* is correct.

An instructor must carry spare ropes for his or her students.

This sentence refers to an unknown instructor, who could be male or female, so the determiners *his* and *her* are required.

Instructors must carry spare ropes for their students.

Sometimes it's clearer to use both the noun and the determiner in the plural form.

Verbs

MOST VERBS ARE ACTION WORDS.

A verb is the most important word in a sentence; without it, the sentence would not make sense. Verbs describe what a person or thing is doing or being.

SEE ALSO	
❰ 22–23 Nouns	
❰ 26–27 Adjectives	
❰ 34–35 Pronouns	
Adverbs	40–41 ❱
Simple tenses	42–43 ❱
Perfect and continuous tenses	44–45 ❱
Irregular verbs	50–51 ❱

Verbs, subjects, and objects

All sentences require both a verb and a subject. The subject (a noun or pronoun) is the person or thing doing the action (a verb). Many sentences also have an object. The direct object (also a noun or pronoun) is the person or thing that is receiving the action.

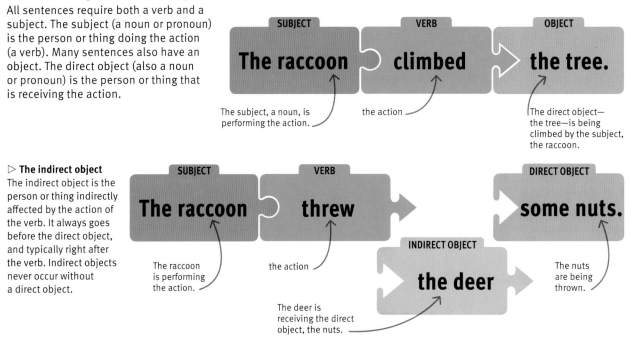

SUBJECT — **The raccoon** — The subject, a noun, is performing the action.

VERB — **climbed** — the action

OBJECT — **the tree.** — The direct object—the tree—is being climbed by the subject, the raccoon.

▷ **The indirect object**
The indirect object is the person or thing indirectly affected by the action of the verb. It always goes before the direct object, and typically right after the verb. Indirect objects never occur without a direct object.

SUBJECT — **The raccoon** — The raccoon is performing the action.

VERB — **threw** — the action

INDIRECT OBJECT — **the deer** — The deer is receiving the direct object, the nuts.

DIRECT OBJECT — **some nuts.** — The nuts are being thrown.

Transitive verbs

Action verbs can be divided into two types—transitive and intransitive. A transitive verb always occurs with an object. It carries an action across from the subject to the direct object. If you can ask and answer the question *who?* or *what?* using the verb, then it is transitive.

This object answers the question "What did the fire destroy?"

A fire destroyed the forest.

| SUBJECT | TRANSITIVE VERB | OBJECT |

Intransitive verbs

Intransitive verbs do not need an object—they make sense on their own. Common intransitive verbs include *arrive*, *sleep*, and *die*. Some verbs, such as *escape*, can be both transitive and intransitive.

Here, *escaped* is used as an intransitive verb—it makes sense without an object.

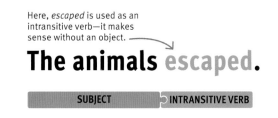

The animals escaped.

| SUBJECT | INTRANSITIVE VERB |

Linking verbs

A linking verb links the subject of a sentence to a word or phrase that describes the subject. Linking verbs either relate to the senses (*feel*, *taste*, *smell*, *look*, *hear*) or to a state of existence (*be*, *become*, *appear*, *remain*). The most common linking verb is *be*.

subject —— This linking verb is a past form of the verb *be*.

This adjective describes the state of mind of the rabbits.

The rabbits were frightened.

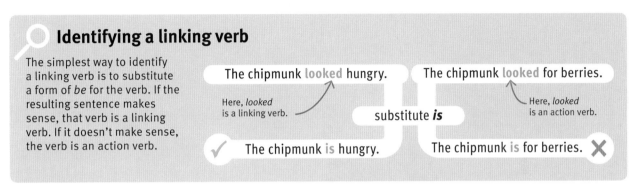

Identifying a linking verb

The simplest way to identify a linking verb is to substitute a form of *be* for the verb. If the resulting sentence makes sense, that verb is a linking verb. If it doesn't make sense, the verb is an action verb.

The chipmunk looked hungry.

Here, *looked* is a linking verb.

substitute *is*

The chipmunk looked for berries.

Here, *looked* is an action verb.

✓ The chipmunk is hungry.

The chipmunk is for berries. ✗

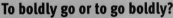

The infinitive

The infinitive is the simplest form of a verb—the form that is used in dictionaries. It can be used on its own, but is almost always preceded by *to*. Unlike verbs, infinitives never change in form. They can be used as nouns, adjectives, or adverbs in a sentence.

The chipmunk needed to eat.

subject

This infinitive is acting like a noun, such as *food*, would act because it is the object of the sentence.

He found a grasshopper to eat.

subject

This infinitive is acting like an adjective, because it is modifying the object of the sentence; it adds the information that the grasshopper is edible.

A well-known exception to the **subject–verb–object** rule comes from the Christian marriage service: "With this ring, **I thee wed**."

REAL WORLD

To boldly go or to go boldly?

Split infinitives occur when an adverb, such as *boldly*, is placed between the infinitive and the preceding *to*. It's preferable to keep the *to* next to the verb, but avoiding a split infinitive can make a sentence awkward. Split infinitives can be used sparingly for emphasis, to avoid confusion, or for a more natural reading order. A famous example is from the opening lines of the 1960s *Star Trek* television series: "To boldly go where no man has gone before."

GLOSSARY

Intransitive verb A verb that does not require an object.

Linking verb A verb, such as *be*, that connects the subject of a sentence to a word or phrase—often an adjective—that describes the subject.

Object The noun or pronoun that is receiving the action of the verb.

Subject The noun or pronoun that is performing the action of the verb.

Transitive verb A verb that must be used with an object.

Adverbs

AN ADVERB MODIFIES A VERB, AN ADJECTIVE, OR ANOTHER ADVERB.

The word *adverb* essentially means "to add to a verb," and this is what adverbs mostly do. They provide information about how, when, where, or how often something is happening, and to what degree.

When and how often?

Adverbs of time indicate when something is happening, while adverbs of frequency indicate how often it is happening. These adverbs modify verbs, and can occupy different positions in a sentence—usually at the beginning or end of a clause.

yesterday   soon
today   now
then   later

adverbs of time

always   rarely
usually   again
sometimes   never

adverbs of frequency

Where?

Adverbs of place work in the same way as adverbs of time and frequency. They modify verbs and tell the reader more about where something is happening.

away   nowhere   there

everywhere

abroad   upstairs

here   out

Yesterday we went out. We left an extremely large dog saw us.

Forming common adverbs

Most adverbs in English are formed by adding the ending -ly to an adjective, but there are some exceptions. Some adjectives, such as *lovely* or *holy*, also end in -ly, so it's important not to confuse these with adverbs.

Adjective ending	Rule	Adverb
-l (beautiful, wonderful)	Add -ly	beautifully, wonderfully
-y (pretty, busy, hungry)	Change -y to -i, then add -ly	prettily, busily, hungrily
-le (comfortable, reputable)	Change -e to -y	comfortably, reputably
-ic (enthusiastic, ecstatic)	Add -ally	enthusiastically, ecstatically
-ly (friendly, daily)	Use an adverbial phrase	in a friendly way, every day

How?

Adverbs that describe how actions are performed are known as adverbs of manner. They are formed from adjectives and modify verbs. These adverbs can be placed before or after the verb, or at the beginning or end of a clause. Like adjectives, most adverbs of manner and frequency can be graded by adverbs of degree, such as *very*, *quite,* or *almost*. These are always placed directly before the adjective or adverb they describe.

This adverb of degree is modifying the adverb of manner *quietly*—it indicates how quietly they left.

We left very quietly

This adverb of manner is at the end of a clause, and is modifying the verb *left*—it is describing how they left.

an extremely **large dog**

This adverb of degree is modifying the adjective *large*—it is explaining how large the dog was.

• Some **adverbs of degree**, such as *just*, *only*, *almost*, and *even*, must be placed immediately in front of the word they are modifying: for example, "I have **just** arrived."

Sentence adverbs

Sentence adverbs are unusual because they do not just modify a verb—they modify the whole sentence or clause containing that verb. They usually express the likelihood or desirability of something happening, and include words like *unfortunately*, *probably*, and *certainly*. They can also be used to influence the reader.

This adverb is modifying a whole clause, meaning "it is unfortunate that an extremely large dog saw us."

unfortunately **an** extremely **large dog saw us**

---

very quietly**, but unfortunately**
We'll run more quickly **next time.**

Comparing adverbs

Like adjectives, adverbs of manner can be compared. To form the comparative, *more* is usually added before the adverb. In the same way, *most* is added before the adverb to form the superlative.

more quickly
most quickly

• *Then* is an **adverb of time,** and should **not** be used as a **conjunction**. When joining two clauses together, use a conjunction such as *and* before *then*.

• **Don't overuse adverbs**. In the phrase "absolutely fabulous," the adverb *absolutely* adds nothing to the adjective *fabulous*, which already implies high levels of enthusiasm for something.

The three **most common adverbs** in English are *not*, *very,* and *too*.

GLOSSARY

Adverbial phrase A group of words such as "in July of last year" that perform the same role as an adverb and answer questions such as: How? When? Where? How often?

Simple tenses

THE TENSE OF A VERB INDICATES WHEN AN ACTION TAKES PLACE.

Unlike most parts of speech, verbs change their form. These different forms, known as tenses, indicate the timing of an action, which is performed by the first, second, or third person.

Picking the right person

Each verb must express a person (first, second, or third), a number (singular or plural), and a tense (past, present, or future). There are three persons in English. These identify who is taking part in a conversation.

The word **tense** comes from the **Latin** word *tempus*, which means **"time."**

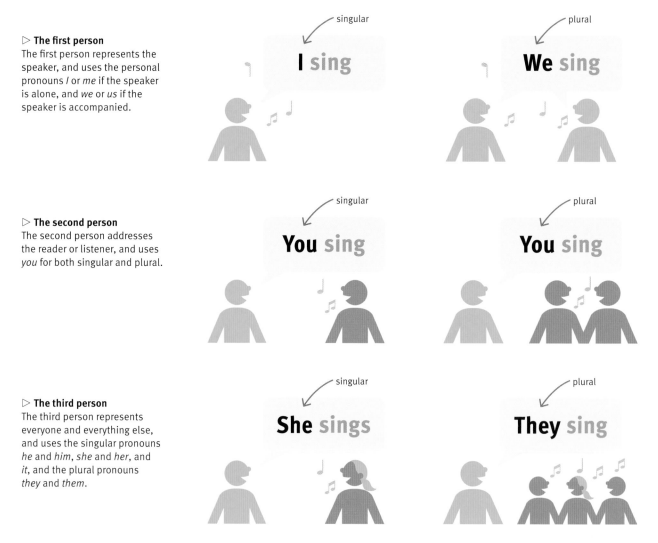

▷ **The first person**
The first person represents the speaker, and uses the personal pronouns *I* or *me* if the speaker is alone, and *we* or *us* if the speaker is accompanied.

singular
I sing

plural
We sing

▷ **The second person**
The second person addresses the reader or listener, and uses *you* for both singular and plural.

singular
You sing

plural
You sing

▷ **The third person**
The third person represents everyone and everything else, and uses the singular pronouns *he* and *him*, *she* and *her*, and *it*, and the plural pronouns *they* and *them*.

singular
She sings

plural
They sing

The present simple tense

The present simple tense is used to express a constant or repeated action that is happening right now. It can also represent a widespread truth: For example, "I smile all the time." Regular verbs in the present tense use the infinitive, except for the third person singular, which uses the infinitive plus the ending -s.

I smile   **We** smile

You smile   **You** smile

She smiles   **They** smile

The third person singular is formed by adding an *s*.

The past simple tense

The past simple tense expresses an action that began and ended in the past. Regular past tense verbs are formed using the infinitive, followed by the ending -ed.

The first, second, and third person take the same form of the verb in the past tense—for both singular and plural.

I laughed   **We** laughed

You laughed   **You** laughed

She laughed   **They** laughed

The future simple tense

The future simple tense is used to express actions that will occur in the future. Regular verbs in the future tense are formed using the auxiliary verb *will*, followed by the infinitive.

I will cry   **We** will cry

You will cry   **You** will cry

She will cry   **They** will cry

The auxiliary verb *will* is used to create the future simple tense.

• Another way of forming the **future simple tense** is to place *am, is,* or *are* before *going to,* followed by the infinitive. This form is useful when the action being described is definitely going to happen. For example, **"It is going to explode."**

• The three basic tenses are the present, the past, and the future. Each of these tenses has a **simple** form, a **continuous** form, a **perfect** form, and a **perfect continuous** form.

GLOSSARY

Auxiliary verb A "helping" verb like *be* or *have* that joins the main verb in a sentence to the subject.

Infinitive The simplest form of a verb: the form that is used in dictionaries.

Perfect and continuous tenses

THESE TENSES GIVE MORE INFORMATION ABOUT WHEN
AN ACTION IS HAPPENING, AND HOW LONG IT GOES ON FOR.

SEE ALSO

❮ 38–39 Verbs
❮ 42–43 Simple tenses
Participles   **46–47 ❯**
Auxiliary verbs   **48–49 ❯**
Irregular verbs   **50–51 ❯**

The perfect tenses refer to actions that are completed over a period
of time. The continuous tenses are used to emphasize that an action
is ongoing at a particular point in time.

GLOSSARY

Auxiliary verb A "helping" verb like
be or *have* that links the main verb in
a sentence to the subject.

Past participle The form of a verb that
usually ends in -ed or -en.

Present participle The form of a verb
that ends in -ing.

The present perfect tense

The perfect tenses describe actions
that span a period of time but have a
known end. The present perfect tense
refers either to an action that happened
at an unspecified time in the past, or to
an action that began in the past and
continues in the present. It is formed
using the past participle, preceded by
the auxiliary verb form *have* or—for
the third person singular—*has*.

This refers to an action
that happened at some
point in the past.

I have disappeared   **We** have disappeared
You have disappeared   **You** have disappeared
She has disappeared   **They** have disappeared

This refers to an
action that began in
the past and continues
in the present.

She has lived here for ten years.

The third person singular is formed
using *has* instead of *have*.

The past perfect tense

The past perfect tense describes an
action that happened in the past before
something else happened. It is formed
in the same way as the present perfect
tense, but using the auxiliary verb form
had before the past participle.

I had escaped   **We** had escaped
You had escaped   **You** had escaped
It had escaped   **They** had escaped

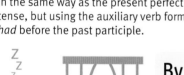

By the time **the guard** noticed, **I** had escaped.

This action finished before
the second action (the
guard noticing) started.

The future perfect tense

The future perfect tense describes an
action that will occur at some point in
the future before another action. For
example, "He will have offended again
before we catch him."

I will have offended   **We** will have offended
You will have offended   **You** will have offended
He will have offended   **They** will have offended

This tense is formed using the past
participle, preceded by *will have*.

The present continuous tense

Continuous or progressive tenses are used to describe actions or situations that are ongoing. The present continuous tense expresses an action that is continuing at the same time that something else is happening. This tense is formed using the present participle, preceded by *am*, *are*, or *is*.

I am hiding
You are hiding
She is hiding

We are hiding
You are hiding
They are hiding

I am hiding in a tree until **it gets** dark.

The action *hiding* is continuing at the same time that it starts to get dark.

The past continuous tense

The past continuous tense describes a past action that was happening at the same time that another action occurred. For example, "They were falling asleep when they heard a loud crash."

I was falling
You were falling
He was falling

We were falling
You were falling
They were falling

This tense is formed in the same way as the present continuous tense, but using *was* or *were* instead of *am*, *is*, or *are*.

The future continuous tense

The future continuous tense describes an ongoing action that is going to happen in the future. Like the other continuous forms, the present participle is used, but it is preceded by *will be*.

I will be watching
You will be watching
She will be watching

We will be watching
You will be watching
They will be watching

Perfect continuous tenses

Like simple continuous tenses, perfect continuous tenses describe ongoing actions. Like perfect tenses, these actions end at some point in the present, past, or future. Perfect continuous tenses are also formed using the present participle.

Tense	Form	Example
Present perfect continuous	have/has been + present participle	I have been hiding since dawn.
Past perfect continuous	had been + present participle	The guard had been searching all day.
Future perfect continuous	will have been + present participle	They will have been following my trail.

REAL WORLD

Verbal dynamism

Some verbs sound strange when they are used in the continuous tenses. For something to be ongoing, it needs to be something active, such as running or eating. Verbs that do not imply an action, but instead refer to a state of affairs—for example, *know*, *own*, *love*, or *feel*—cannot be used in the continuous tenses. Although it has become a familiar expression, the slogan "I'm lovin' it" is grammatically wrong. Maybe that's why everyone remembers it.

Participles

PARTICIPLES ARE FORMED FROM VERBS.

There are two participles: the past and the present. They are used with auxiliary verbs like *have* and *be* to form tenses, and on their own as adjectives. The present participle can also be used as a noun.

Past participles as verbs

Combined with the auxiliary verb *have*, past participles are used to form the perfect tense of a verb. Regular past participles are formed in the same way as the simple past tense, using the infinitive, plus the ending -ed. Common irregular past participle endings include -en, -t, or -n. The past participle of a few verbs is the same as the infinitive, and some, such as *tell*, change their spelling completely.

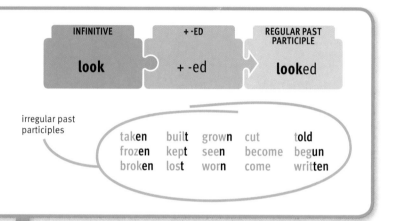

irregular past participles

tak**en**	buil**t**	grow**n**	cut	**told**
froz**en**	kep**t**	see**n**	become	beg**un**
brok**en**	los**t**	wor**n**	come	writ**ten**

Josh had looked everywhere for
been hoping to do some ice-

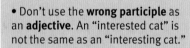

• Don't use the **wrong participle** as an **adjective**. An "interested cat" is not the same as an "interesting cat."

GLOSSARY

Auxiliary verb A "helping" verb like *be* or *have* that joins the main verb in a sentence to the subject.

Gerund The name given to the present participle when it is used as a noun.

Linking verb A verb that joins the subject of a sentence to a word or phrase that describes the subject.

Present participles as verbs

Present participles are used with the auxiliary verb *be* to form verbs in the continuous tense. They are formed using the infinitive and the ending -ing. Unlike past participles, all present participles have the same ending. If the infinitive ends in a silent -e (for example, *hope*), the -e is dropped before the -ing ending is added.

Past participles as adjectives

Past participles can be used on their own as adjectives to modify nouns. They are placed either before the noun or pronoun they describe, or after it, following a linking verb.

This past participle is being used as an adjective before the noun it describes (*skates*).

his broken skates

His skates were broken.

Here, the past participle is being used as an adjective after the noun it describes (*skates*), following the linking verb *were*.

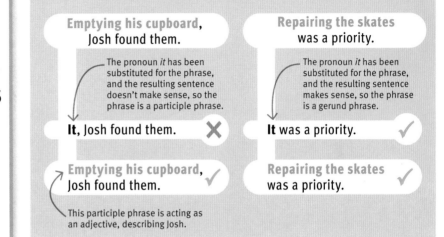

Identifying a gerund phrase

Participle phrases act as adjectives, whereas gerund phrases act as nouns, which can be described by adjectives. Since gerund phrases are always singular, it is possible to check whether a phrase is a gerund phrase by substituting the pronoun *it*.

Emptying his cupboard, Josh found them.

The pronoun *it* has been substituted for the phrase, and the resulting sentence doesn't make sense, so the phrase is a participle phrase.

It, Josh found them. ✗

Emptying his cupboard, ✓ Josh found them.

This participle phrase is acting as an adjective, describing Josh.

Repairing the skates was a priority.

The pronoun *it* has been substituted for the phrase, and the resulting sentence makes sense, so the phrase is a gerund phrase.

It was a priority. ✓

Repairing the skates ✓ was a priority.

his broken skates. He had skating, but they were missing.

Present participles as nouns

When the present participle of a verb is used as a noun, it is called a gerund. Like nouns, a gerund (one word) or a gerund phrase (multiple words) can be used as the subject or object of a sentence.

subject

He wanted to do some ice-skating.

The gerund phrase *ice-skating* is acting as the object of this sentence.

Present participles as adjectives

Like past participles, present participles can be used as adjectives. They can be placed before or after the noun or pronoun that they modify.

This present participle is being used as an adjective after the pronoun it describes (*they*), following the linking verb *were*.

They were missing.

the missing skates

This present participle is formed from the verb *miss*, and is describing the noun *skates*.

Auxiliary verbs

SOME VERBS HELP TO FORM OTHER VERBS.

Often called "helping verbs," auxiliary verbs can be used in front of other verbs to form tenses, negative sentences, and the passive voice, or to express different moods.

Helpful properties

Auxiliary verbs are known as helping verbs because they perform several different roles. Their main job is to help form different tenses, but they are also used to create negative sentences, turn statements into questions, and add emphasis to speech.

Must is the **only verb** in English to have a **present** but **no past** form.

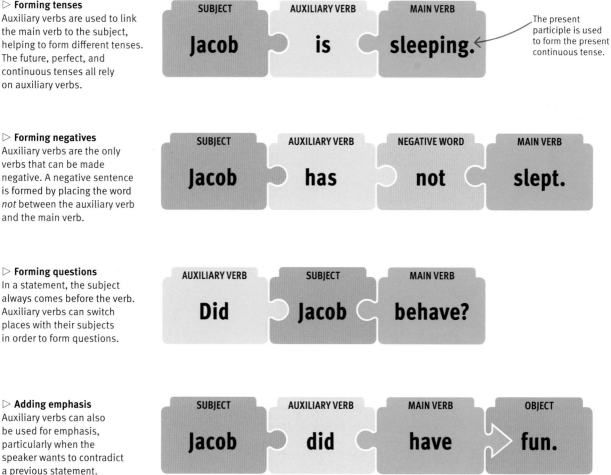

▷ **Forming tenses**
Auxiliary verbs are used to link the main verb to the subject, helping to form different tenses. The future, perfect, and continuous tenses all rely on auxiliary verbs.

SUBJECT — **Jacob** AUXILIARY VERB — **is** MAIN VERB — **sleeping.**

The present participle is used to form the present continuous tense.

▷ **Forming negatives**
Auxiliary verbs are the only verbs that can be made negative. A negative sentence is formed by placing the word *not* between the auxiliary verb and the main verb.

SUBJECT — **Jacob** AUXILIARY VERB — **has** NEGATIVE WORD — **not** MAIN VERB — **slept.**

▷ **Forming questions**
In a statement, the subject always comes before the verb. Auxiliary verbs can switch places with their subjects in order to form questions.

AUXILIARY VERB — **Did** SUBJECT — **Jacob** MAIN VERB — **behave?**

▷ **Adding emphasis**
Auxiliary verbs can also be used for emphasis, particularly when the speaker wants to contradict a previous statement.

SUBJECT — **Jacob** AUXILIARY VERB — **did** MAIN VERB — **have** OBJECT — **fun.**

Primary auxiliary verbs

The verbs *be*, *have,* and *do* are known as the primary auxiliary verbs. Primary auxiliary verbs can be used as the main verb in a sentence, or they can be used with participles to form tenses. These verbs also have participles of their own. Auxiliary verbs are irregular verbs, and are irregular even in the present tense.

Verb form	be	have	do
Infinitive	be	have	do
First person (present)	am, are	have	do
Second person (present)	are	have	do
Third person (present)	is, are	has, have	does, do
Past participle	been	had	done
Present participle	being	having	doing

- Only the **primary auxiliaries**—*be*, *have*, and *do*—can **change** their form. **Modal auxiliaries** always take the **same form**.

- *Might* is the past tense of *may*, so *might* is always used when talking about something that might have happened previously.

- Sometimes modal auxiliaries are used to add **emphasis** to a decision or a command. Using *will* instead of *am going to* for the **first person** future tense makes a statement sound more determined: for example, "I **will** go to the party."

Modal auxiliary verbs

Common auxiliary verbs that cannot be used on their own are known as modal auxiliary verbs. These include *can*, *will*, *should*, *may*, and *must*, and they are used with action verbs to express a command, an obligation, or a possibility. Modal auxiliaries are unusual because they do not have an infinitive form or participles, nor—unlike primary auxiliaries and regular verbs—do they take the ending -s for the third person singular.

The third person singular modal auxiliary does not take an -s; "he cans" doesn't make sense.

Modal auxiliary	Use	Example
can	Used to express a person's ability to do something.	I can run fast.
could	Used to show possibility; also the past form of *can*.	I could run faster.
may	Used to ask permission to do something, or to express a possibility.	May I come?
might	Used to express a small possibility; also the past form of *may*.	I might run away.
must	Used to indicate a strong obligation.	I must come.
ought	Used to express a sense of obligation.	I ought to stay.
shall	Used to form the future simple tense, and to show determination.	I shall run faster.
should	Used to express obligation.	I should come.
will	Used to form the future simple tense, and to show determination or issue a command.	You will come!
would	Used to express a polite question or a wish, or to indicate the consequence of a conditional sentence; also the past form of *will*.	Would you like to come? I would love to come. If I were to come, I would have fun.

Irregular verbs

SOME VERBS HAVE ONE OR MORE IRREGULAR FORMS.

The past tense and past participles of all regular verbs are formed in the same way. By contrast, irregular verbs are unpredictable, and take a variety of verb endings. Some change their spelling completely. It is essential to learn these.

SEE ALSO

❰ **38–39** Verbs
❰ **42–43** Simple tenses
❰ **44–45** Perfect and continuous tenses
❰ **46–47** Participles
❰ **48–49** Auxiliary verbs

Forming irregular verbs

The simple past tense and past participle of regular verbs are formed using the ending -ed (or -d, if the infinitive form already ends in -e). Irregular verbs do not follow this pattern. They take different endings, and the vowel of a verb often changes to form the past tense.

• **Auxiliary verbs** are **irregular**, and—unlike other irregular verbs—the verbs *be*, *have*, and *do* are irregular **even in the present tense**.

regular simple past tense of *discover*, with the ending -ed

Grace discovered her shoes a week after her sister had swiped them.

regular past participle of *swipe*, with the ending -d

Some of the **most common verbs** in the **English** language are **irregular** verbs.

irregular simple past tense of *find*

Grace found her shoes a week after her sister had stolen them.

irregular past participle of *steal*

GLOSSARY

Auxiliary verb A "helping" verb like *be* or *have* that joins the main verb in a sentence to the subject.

Infinitive The simplest form of a verb: the form that is used in dictionaries.

Past participle The form of a verb that usually ends in -ed or -en. It is used with the auxiliary verbs *have* and *will* to form the perfect tenses.

🔍 Identifying when to use *lie* and *lay*

The irregular verbs *lie* and *lay* are often mixed up in everyday speech. The past tense of the verb *lie* (meaning "to be in a resting position") is the same as the infinitive form of the verb *lay* (meaning "to place something" or "to enforce"). The mistake most speakers make is to use the past tense form of *lie*—"lay"—when the present tense or infinitive form is required.

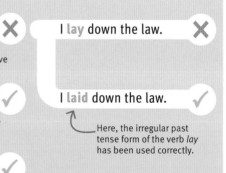

I need to lay down. ✗

It is clear from the context of the sentence that the infinitive *lie* is required, rather than the infinitive *lay*.

I need to lie down. ✓

Here, the irregular past tense form of the verb *lie* has been used correctly.

I lay down. ✓

I lay down the law. ✗

I laid down the law. ✓

Here, the irregular past tense form of the verb *lay* has been used correctly.

Common irregular verbs

Many well-known verbs do not take the standard ending -ed when they are used in the past tense or as past participles. The past tense forms and past participles of some irregular verbs look very different from the infinitive form. All of these verb forms have to be learned.

Infinitive form	Simple past tense	Past participle
be	was/were	been
become	became	become
begin	began	begun
blow	blew	blown
break	broke	broken
bring	brought	brought
build	built	built
buy	bought	bought
catch	caught	caught
choose	chose	chosen
come	came	come
cost	cost	cost
creep	crept	crept
cut	cut	cut
do	did	done
draw	drew	drawn
drink	drank	drunk
drive	drove	driven
eat	ate	eaten
fall	fell	fallen
feel	felt	felt
find	found	found
fly	flew	flown
freeze	froze	frozen
get	got	got or gotten
give	gave	given
go	went	gone
grow	grew	grown
hang	hung	hung
have	had	had
hear	heard	heard
hold	held	held
keep	kept	kept
know	knew	known
lay	laid	laid

Infinitive form	Simple past tense	Past participle
lead	led	led
leave	left	left
let	let	let
lie	lay	lain
lose	lost	lost
make	made	made
mean	meant	meant
meet	met	met
mistake	mistook	mistaken
pay	paid	paid
put	put	put
ride	rode	ridden
rise	rose	risen
run	ran	run
say	said	said
see	saw	seen
sell	sold	sold
send	sent	sent
set	set	set
shake	shook	shaken
sit	sat	sat
sleep	slept	slept
speak	spoke	spoken
spend	spent	spent
spin	spun	spun
stand	stood	stood
steal	stole	stolen
stick	stuck	stuck
swear	swore	sworn
swim	swam	swum
take	took	taken
teach	taught	taught
tear	tore	torn
tell	told	told
think	thought	thought
throw	threw	thrown
understand	understood	understood
wear	wore	worn
weep	wept	wept
win	won	won
write	wrote	written

Verb agreement

THE NUMBER OF THE SUBJECT DICTATES THE NUMBER OF THE VERB.

Like nouns and pronouns, a verb can be singular or plural in number, but it must match the subject to which it relates. Sometimes it's hard to know whether a noun is singular or plural, leading to errors in verb agreement.

SEE ALSO

❮ 22–23 Nouns
❮ 24–25 Plurals
❮ 34–35 Pronouns
❮ 36–37 Number and gender
❮ 38–39 Verbs
❮ 42–43 Simple tenses
Prepositions   60–61 ❯

Singular or plural?

The key to correct verb agreement is to follow this simple rule: If the subject is singular, the verb must be singular; if the subject is plural, the verb must also be plural.

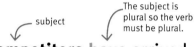

subject

The subject is plural so the verb must be plural.

The **competitors** have arrived, and the **Mighty Musclemen contest** is about to start.

subject

The subject is singular so the verb must be singular.

• Some nouns sound plural but are actually treated as **singular**. These include *mathematics* and *politics*, as well as **proper nouns** such as *United States* or *Philippines*.

Identifying the subject

One problem occurs when the wrong word is identified as the subject. This often happens when the subject and verb are separated by a prepositional phrase. When the prepositional phrase is removed from the sentence, it becomes clear which noun or pronoun is the true subject.

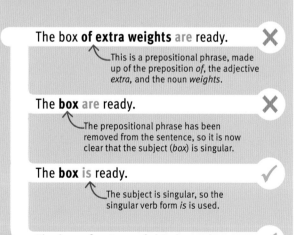

The box **of extra weights** are ready.   ✗

This is a prepositional phrase, made up of the preposition *of*, the adjective *extra*, and the noun *weights*.

The **box** are ready.   ✗

The prepositional phrase has been removed from the sentence, so it is now clear that the subject (*box*) is singular.

The **box** is ready.   ✓

The subject is singular, so the singular verb form *is* is used.

The **box of extra weights** is ready.   ✓

The prepositional phrase has been put back into the sentence, and the verb now agrees with the subject.

Collective nouns

Most collective nouns (for example, *class* or *crowd*) are singular words, because they can be made plural (*classes*, *crowds*). However, some collective nouns, including *team*, *staff*, and *couple*, can be singular or plural. A good general rule to follow is to consider whether the noun is acting as a unit or whether the noun is made up of individuals acting in different ways.

My **team** has won.

Here, the team represents a unit, so the singular form of the verb is used.

The **team** are divided in their feelings.

Here, the individual members of the team are acting in different ways, so the plural form of the verb is used.

Multiple subjects

If a sentence contains more than one noun, and these nouns are joined by *and*, they almost always take a plural verb. These are known as compound subjects. Phrases such as *along with* and *as well as* separate the subjects, however. In these cases, the verb should agree with the first subject, regardless of whether the second subject is singular or plural. By contrast, if a singular subject is joined to a plural subject and separated by *or* or *nor*, the verb agrees with the nearest subject.

• When the phrase ***the number of*** precedes the subject of a sentence, the subject is considered to be singular: "The number of weights used **is** variable." By contrast, the phrase ***a number of*** makes a subject plural: "A number of different weights **are** used."

• Expressions of **quantity**, such as **time, money, weight,** or **fractions,** are treated in the same way as **collective nouns.** For example, "**Half** of Tyler's allowance **is** spent on exercise equipment."

Tyler and his brother **Matt** are competing.

◁ **Compound subjects**
The subjects *Tyler* and *Matt* are acting together, and are joined by *and*, so they take the plural form.

Matt's **size as well as** his **strength** is awesome.

◁ **Separate subjects**
The subjects *size* and *strength* are acting separately, so the verb is singular to match the first subject, *size*.

Neither Tyler's **neck nor** his **arms** are small.

◁ **Mixed subjects**
The plural subject *arms* is closer to the verb than the singular subject *neck*, so the verb is plural. With mixed subjects, always put the plural subject closest to the verb.

Indefinite pronouns

Most indefinite pronouns can be easily identified as singular or plural. *Both*, *several*, *few*, and *many*, for example, are always plural. Some, however, are singular words that refer to plural things. These include *each*, *everyone*, and *everything*.

▽ **Agreeing with prepositional phrases**
Five indefinite pronouns can be singular or plural, depending on the context. These are *all*, *any*, *most*, *none*, and *some*. Only when these pronouns occur do prepositional phrases determine whether a verb should be singular or plural.

Number	Indefinite pronoun
singular	everybody, everyone, everything, somebody, someone, something, anybody, anyone, anything, nobody, no one, nothing, neither, another, each, either, one, other, much
plural	both, several, few, many, others
singular or plural	all, any, most, none, some

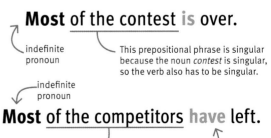

Most of the contest **is** over.

indefinite pronoun

This prepositional phrase is singular because the noun *contest* is singular, so the verb also has to be singular.

indefinite pronoun

Most of the competitors **have** left.

This prepositional phrase is plural, because the noun *competitors* is plural.

The verb is plural to match the prepositional phrase.

Voices and moods

SENTENCES IN ENGLISH CAN BE EXPRESSED
IN DIFFERENT VOICES AND DIFFERENT MOODS.

There are two voices in English. These determine whether
the subject of a sentence is performing or receiving an action.
Mood is the form of the verb that conveys the attitude in which
a thought is expressed.

The active voice

Verbs can be used in two different ways.
These are known as voices. The active
voice is simpler than the passive voice.
In an active sentence, the subject
is performing the action of the verb,
and the object is receiving it.

The snake is performing
the action of attacking.

The action is
being performed.

The boy is
receiving
the action.

Subject   **Verb**   **Object**

The snake attacked the boy.

The passive voice

In a passive sentence, the word order
is reversed so that the subject is
receiving the action and the object
is performing it. The passive voice is
formed using the auxiliary verb *be*
followed by a past participle. The
performer of the action is either
identified using the preposition
by or not included at all.

The boy is now the
subject, but he is still
receiving the action.

The action is
being performed.

The snake is still
performing the action,
but it is now the object.

This preposition
indicates who or
what is performing
the action: the snake.

Subject   **Verb**   **Object**

The boy was attacked by the snake.

The object has been
removed from this
sentence, but it
still makes sense.

Subject   **Verb**

The boy was attacked.

past tense form of the
auxiliary verb *be*

past participle of the
regular verb *attack*

REAL WORLD

Passive persuasion

The passive voice is often used on
official signs, because it is perceived
as less confrontational than the active
voice. In these situations, it is also
often unnecessary to state who is
performing the action.

Danger

Pedestrians are
not permitted
beyond this point

The indicative mood

There are three main moods in English. Most verbs are used in the indicative mood, which indicates an actual condition, as opposed to an intended, expected, or believed condition. This mood is used to state facts.

This sentence states a fact—something that was the case at some point in the past—so it is in the indicative mood.

The boy was terrified.

The imperative mood

The imperative mood is used to give commands or make requests. Exclamations are often in the imperative mood; these always end with an exclamation point.

This command is also an exclamation.

This is a request.

Go away! Please leave me alone.

The subjunctive mood

The subjunctive mood is rarely used in English, and it can only be identified in the third person form or with the verb *be*. It is used after verbs and phrases that express an obligation or a desire, such as *demand*, *require*, *suggest*, or *it is essential that*, and it indicates that the obligation or desire may not be fulfilled.

> **GLOSSARY**
>
> **Auxiliary verb** A "helping" verb like *be* or *have* that links the main verb in a sentence to the subject.
>
> **Exclamation** A sentence that expresses a strong emotion, such as surprise, or a raised voice, and ends with an exclamation point.
>
> **Modal auxiliary verb** An auxiliary verb that is used with an action verb to express a command, an obligation, or a possibility.
>
> **Past participle** The form of a verb that ends in -ed or -en. It is used with the auxiliary verb *be* to form the passive voice.

▷ **Third person**
To form most subjunctive verbs, the final *s* is removed from the third person form.

He demanded that the zookeeper remove the snake.

The present subjunctive follows the verb phrase *demanded that*. It is used because the zookeeper might not remove the snake.

▷ **Exception**
The main exception is the verb *be*, which takes the form *be* for the present tense and *were* for the past tense.

The zookeeper requested that the boy be quiet.

The present subjunctive follows the verb phrase *requested that*. The zookeeper wants the boy to be quiet, but the boy might not be quiet.

🔍 Identifying the subjunctive in conditional sentences

Conditional sentences are used to indicate that the action of a main clause ("going to the beach") can only happen if a certain condition, contained in a subordinate clause, is fulfilled ("if the weather is hot"). Most conditional sentences start with *if* or *unless*. If the action being described is almost certain to happen, the indicative mood is used. If the action being described is hypothetical (impossible to predict), the past tense form of the subjunctive mood should be used.

Many conditional sentences start with *if*.

If the weather...

They will almost certainly go to the beach if the weather is hot, so the indicative mood is used.

If the weather **is** hot, we **will go** to the beach. ✓

If the weather **were** hot, we **would be** happier. ✓

The weather is not hot, so the belief that they would be happier is a hypothetical situation, which requires the subjunctive verb form *were*.

The modal auxiliary verb *would* usually appears in conditional sentences with the subjunctive.

Phrasal verbs

NEW VERBS ARE FORMED BY ADDING AN ADVERB OR
A PREPOSITION TO AN EXISTING VERB.

A phrasal verb is a compound of a verb and an adverb, a verb and
a preposition, or a verb, an adverb, and a preposition. Phrasal verbs
work like regular verbs, but they are mostly used in informal speech.

Adverb phrasal verbs

Composed of an existing verb
followed by an adverb, an adverb
phrasal verb works in the same way
as a regular verb—as a single unit.
The adverb is essential to the
phrasal verb's meaning, either
intensifying the sense of the
preceding verb or changing its
meaning entirely. Adverbs like
up, *down*, *out*, or *off* are often
used to form phrasal verbs.

The adverb *up* changes the
meaning of the verb *get*,
resulting in a phrasal verb
that means "to rise, usually
after sleeping," rather than
"to receive or obtain."

I got up early.

adverb phrasal verb

Most **new verbs** in
the **English** language
are **phrasal verbs**.

- The small words used to form
phrasal verbs—**adverbs** and
prepositions—are often known
as **particles**.
- Phrasal verbs are **never
hyphenated**.

I got up early because Daniel
We ran into Paulo, who was

Prepositional phrasal verbs

Prepositional phrasal verbs consist of
a verb followed by a preposition, such
as *by*, *after*, *in*, *on*, or *for*. The preposition
links the verb to the noun or pronoun that
follows—the direct object. Prepositional
phrasal verbs are always transitive, but
unlike adverb phrasal verbs, prepositional
phrasal verbs cannot usually be separated
by the direct object (see "Word order").

talk about

stand by

listen to

call on

take after

wait for

run into

Versatile verbs

Only a handful of adverbs and
prepositions are needed to
create a range of phrasal verbs
with different meanings. Using
a different phrasal verb can
completely change the
meaning of a sentence. For
example, "Paulo is looking
after the game" means that
he is in charge of the game.

GLOSSARY

Direct object The noun or pronoun that is receiving the action of the verb.
Intransitive verb A verb that does not require an object.
Transitive verb A verb that must be used with an object.

Word order

Like regular verbs, phrasal verbs can be transitive or intransitive. Transitive phrasal verbs require a direct object to receive the action, while intransitive phrasal verbs, such as *get up* or *eat out*, make sense without an object. The verb and adverb in a transitive adverb phrasal verb can usually be separated by the direct object.

Daniel was taking me out for lunch.

direct object

This adverb phrasal verb is transitive, so it can be separated by the direct object.

Identifying when a phrasal verb can be separated

Some transitive phrasal verbs can be separated by a direct object; others cannot be separated. A simple way to test whether a phrasal verb is separable or inseparable is to place the pronoun *it* (representing the direct object) between the verb and the adverb or preposition. If the resulting phrase makes sense, that phrasal verb can be separated.

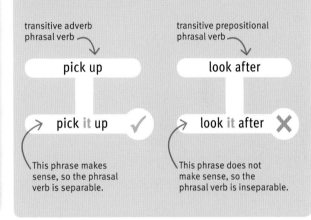

transitive adverb phrasal verb

pick up

pick it up ✓

This phrase makes sense, so the phrasal verb is separable.

transitive prepositional phrasal verb

look after

look it after ✗

This phrase does not make sense, so the phrasal verb is inseparable.

was taking me out for lunch.
looking forward to the game.

look forward to
look over
look out
look through
look at
look after

Adverb-prepositional phrasal verbs

Some phrasal verbs are made up of a verb, followed by an adverb and a preposition. Like prepositional phrasal verbs, these must have a direct object, and the parts of the phrasal verb cannot be separated by this object.

Paulo was looking forward to the game.

verb

adverb   preposition   direct object

Conjunctions

A CONJUNCTION CONNECTS WORDS, PHRASES, AND CLAUSES.

Also known as connectives, conjunctions are used to link two or more parts of a sentence. These parts can be of equal importance, or a main clause can be linked to a subordinate clause using a subordinator.

• Relative pronouns such as **who**, **whom**, **which**, and **that** are used in the same way as subordinators.

• It's a good idea to avoid starting a sentence with conjunctions like **because** or **and**, because this practice often results in **incomplete sentences**.

Coordinating conjunctions

Without conjunctions, writing would be made up of numerous short sentences. Conjunctions are used to create longer sentences, preventing text from becoming stilted. Coordinating conjunctions are used to link words, phrases, or clauses of equal importance. They include the words *and*, *but*, *or*, *nor*, *yet*, *for,* and *so*.

roses and sunflowers

This coordinating conjunction is being used to link two types of flowers.

Flora tried to water her roses and

She cut both the hedge and the

• Never use a comma to link two main clauses. **Main clauses** should only be linked using a **conjunction**, a **semicolon**, or a **colon**.

GLOSSARY

Main clause A group of words that contains a subject and a verb and makes complete sense on its own.

Subordinate clause A group of words that contains a subject and a verb but depends on a main clause for its meaning.

Pairs of conjunctions

Conjunctions can be single words or phrases, and they often appear in pairs. Pairs such as *both–and*, *either–or*, and *not only–but also* are sometimes known as "correlative conjunctions" because the conjunctions work together. The two parts must be placed directly before the words they are joining.

pair of conjunctions

She cut both the hedge and the tree.

nouns being joined by the pair

Identifying when to use a semicolon

Adverbs such as *however*, *accordingly*, *besides*, and *therefore* can also be used as conjunctions to join two main clauses. Unlike coordinating conjunctions and subordinators, these adverbs must be preceded by a semicolon and followed by a comma.

two main clauses

She was confident. She hadn't cut the hedge before.

coordinating conjunction separating two main clauses

She was confident, **but** she hadn't cut the hedge before.

This adverb is being used as a conjunction, so it must be preceded by a semicolon and followed by a comma.

She was confident; **however**, she hadn't cut the hedge before.

Coordinating multiple subjects

When a coordinating conjunction is used to link two main clauses with different subjects, a comma should be placed before the conjunction. This helps to show where one main clause ends and another begins.

first main clause

first subject

Flora tried to water her roses and sunflowers, but the hose burst.

A comma and coordinating conjunction separate the two main clauses.

second subject

second main clause

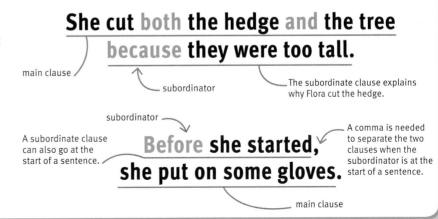

sunflowers, but the hose burst.
tree because they were too tall.

Subordinators

Subordinators or subordinating conjunctions are used to connect words, phrases, and clauses of unequal importance. A subordinate clause adds information to a main clause, explaining why, where, or when something is happening. Subordinate clauses start with subordinators like *before*, *if*, *because*, *although*, and *while*, and can be placed at the beginning or end of a sentence.

She cut both the hedge and the tree because they were too tall.

main clause

subordinator

The subordinate clause explains why Flora cut the hedge.

subordinator

A subordinate clause can also go at the start of a sentence.

Before she started, she put on some gloves.

A comma is needed to separate the two clauses when the subordinator is at the start of a sentence.

main clause

Prepositions

PREPOSITIONS CONNECT NOUNS AND PRONOUNS TO OTHER WORDS IN A SENTENCE.

Prepositions never appear alone. They are short words that convey the relationship of a noun or pronoun to another part of a sentence—often the physical position of one thing in relation to another.

Simple prepositions

Prepositions are common in written and spoken English. They usually appear as part of a prepositional phrase, and include words like *for*, *about*, *with*, *of,* and *on*. A prepositional phrase is made up of a preposition followed by its object, which is a noun, pronoun, or noun phrase.

preposition — adjective

for a long bicycle ride

article — noun phrase and object of the preposition

• In **formal writing**, **sentences** should **not end** with **prepositions**, but this practice is common in spoken English. "What are you talking about?" is a good example.

• **Prepositional phrases** only ever contain the **object** of a clause. They never contain the subject. In the sentence "They sped **down a hill**," *hill* is the object, and *they* is the subject.

Daisy went for a long bicycle a hill and through a stream

Winston Churchill, objecting to strict rules about **prepositional word order**, famously said, "That is nonsense **up with which** I shall not put."

Parallel prepositions

Writers can improve their sentences by using consistent language. If different prepositions are required for different nouns, they must all be included in the sentence. If one preposition is being used to introduce a series of nouns, it only needs to be used before the first noun. The same preposition can be used before each noun, but this is repetitive.

The noun objects *hill* and *stream* require different prepositions, so both must be included in the sentence.

They raced down a hill and through a stream.

This preposition applies to both nouns, so it only needs to appear before the first item in this list.

They sped through a stream and a forest.

Identifying prepositional phrasal verbs

A prepositional phrasal verb is made up of a verb followed by a preposition. This type of verb must have an object, but the preposition cannot be separated from its verb by this object. If the preposition part of a prepositional phrasal verb is removed, the sentence will not make sense.

Daisy was **annoyed** and **afraid** of Ed's poor cycling skills. ✗

If the phrase *and afraid* is removed, the sentence does not make sense.

Daisy was **annoyed** of Ed's poor cycling skills. ✗

This phrasal verb does make sense on its own.

Daisy was **afraid** of Ed's poor cycling skills. ✓

The correct preposition has been added into the sentence.

object, a noun phrase

Daisy was **annoyed** by and **afraid** of Ed's poor cycling skills. ✓

Using prepositional phrases

Prepositional phrases can be used like adjectives and adverbs to modify nouns or verbs. They can offer more detail about an object so that the reader knows what or whom is being referred to, or they can point to where something is, or when or why something happened.

This prepositional phrase is working as an adjective because it is describing a noun, *eagle.*

Daisy saw an eagle in a tree.

This prepositional phrase is working as an adverb, because it is describing where they raced.

They raced down a hill.

ride with Ed. They raced down and stopped next to a bridge.

Complex prepositions

Sometimes simple prepositions are used with one or two other words to form complex prepositions, which act as a single unit. Like one-word prepositions, these come before nouns or pronouns in prepositional phrases and can act as adjectives or adverbs.

except for

next to

out of

as for

in front of

in spite of

along with

GLOSSARY

Adjective prepositional phrase A prepositional phrase that describes a noun.

Adverb prepositional phrase A prepositional phrase that describes a verb.

Noun phrase A phrase made up of a noun and any words that are modifying that noun, such as articles or adjectives.

Object The noun or pronoun that is receiving the action of the verb.

Prepositional phrasal verb A verb followed by a preposition, which together act as a single unit.

Prepositional phrase A preposition followed by a noun, pronoun, or noun phrase that together act as an adjective (describing a noun) or an adverb (describing a verb) in a sentence.

Interjections

INTERJECTIONS ARE WORDS OR PHRASES THAT
OCCUR ALONE AND EXPRESS EMOTION.

Interjections are considered a part of speech, but they play no
grammatical role in a sentence. They are single words or phrases
that are used to exclaim, protest, or command, and rarely appear
in formal writing.

Emotional words

Interjections occur frequently in spoken English. They are
useful in informal writing—particularly in narratives or
scripts—since they help convey the emotions of a character,
but they are only used in formal writing as part of a direct
quotation. New interjections to describe different emotions
are invented all the time, and they vary from region to region.

Emotion	Interjection
pain	ouch, ow, oh
disgust	yuck, ugh, ew
surprise	eek, yikes, ooh, wow, eh, well, really
elation	hooray, yippee, ha, woo-hoo, whoopee
pleasure	mmm, yeah
relief	phew, whew, whoa
boredom	blah, ho-hum
embarrassment	ahem, er
disappointment	aw, meh, pfft
dismay	oh no, oh, oops
panic	help, ah, uh oh
irritation	hmph, huh, hey, oy
disapproval	tsk-tsk, tut-tut
realization	aha, ah
pity	dear, alas, ahh
doubt	hmm, er, um

👍 • **Use interjections in moderation,**
or not at all. They rarely improve a
piece of writing.

Using interjections

Interjections that express strong emotions such as
dismay or surprise usually function as exclamations,
appearing alone as single words or phrases followed
by an exclamation point. Milder emotions tend to be
expressed using an interjection followed by a comma.

Uh oh! ← This is an exclamation, because
it expresses a strong emotion
(panic). It is punctuated with an
exclamation point.

This mild interjection has
been incorporated into a
sentence; it is separated
from the main part of the
sentence by a comma.

Phew, that
was scary.

Eureka!

Albert Einstein is reputed to have uttered the interjection *Eureka!* on coming up with his special theory of relativity. *Eureka* is a Greek word, meaning "I have found it." Similar moments of revelation may be marked by interjections like *aha!* or *hooray!*—the benefit being that a single-word interjection conveys much more emotion than a simple sentence.

Greetings

Everyday greetings like *hello, hi, goodbye,* and even *yoo-hoo* are interjections, functioning on their own or as part of a sentence. Like other interjections, if a greeting is removed from a sentence, the meaning of that sentence is not affected.

Interruptions and introductions

Many English speakers use the interjections *er* or *um* to fill pauses in their speech, such as when they are unsure of what to say. These are sometimes called hesitation devices. *Yes, no,* and variations of the two are also interjections, as are other introductory expressions such as *indeed* and *well*. These can be used alone in response to a question or statement.

I, er, have no idea what has happened to, um, the snake charmer.

Commas are used on either side of a mild interjection such as a hesitation device if it appears in the middle of a sentence.

Yes, he's been gone for ages. Where is he?

The interjections *yes* and *no* are used at the start of a sentence, followed by a comma, or on their own.

Asides

Interjections are often used in parentheses to indicate an aside or an action. This is particularly useful in a play script, because it indicates the tone of a sentence and gives directions to the actors.

The snake charmer is (cough!) temporarily unavailable.

This aside tells the speaker to pause and cough—in this case, indicating that the speaker doesn't necessarily believe what he or she is saying.

Hello, what are you doing?

This interjection is used to mean "be quiet!"

Shh! I'm concentrating.

Phrases

A PHRASE IS A GROUP OF WORDS THAT MAKE UP PART OF A SENTENCE.

Phrases add information to a sentence, but they only make complete sense as part of a sentence. A phrase does not contain a verb, and it can perform the function of an adjective, an adverb, or a noun.

Adjective phrases

Like adjectives, adjective phrases describe nouns or pronouns. An adjective phrase usually starts with an adverb or a preposition. It can be placed before or after the noun or pronoun it describes.

very red-faced

adverb

This adjective phrase is made up of an adverb followed by an adjective, and it can be used after the noun it describes.

the very red-faced drummer

This adjective phrase can also be placed before the noun it describes.

of the band

preposition

This is an adjective phrase because it is giving more information about the members, a noun.

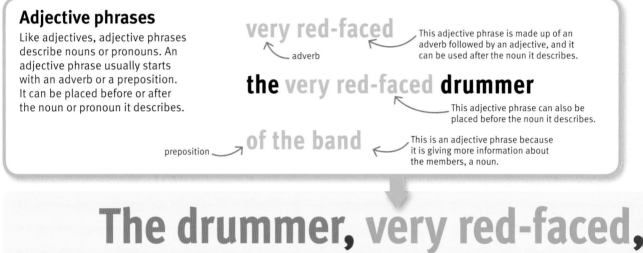

The drummer, very red-faced,
The shocked members of the band

• **Phrases** can be used **instead of one-word adjectives** or **adverbs** to make a piece of writing more **interesting**.

Most **dictionary definitions** are **adjective phrases**.

Noun phrases

A noun phrase is made up of a noun and any words that are modifying that noun, including articles, determiners, and adjectives or adjective phrases. Noun phrases work in exactly the same way as nouns in a sentence.

This is a noun phrase because it is performing the action of the verb—hiding. This noun phrase is the subject of the sentence.

the shocked members of the band

This adjective phrase forms part of the noun phrase.

the drummer

article

This is a simple noun phrase consisting of an article and a noun.

Adverbial phrases

Like adverbs, adverbial phrases describe verbs, adjectives, and other adverbs. They answer questions such as: How? When? Why? Where? How often?

angrily across the stage

This is an adverbial phrase because it is describing how ("angrily") and where ("across the stage") the drummer strode.

behind their instruments

This is an adverbial phrase because it is describing where the members of the band hid.

strode angrily across the stage.
hid behind their instruments.

Prepositional phrases

Prepositional phrases are the most common type of phrase, but they always act as either adjectives or adverbs in a sentence, modifying nouns or verbs. They are therefore contained within—or make up—adjective or adverbial phrases. A prepositional phrase is made up of a preposition, along with the noun or noun phrase that follows it.

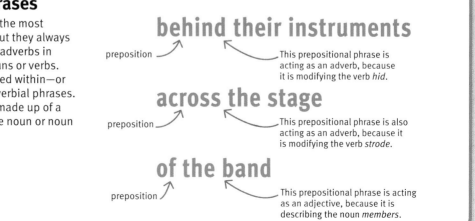

behind their instruments

preposition

This prepositional phrase is acting as an adverb, because it is modifying the verb *hid*.

across the stage

preposition

This prepositional phrase is also acting as an adverb, because it is modifying the verb *strode*.

of the band

preposition

This prepositional phrase is acting as an adjective, because it is describing the noun *members*.

Clauses

A CLAUSE IS THE KEY ELEMENT OF A SENTENCE.

A clause is a group of words that contains a subject and a verb. It can form part of a sentence, or a complete simple sentence. Clauses can be main or subordinate, and they can behave like adjectives or adverbs.

Main clauses

Also known as an independent clause, a main clause includes a subject and a verb and expresses a complete thought. Main clauses are the same as simple sentences, because they have to make sense on their own.

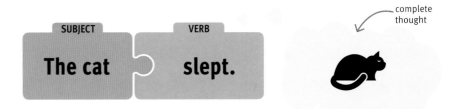

Subordinate clauses

A subordinate clause (also called a dependent clause) contains a subject and a verb, but it does not make sense on its own. It depends on a main clause for its meaning. Subordinate clauses often explain or add more information about where or when things happen, or how they are done. Relative and adverbial clauses are types of subordinate clause.

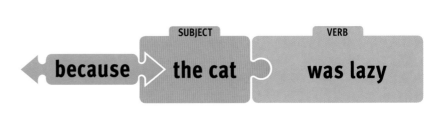

Identifying main and subordinate clauses

Both main and subordinate clauses have a subject and a verb, but only main clauses make sense on their own. The easiest way to identify a subordinate clause is to look for relative pronouns, such as *which* or *that*, or subordinators, such as *because* or *although*.

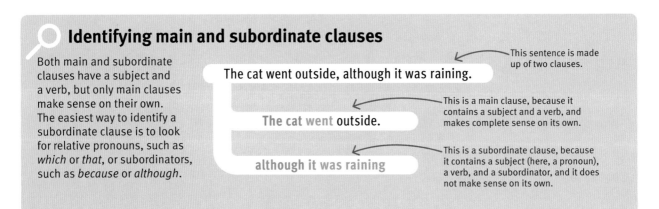

The cat went outside, although it was raining.

This sentence is made up of two clauses.

The cat went outside.

This is a main clause, because it contains a subject and a verb, and makes complete sense on its own.

although it was raining

This is a subordinate clause, because it contains a subject (here, a pronoun), a verb, and a subordinator, and it does not make sense on its own.

Relative clauses

Relative clauses are also known as adjective clauses, and they are a type of subordinate clause. Like adjectives and adjective phrases, relative clauses describe nouns and pronouns. Unlike adjectives, they can only be placed after the noun or pronoun they are modifying. Relative clauses always start with one of the relative pronouns *who*, *whom*, *whose*, *which,* or *that*, which acts as the subject or the object of the clause.

▽ **Subject**
The relative pronoun *which* is the subject of this relative clause, which describes a noun.

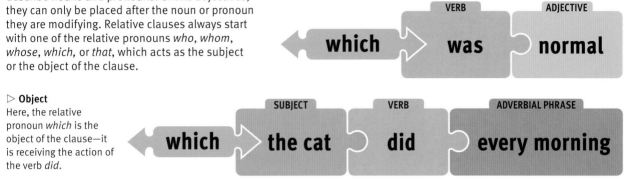

▷ **Object**
Here, the relative pronoun *which* is the object of the clause—it is receiving the action of the verb *did*.

Adverbial clauses

An adverbial clause is a type of subordinate clause that behaves like an adverb. It gives additional information about how, when, where, and why something is happening. Adverbial clauses start with subordinators such as *because*, *although*, *after*, *while*, since, *as,* and *until*.

▷ **Why?**
This adverbial clause explains why the cat did something, but it does not make sense without a main clause.

▷ **When?**
This adverbial clause explains when the cat did something, but it does not make sense without a main clause.

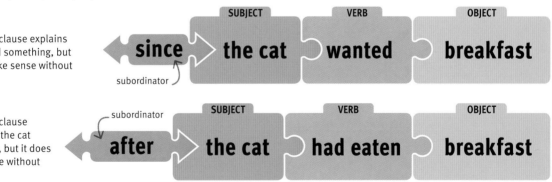

GLOSSARY

Adverbial phrase A group of words that behave in the same way as an adverb and answer questions such as: How? When? Why? Where? How often?

Object The person or thing that is receiving the verb's action.

Relative pronoun A pronoun that links one part of a sentence to another by introducing a relative clause, which describes an earlier noun or pronoun.

Subject The person or thing that is performing the action.

Subordinator A conjunction used to connect words, phrases, and clauses of unequal importance.

• A **main clause** can be turned into a **subordinate clause** by adding a **subordinator**—for example, "**because** the cat slept."

Sentences

THERE ARE MANY DIFFERENT TYPES OF SENTENCES, VARYING IN COMPLEXITY.

A sentence is a unit of written language that contains a subject and a verb and makes complete sense on its own. It must begin with a capital letter and end with a period, exclamation point, or question mark.

Simple sentences

A simple sentence is the same as a main clause. It must have a subject and one main verb, and it must express a single idea. The subject is the person or thing that does the action (the verb), but one subject can be made up of more than one person or thing. Most simple sentences also include an object, which is the person or thing receiving the action.

capital letter

The chef cooked.

A period ends the sentence.

subject verb

Descriptive words and phrases can be added to give more information, but if there is still only one verb, it remains a simple sentence.

The chef and his friends ate the delicious meal.

The subject can represent more than one person or thing.

object

Statements

A statement is a sentence that conveys a fact or piece of information. The subject always comes before the verb. Most simple sentences are statements, and statements end with a period.

The pie had exploded.

This is a statement because it states a fact and ends with a period.

- **Shorter sentences** tend to be **more effective** at getting a message across.
- It's important to **vary the sentence construction** in a piece of writing, so that it does not become monotonous.
- **Simple sentences** can be used to **create tension** in a story.

Questions

A question is a sentence that asks for information and ends with a question mark. Unlike a statement, the subject is placed after the verb. Only auxiliary verbs can change places with their subjects, so a question must include an auxiliary verb like *be*, *do*, or *can*. Many questions also start with question words such as *why*, *when*, *where*, and *how*.

question word   subject   main verb

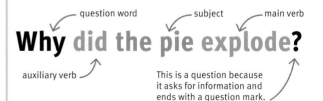

Why did the pie explode?

auxiliary verb

This is a question because it asks for information and ends with a question mark.

Identifying a sentence

A main clause becomes a sentence once it starts with a capital letter and ends with a period, question mark, or exclamation point. All sentences must have a subject and a verb, and make sense without any additional information.

This is not a sentence because it doesn't have a subject, nor does it make sense, and because the question word *what* at the beginning indicates that a question is being asked.

✗ the chef loves cooking

This is not a sentence because it does not begin with a capital letter and end with a period.

✓ The chef loves cooking.

✗ What is.

✓ What is he cooking?

✗ something is burning!

This is not a sentence because it does not start with a capital letter.

✓ Something is burning!

Commands

A command is a sentence that gives an order or an instruction. Instructions are most effective when they are written in simple sentences. The subject in a command is implied, rather than present—it is the person who is receiving the command. Orders usually end with an exclamation point, while instructions tend to end with a period.

This sentence gives an order, so it ends with an exclamation point.

Do not open the oven!

The implied subject is the person who is being told not to open the oven.

Please do not touch the pie.

The implied subject is the person who is being asked not to touch the pie.

This sentence gives a polite instruction, so it ends with a period.

Exclamations

An exclamation works in the same way as a statement, but it expresses a strong emotion, such as surprise or horror. Exclamations always end with an exclamation point.

The pie had exploded!

The use of an exclamation point instead of a period adds emotion to a statement, making it seem more dramatic.

The **shortest complete sentence** in the **English** language is **"I am."**

"Careful you must be..."

When the simple rules of sentence construction are not followed, sentences become very hard to understand. The *Star Wars* character Yoda's speech is a good example. Instead of speaking in sentences that follow the subject–verb–object pattern, Yoda muddles his sentences so that the object comes first, followed by the subject, and then the verb. The result is confusing.

GLOSSARY

Auxiliary verb A "helping" verb like *be* or *have* that joins the main verb in a sentence to the subject.

Main clause A group of words that contains a subject and a verb and makes complete sense on its own.

Object The person or thing that is receiving the action of the verb.

Subject The person or thing that is performing the action of the verb.

Compound sentences

A COMPOUND SENTENCE IS A SENTENCE THAT HAS MORE THAN ONE MAIN CLAUSE.

Compound sentences are made up of two or more main clauses, but no subordinate clauses. The main clauses are linked using conjunctions, and the resulting sentence conveys different ideas of equal importance.

Joining main clauses

Compound sentences are a useful way of connecting two or more ideas of equal importance. They help improve the flow of a piece of writing, as many successive simple sentences can be uncomfortable to read. To form most compound sentences, two main clauses—each containing a subject and a verb—are joined together using a coordinating conjunction like *and*, *but*, or *so*. A comma is used before the coordinating conjunction to separate the two clauses.

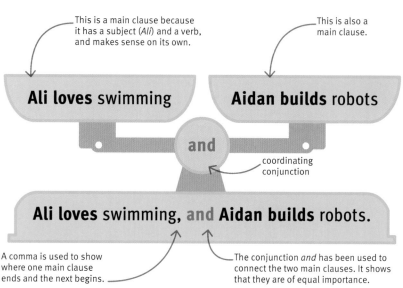

This is a main clause because it has a subject (*Ali*) and a verb, and makes sense on its own.

This is also a main clause.

Ali loves swimming

Aidan builds robots

and

coordinating conjunction

Ali loves swimming, **and Aidan builds** robots.

A comma is used to show where one main clause ends and the next begins.

The conjunction *and* has been used to connect the two main clauses. It shows that they are of equal importance.

Using conjunctions

There are seven main coordinating conjunctions, and these are used in different ways. The conjunction *and* is used to join two things that are alike, or to show that one thing follows the other. *But* is used to contrast one idea with another, while *so* indicates that the second thing occurs as a result of the first. *Yet* is used to mean "nevertheless," *or* and *nor* are used to link alternatives, and *for* is used in compound sentences to mean "because."

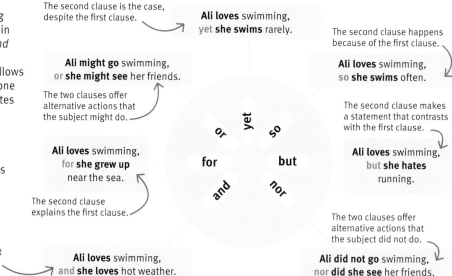

The second clause is the case, despite the first clause.

Ali loves swimming, **yet she swims** rarely.

The second clause happens because of the first clause.

Ali loves swimming, **so she swims** often.

Ali might go swimming, **or she might see** her friends.

The two clauses offer alternative actions that the subject might do.

The second clause makes a statement that contrasts with the first clause.

Ali loves swimming, **but she hates** running.

Ali loves swimming, **for she grew up** near the sea.

The second clause explains the first clause.

or yet so for but and nor

The two clauses give similar information that is of equal importance.

Ali loves swimming, **and she loves** hot weather.

The two clauses offer alternative actions that the subject did not do.

Ali did not go swimming, **nor did she see** her friends.

Joining multiple main clauses

Sometimes three (or more) main clauses are joined together. If the resulting sentence is a list of main clauses containing similar ideas, a comma is used to separate the first two main clauses, and a conjunction is used before the third clause.

A comma is used to separate the first two main clauses in a list of three clauses.

Ali loves swimming, **Aidan builds** robots, **and Sophie enjoys** reading.

A coordinating conjunction is used to join the third main clause to the second main clause.

Using semicolons

Another way to form a compound sentence is to link two main clauses using a semicolon. A semicolon performs the same role as a conjunction, and can therefore be replaced by a conjunction. It shows that two clauses are closely related and equally important.

The two main clauses are giving two different, but closely related, pieces of information about Aidan, so they can be linked using a semicolon.

Aidan builds robots; **he** also **repairs** motorcycles.

The same two clauses can also be linked using a conjunction.

Aidan builds robots, **and he** also **repairs** motorcycles.

Using colons

A colon can also be used to form a compound sentence. Rather than connecting two similar ideas, a colon is used to show that the second main clause is an explanation of the first main clause. Unlike a semicolon, a colon cannot be replaced by a conjunction.

Aidan has an unusual hobby: **He builds** robots.

These two main clauses are linked using a colon, because the second clause is an explanation of the first clause.

GLOSSARY

Coordinating conjunction A word that connects words, phrases, and clauses of equal importance.

Main clause A group of words that contains a subject and a verb and makes complete sense on its own.

Subject The person or thing that is performing the action of the verb.

Subordinate clause A group of words that contains a subject and a verb but depends on a main clause for its meaning.

• **Never use a comma to join two main clauses.** Main clauses can only be connected using a conjunction, a semicolon, or a colon.

• If the two **main clauses** use the **same subject** and are linked using a **conjunction**, the subject can be left out of the second clause. If the sentence is short, no comma is required before the conjunction. For example, "Ali loves swimming **but** hates running."

Complex sentences

A COMPLEX SENTENCE CONTAINS AT LEAST ONE
SUBORDINATE CLAUSE.

Unlike a compound sentence, which contains only main clauses,
a complex sentence is made up of a main clause and one or more
subordinate clauses. The subordinate clause depends on the main
clause for its meaning.

Ranking ideas

Complex sentences are useful because they can be used to
indicate that one idea is more important than another. The
secondary idea is contained in a subordinate clause, which
has a subject and a verb, but does not make sense without
the main clause to which it is attached. Subordinate clauses
add information to main clauses.

main clause

Zoe put on her coat ⤺
because it was cold.

This is a subordinate clause
because it explains why Zoe
put on her coat, but does not
make sense on its own.

Linking subordinate clauses

Subordinate clauses usually start with
a relative pronoun such as *which* or *that*,
a participle such as *dancing* or *shouting*,
or a subordinator such as *because* or
although. Many subordinators, including
where, *when,* and *while*, give a clear
indication of the type of information
they are offering.

MAIN CLAUSE

**Zoe had fun at
the dance class**

SUBORDINATE CLAUSES

where she met a new friend.

which finished late.

while the music played.

although she was tired.

until it was time to go home.

dancing with her friends.

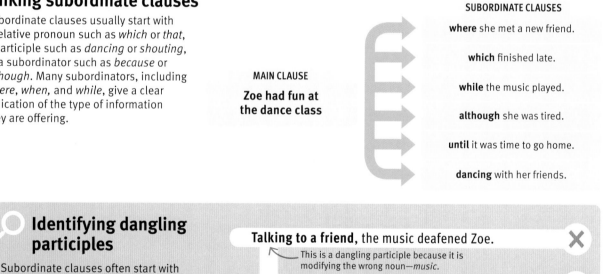

Identifying dangling participles

Subordinate clauses often start with
a participle, which describes the action
being performed by the subject of the
main clause. If a subordinate clause
that starts with a participle is put in
the wrong place in a sentence, it is
described as "dangling," because
it has no subject to hold on to. The
clause should always be placed next
to the subject it describes.

Talking to a friend, the music deafened Zoe. ✗
This is a dangling participle because it is
modifying the wrong noun—*music.*

The music was **talking to a friend.** ✗
Check which noun the subordinate clause is modifying
by moving the noun so that it relates to the clause.

Zoe was **talking to a friend.** ✓
The correct noun is now
being modified.

Talking to a friend, Zoe was deafened by the music. ✓
Rewrite the sentence so that the correct
noun is next to the subordinate clause.

Clause order

Subordinate clauses that start with relative pronouns always follow the noun or pronoun they are describing. If a subordinate clause starts with a subordinator or a participle, however, it can occupy different positions in a sentence.

The subordinate clause is separated from the main clause by a subordinator, so no comma is required.

▷ Ending a sentence
When a subordinate clause is placed at the end of a sentence, no comma is required to separate the clauses unless the sentence is long and would otherwise be confusing.

Rob hid in a corner **because he hated dancing.**

This subordinate clause is at the beginning of the sentence, so a comma is required to separate the two clauses.

▷ Starting a sentence
If the subordinate clause is placed at the start of a sentence, however, it must be separated from the main clause that follows by a comma.

Until the class was over, Rob hid in a corner.

This subordinate clause has split the main clause into two parts, so commas are required to show which parts belong to which clauses.

▷ Sitting in the middle
Similarly, if a subordinate clause breaks up a main clause, a comma is required at the start and end of the clause to separate it from the main clause.

Rob, **feeling bored,** hid in a corner.

Multiple subordinate clauses

As long as a complex sentence contains at least one main clause, more than one subordinate clause can be used. The easiest way to construct a complex sentence is to start with a main clause and then add the subordinate clauses, one at a time.

Tim missed the class.

main clause

A subordinate clause has been added to make this a complex sentence.

Although he loved dancing, Tim missed the class.

main clause

subordinate clause

main clause

Although he loved dancing, Tim missed the class, **which was full.**

A second subordinate clause has been added.

GLOSSARY

Main clause A group of words that contains a subject and a verb and makes complete sense on its own.

Relative pronoun A pronoun that links one part of a sentence to another by introducing a relative clause, which describes an earlier noun or pronoun.

Subject The person or thing that is performing the action of the verb.

Subordinate clause A group of words that contains a subject and a verb but depends on a main clause for its meaning.

Subordinator A conjunction used to connect words, phrases, and clauses of unequal importance.

Using clauses correctly

CLAUSES MUST BE PUT IN A CERTAIN ORDER FOR A SENTENCE
CONTAINING SEVERAL CLAUSES TO MAKE SENSE.

A main clause must make complete sense on its own, while
a subordinate clause only makes sense when it is connected
to a main clause. When clauses are put in the wrong place
in a sentence, the meaning of that sentence changes.

Breaking sentences down

Certain rules must be followed for a complex
sentence to make sense. If a sentence is
broken down into its component parts, it has
to be clear which clause refers to which
subject. Each clause must have its own
subject and verb, and a main clause must
express a complete thought.

This is a main clause because
it makes sense on its own.

This subordinate clause explains
why Lauren (the subject of the
sentence) was upset.

Lauren was upset **because she had lost her swimsuit,** which was new.

This subordinate clause is placed at
the end of the sentence because it
describes the swimsuit, not Lauren.

Identifying a misplaced clause

If a clause describes someone or something, it needs to be placed as
close as possible to the person or thing it describes. Sometimes a
phrase or another clause gets in the way, and the whole meaning of
a sentence changes as a result. When this happens, the sentence
should be reworded so that the potentially confusing clause is
placed next to the person or thing that it describes.

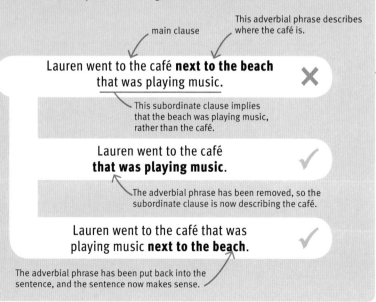

main clause

This adverbial phrase describes
where the café is.

Lauren went to the café **next to the beach**
that was playing music. ✕

This subordinate clause implies
that the beach was playing music,
rather than the café.

Lauren went to the café
that was playing music. ✓

The adverbial phrase has been removed, so the
subordinate clause is now describing the café.

Lauren went to the café that was
playing music **next to the beach.** ✓

The adverbial phrase has been put back into the
sentence, and the sentence now makes sense.

GLOSSARY

Adverbial phrase A group of words
such as "in July of last year" that
perform the same role as an adverb and
answer questions such as: How? When?
Why? Where? How often?

Main clause A group of words that
contains a subject and a verb and
makes complete sense on its own.

Subject The person or thing that is
performing the action of the verb.

Subordinate clause A group of words
that contains a subject and a verb
but depends on a main clause for
its meaning.

Split subject and verb

Some subordinate clauses can be placed in the middle of a sentence, separating the different parts of a main clause. If the subject of a sentence is too far away from its verb, the meaning of that sentence will be difficult to follow, so long subordinate clauses are best placed at the beginning or end of a sentence.

▷ **Separated**
This sentence is hard to follow, because the verb, *felt*, is separated from its subject, *Lauren*, by a long subordinate clause.

Lauren, after walking to the café, buying two scoops of ice cream, and eating them hungrily, **felt ill.**

▷ **Reunited**
The sentence has been reorganized so that the subject of the main clause, *Lauren*, is now next to its verb.

After walking to the café, buying two scoops of ice cream, and eating them hungrily, **Lauren felt ill.**

Avoiding sentence fragments

Sentence fragments are parts of sentences that do not contain all the pieces needed to make a complete sentence. In the context of a conversation, sentence fragments can be meaningful. Once the context has been removed, however, sentence fragments make no sense at all, so they are rarely used in writing.

▽ **Recognizing fragments**
Many sentence fragments do not contain a subject or a verb, and they only make sense in context: for example, as the answer to a question.

What would you like?

Vanilla-and-fudge ice cream.

sentence fragment

▽ **Making sentences**
If a sentence fragment has been removed from its context, the subject and verb need to be reinstated. A written sentence should never have to rely on the sentences around it for its sense.

subject

I would like vanilla-and-fudge ice cream.

verb

Managing modifiers

A MODIFIER IS A WORD, PHRASE, OR CLAUSE THAT
DESCRIBES ANOTHER WORD, PHRASE, OR CLAUSE.

Used correctly, modifiers make sentences more descriptive and
therefore more interesting. If a modifier is put in the wrong place in
a sentence, however, it can alter the whole meaning of that sentence.

SEE ALSO
❮ **26–27** Adjectives
❮ **40–41** Adverbs
❮ **46–47** Participles
❮ **64–65** Phrases
❮ **66–67** Clauses
❮ **74–75** Using clauses correctly

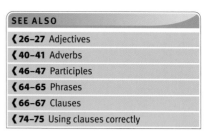

Misplaced adverbs

Common one-word modifiers include the adverbs
only, *almost*, *just,* and *nearly*. These adverb modifiers
are usually placed right before the word they modify.
If a modifier is in the wrong place, the intended
meaning may not be clear, and the modifier may
end up modifying the wrong person or thing.

This means that I spoke to Maria very
recently, and asked her to lunch.

I just asked Maria to lunch.

I asked just Maria to lunch.

This means that I asked Maria
to lunch, and no one else.

This means that I was
tempted to eat a whole pie,
but I didn't eat any of it.

I almost ate a whole pie.

This means that I ate the
pie, and ate most of it.

I ate almost a whole pie.

The comedian Groucho Marx
humorously used a **misplaced
modifier**: "One morning I shot an
elephant **in my pajamas**. How he got
into my pajamas I'll never know."

Misplaced adjectives

Like adverb modifiers, adjective modifiers should be
placed as close as possible to the person or thing they
describe. Misplaced adjectives tend to occur when
a noun is described by several words.

This adjective is describing a
silver woman, not a silver bracelet.

Jim found a silver woman's bracelet.

Jim found a woman's silver bracelet.

The adjective is now describing a silver
bracelet that belongs to a woman.

GLOSSARY

Dangling participle When a modifying phrase or clause
that starts with a participle is put in the wrong place in
a sentence, it is described as "dangling," because it has
no subject to hold on to.

Main clause A group of words that contains a subject and
a verb and makes complete sense on its own.

Misplaced modifier A modifier that has been placed so
far from the person or thing it is intended to modify that
it appears to modify a different person or thing.

Participle The form of a verb that ends in -ing (present
participle) or -ed or -en (past participle).

Subject The person or thing that is performing the
action of the verb.

Subordinate clause A group of words that contains a subject
and a verb but depends on a main clause for its meaning.

Misplaced prepositional phrases

Prepositional phrases often end up in the wrong place. If a modifier is a phrase, it should still be placed next to the person or thing it is modifying. If a prepositional phrase is placed elsewhere in a sentence, it may not convey the intended message.

Laura went for a walk with the dog **in her new boots**.

This prepositional phrase is modifying the dog, so the dog is wearing the new boots.

Laura went for a walk **in her new boots** with the dog.

This prepositional phrase is now modifying the main clause, "Laura went for a walk," so it is Laura who is wearing the boots.

- When writing, always **reread** a finished piece of text before showing it to anyone. As the writer, it's **easy to overlook** potentially **amusing** or **misleading word order**.
- A good way to check for **misplaced modifiers** in a sentence is to **single out** any **modifying words** or phrases by **underlining** or **highlighting** them. It is then easier to see which modifiers relate to which nouns, and **move** any that are in the **wrong place**.

Identifying squinting modifiers

If a modifier is placed between two phrases or clauses, it can be difficult to figure out which phrase or clause it relates to. This type of modifier is often referred to as a squinting modifier, because it looks in two different directions at the same time. The only way to resolve this ambiguity is to move the modifier so that there can be no confusion.

This adverb could be modifying the verb *swim*, in which case the sentence is saying that the people who often swim are the ones who will get stronger.

People who swim **often** will get stronger. ✗

Alternatively, *often* could be modifying the phrase "will get stronger," in which case the sentence is saying that people in general will often get stronger if they swim.

People who **often** swim will get stronger. ✓

The modifying adverb has been moved so that there is no ambiguity, and the people who often swim are the ones who will get stronger.

People who swim will **often** get stronger. ✓

The modifying adverb has been moved to avoid confusion, and the sentence is saying that people in general will often get stronger if they swim.

Dangling participles

Subordinate clauses that start with a participle often cause confusion. This type of clause must be next to its subject, which should also be the subject of the sentence. If the clause is put in the wrong place, it will modify the wrong thing; similarly, if the intended subject is left out of a sentence, that sentence will not make sense. When these errors occur, they are known as dangling participles.

Driving past, the camel was asleep.

In this sentence, the sleeping camel is doing the driving. The intended subject (the person who was driving) has been left out of the sentence.

Driving past, he saw a sleeping camel.

The sentence has been reworded so that the participle *driving* now modifies a subject, *he*, which is also the subject of the sentence.

Commonly misused words

SOME GRAMMATICAL ERRORS OCCUR FREQUENTLY.

It's common to make grammatical mistakes when speaking, but when these mistakes are transferred to writing, the meaning of a sentence is often affected. Most of these problems result from confusion between two words.

That or *which*?

Use *that* for restrictive relative clauses, which introduce essential information, and *which* for nonrestrictive relative clauses, which introduce additional, nonessential information.

The cats **that are black** are sleeping.

The cats, **which are black**, are sleeping.

May or *might*?

The auxiliary verb *may* implies a possibility that something will happen, while *might* indicates a real uncertainty. If something is unlikely to happen, use *might*.

I **may** go for a swim later.

You **might** encounter a shark.

Can or *may*?

Can refers to a person's ability to do something, whereas *may* is used to ask permission. These auxiliary verbs are not interchangeable.

Can you cook?

May I come?

I or *me*?

The simplest way to know which pronoun to use is to remove the other person from the sentence. It should then become obvious. Always remember to put the other person or people first.

Isabella, Rosie, and I went to a café.

"I went to a café" makes sense, so this is correct.

Rosie bought coffee for Isabella and **me**.

"Rosie bought coffee for me" makes sense, so this is correct.

Who or *whom*?

Think of *who* as representing *he* or *she*, and *whom* as representing *him* or *her*. If in doubt, rephrase the sentence and substitute *he/she* or *him/her*.

Finn, **who** loved snow, went outside.

The substituted clause would be "he loved snow."

Finn found Greg, **whom** Finn had telephoned earlier.

The substituted clause would be "Finn had telephoned him."

Whether or *if*?

Whether does not mean the same thing as *if*. *Whether* is used in sentences where there are two or more alternatives, while *if* can only be used when there are no alternatives.

She couldn't decide **whether** to run **or** hide.

She doesn't know **if** anything will happen.

Its or *it's*?

Use the possessive determiner *its* when describing a thing that belongs to something, and the contraction *it's* to represent *it is*.

It's back! **its** back

Could have or *could of*?

In speech, the contracted form of *could have*, *could've*, is often mistakenly interpreted as *could of*. *Could of* is wrong and should never be used.

You **could have** told me!

Fewer or *less*?

Fewer is used for things that can be counted, while *less* is used for hypothetical quantities—things that cannot be counted.

I got **fewer** than ten birthday presents this year.

I have **less** work to do than he has.

Bring or *take*?

If an object is being moved toward the subject, the verb *bring* should be used. If it is being moved away, the verb *take* should be used.

Should I **bring** a book to read?

You can **take** one of my books.

Good or *well*?

Good is an adjective, so it is used to describe nouns. *Well* is mostly used as an adverb to describe verbs, adjectives, or other adverbs. However, it can also be used as an adjective to mean "healthy." *Good* does not mean "healthy," so it shouldn't be used in that sense.

A **good** chef eats **well**, so stays **well**.

This adjective is describing the noun *chef*.

This adverb is describing the verb *eats*.

This adjective means "healthy."

Literally

Literally means "actually" or "in a real sense." It should only be used to describe things exactly as they happened. Anything else is figurative, not literal.

I **literally** erupted with laughter!

Negatives

A NEGATIVE TURNS A POSITIVE STATEMENT INTO A NEGATIVE ONE.

In order to show that something is incorrect or untrue in English, a positive statement has to be turned into a negative one—usually by adding the word *not* after an auxiliary verb. Double negatives should be avoided.

REAL WORLD

Satisfied?

When British rock band the Rolling Stones sang "I can't get no satisfaction" in 1965, they canceled the negative *can't* out with the negative *no*. But despite the double negative, the meaning was clear, and listeners worldwide understood the band to be thoroughly dissatisfied.

Forming negative sentences

Auxiliary verbs are the only verbs that can be made negative. If a sentence does not contain an auxiliary verb, one must be added. The negative word *not* is then placed directly after the auxiliary verb. The resulting combination is known as a negative auxiliary.

AUXILIARY VERB	NEGATIVE WORD	MAIN VERB
had is will	not	been going go

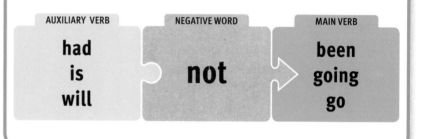

Frank had not been to a German believe he wouldn't try a curried

Contractions

In negative sentences, the auxiliary verb and the negative word *not* can be combined and shortened to form contractions, with an apostrophe to represent the missing letter or letters. Common negative contractions include *haven't* (have not) and *can't* (cannot).

Auxiliary verb	Negative word	Contraction
would	not	wouldn't
do	not	don't
should	not	shouldn't
could	not	couldn't
will	not	won't

Most negative contractions are formed by joining the two words and removing the *o* from *not*.

There are some exceptions: Here, the *i* from *will* has also been changed to *o*.

Identifying a double negative

A double negative is when two negative words appear in a single clause. Although the two negative words are usually intended to convey a single negative thought—and this usage is understood in colloquial English—in reality, one negative plus another negative equals a positive. If a clause includes two negative words, one of them should be removed.

There is now only one negative in the sentence, so it conveys its intended meaning.

There are two negatives in this sentence, so the resulting meaning is that Frank did want more food.

Frank **didn't** want **no** more food. ✘

didn't   no

✓ Frank **didn't** want more food.   Frank **wanted no** more food. ✓

The past tense auxiliary verb form *did* has been removed, so the verb *want* has to be put in the past tense.

There is now only one negative in the sentence, so it conveys its intended meaning.

• *Not* is the most common negative word, but other words can be used in the same way. These range from *never* and *no*, the most forceful, to *seldom*, *barely*, and *hardly*, which reflect smaller degrees of negativity.

Negative pronouns

Some indefinite pronouns are already in a negative form, and therefore don't need to be made negative using *not*. These include *nobody*, *no one*, *nothing*, and *none*.

There is no need to add the word *not* after this auxiliary verb, because *nobody* is a negative word.

Nobody could believe he wouldn't try a curried sausage.

Nobody is a singular pronoun, so the verb must be singular.

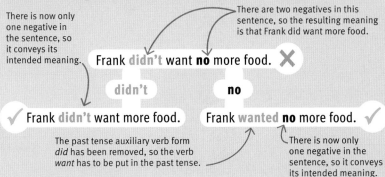
restaurant before. **Nobody could** sausage. He **disliked** spicy food.

Positive thinking

Most statements use fewer words and are more convincing if they are written in a positive way. Even negative words can be used in a positive sentence structure.

This negative word means "did not like," but it can be used in a positive sentence.

He disliked spicy food.

Negative structure	Positive structure
did not like	disliked
was not honest	was dishonest
did not pay attention	ignored
could not remember	forgot
did not start on time	started late
is not attractive	is unattractive

Relative clauses

ALSO KNOWN AS ADJECTIVE CLAUSES, RELATIVE CLAUSES MODIFY NOUNS.

Relative clauses add information to a sentence using the relative pronouns *who*, *whom*, *whose*, *that,* and *which*. Restrictive relative clauses add essential details, while nonrestrictive clauses add nonessential details.

• Make sure that the **relative clause** is **next** to the **noun** or **pronoun** that it is **modifying**. Otherwise, it may end up modifying the wrong person or thing.

• Sometimes a relative clause can be used to **modify** the **rest of the sentence**, rather than a single noun or pronoun. In the following sentence, the relative clause is describing the whole first part of the sentence: "Joe did not look sorry, **which was normal."**

Nonrestrictive relative clauses

There are two types of relative clauses: nonrestrictive and restrictive. Also known as "nondefining" or "nonessential" clauses, nonrestrictive relative clauses offer additional information about a noun. They are separated from the rest of a sentence by commas, because the information they provide is supplementary, rather than essential.

Nonrestrictive clauses require commas.

The principal, who hated chaos, felt calm.

This nonrestrictive relative clause gives more detail about the principal, but it can be removed without affecting the meaning of the sentence.

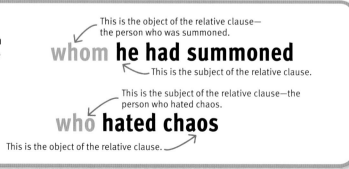

**The principal, who hated chaos, felt
Joe, whom he had summoned. Joe**

Relative pronouns

Relative clauses always follow the noun or pronoun that they modify. They start with one of five relative pronouns, which act as either the subject or the object of the relative clause. *Who* always acts as the subject, while *whom* always acts as the object. The relative pronouns *who*, *whom,* and *whose* are used to refer to people, while *which* and *that* are used to refer to things.

This is the object of the relative clause—the person who was summoned.

whom he had summoned

This is the subject of the relative clause.

This is the subject of the relative clause—the person who hated chaos.

who hated chaos

This is the object of the relative clause.

Identifying when a pronoun can be omitted

Sometimes a relative pronoun can be omitted from a relative clause without affecting the sense of a sentence. This only works if the pronoun is the object of the clause—the person or thing receiving the action.

restrictive relative clause

Joe had to clean up the mess that **the toad had made**. ✓

This is the object of the relative clause, so it can be omitted without changing the meaning of the sentence.

that the toad had made

subject

Joe had to clean up the mess **the toad had made**. ✓

The sentence makes sense without the relative pronoun and object *that*.

• Although *whom* is grammatically correct, *who* is almost always used instead in **everyday** English.

GLOSSARY

Clause A grammatical unit that contains a subject and a verb. Sentences are made up of one or more clauses.

Object The person or thing that is receiving the action of the verb.

Relative pronoun A pronoun that links one part of a sentence to another by introducing a relative clause, which describes an earlier noun or pronoun.

Subject The person or thing that is performing the action of the verb.

Which or *that*?

Historically *which* and *that* were interchangeable, and could be used for either type of relative clause. It is now usual practice to use *that* for restrictive clauses (see below) and *which* for nonrestrictive clauses. This helps to differentiate one type of information from the other.

The principal felt calm, which **was unusual.**

This is a nonrestrictive relative clause, because it gives extra—but not essential—information about the principal.

Joe held the toad that **had escaped.**

This is a restrictive relative clause, because it helps to identify which toad is being described.

calm, which **was unusual. He eyed**
held the toad that **had escaped.**

Restrictive relative clauses

Restrictive relative clauses are sometimes called "defining" or "essential" clauses, because they identify who or what is being referred to and are therefore vital to the meaning of a sentence. Restrictive clauses are not separated from the rest of a sentence by commas.

Joe held the toad
that **had escaped.**

This relative pronoun is acting as the subject of the relative clause— the thing that did the escaping.

This is a restrictive relative clause—it identifies which toad had escaped.

Idioms, analogies, and figures of speech

CERTAIN DEVICES ARE USED TO MAKE SPEECH AND WRITING MORE INTERESTING AND PERSUASIVE.

Figures of speech are used to create different effects, usually to emphasize a point or help an audience visualize something. Idioms would be meaningless if they were not familiar expressions, while analogies are a useful tool for explaining things.

SEE ALSO	
Writing to describe	**208–209)**
Writing from personal experience	**210–211)**
Writing a narrative	**212–213)**

The word *metaphor* comes from the **Greek** word *metapherin*, which means **"transfer."**

Idioms

An idiom is a word or phrase that means something completely different from the word or words it is made up of. The meanings of idioms have little or no relation to the literal meanings of their component parts, but they make sense because they are familiar expressions. Different regions have different idioms.

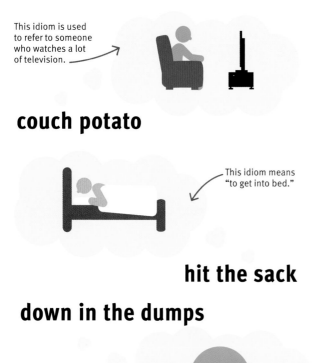

This idiom is used to refer to someone who watches a lot of television.

couch potato

This idiom means "to get into bed."

hit the sack

down in the dumps

This idiom is used to refer to someone who is feeling miserable.

Analogies

Analogies are used to explain what something is by likening that thing to another thing and identifying similarities. An analogy is not a figure of speech, but it works like an extended metaphor or simile: It compares an unfamiliar thing to a familiar thing, and then lists the shared characteristics. Baking a cake, for instance, can be used as an analogy for writing. Both require careful planning and specific ingredients, and are designed to suit a particular audience.

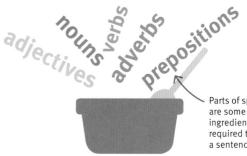

adjectives nouns verbs adverbs prepositions

Parts of speech are some of the ingredients required to create a sentence.

REAL WORLD

Avoiding clichés

Clichés are expressions or ideas that have been overused to the point where they have almost lost their original meanings and serve only to annoy the reader. Clichés such as "best-kept secret," "expect the unexpected," and "the best just got better" are common in slogans and advertisements, but it is always more effective to write something original.

WELCOME TO ALGIERS FOUNDED 1719 leans' Best Kept Secret

Figures of speech

Figures of speech are useful language tools that allow a writer or speaker to persuade, emphasize, impress, or create a mental image. Words and phrases are used out of their literal contexts to create different, heightened effects. When a person claims to be "starving," for example, that person is unlikely to be dying of hunger; rather, he or she is simply very hungry.

• Try to **invent new, interesting metaphors** when writing rather than copying existing ones.

Alliteration
The same letter or sound is used at the start of multiple words for effect.

Catherine **c**arefully **c**ombined **c**old **c**offee **c**ake and **k**iwi fruit.

Simile
The words *like* or *as* are used to compare two things.

She is **as** plump **as** a peach, but she moves **like** a ballerina.

Metaphor
One thing is described as being a different thing, resulting in a comparison between the two.

Her cheeks **are** sun-blushed apples.

Euphemism
A mild word or phrase is substituted for a word or phrase that might cause offense.

She has **ample** proportions (she is overweight).

Pun
Also known as word play, the multiple meanings of a word are used to create humor.

She gave me her measurements as **a round figure**.

Hyperbole
A statement is grossly exaggerated.

She said she could **eat a rhinoceros**.

Personification
An object or animal is given human qualities.

The food **called** to her.

Oxymoron
Two terms are used together that contradict each other.

The pie looked **terribly tasty**.

Onomatopoeia
A word is used that mimics the sound of what it stands for.

She **burped** noisily.

Anaphora
A word or phrase is repeated at the start of successive clauses for emphasis.

She ate the pie; **she ate** the cake; **she ate** the kiwi fruit.

Irony
One thing is said but the opposite thing is meant, usually for humor or emphasis.

I admired her **charming** table manners (her manners were poor).

Understatement
Something is made out to be smaller or less important than it really is.

She said she had enjoyed her **light lunch**.

Colloquialisms and slang

COLLOQUIALISMS AND SLANG ARE FORMS OF INFORMAL SPOKEN LANGUAGE.

Colloquialisms are words or phrases that are used in ordinary, informal speech. Slang is even less formal, and is often only recognized by the members of a particular group. Slang includes words or phrases that may be considered taboo.

Colloquialisms

English speakers use a variety of informal words and phrases that differ from region to region but are recognized by most native speakers. These words and phrases are called colloquialisms, which stems from the Latin word for "conversation."

Colloquialisms are an important part of relaxed conversation (known as colloquial speech), but they should not be used in formal speech or writing. Most colloquialisms are labeled in dictionaries as "informal" or with the abbreviation "colloq."

Some slang terms are used so often that they become **universal**—the slang word **cool**, meaning **"fashionable"** or **"great,"** is one example.

fella
dude   fellow
chap guy
geezer
gent
buddy
man

scratch
loot   dough
greenbacks
bread
moola bones
money

Rhyming slang

Rhyming slang, also known as Cockney rhyming slang, originated in the East End of London in the nineteenth century. It is formed by replacing a common word with a phrase that rhymes with it. Often, the rhyming part of this phrase is then removed, so the resulting slang term bears little or no resemblance to the original common word. The word *phone*, for example, is translated into rhyming slang as the phrase "dog and bone," which is then shortened to "dog."

Shortened forms

Some words have both a formal meaning and a colloquial meaning. The word *kid*, for example, can refer to a baby goat or, informally, to a child. Colloquialisms are often shorter and easier to say than the word or words they represent. Common colloquialisms therefore include shortened forms of longer words and words that have been combined. They also include abbreviations, such as *ROFL* ("rolling on the floor laughing"), which are used in text messages and e-mail chats in place of longer expressions.

Shortened form	Formal term
'cos	because
ain't	is not
gonna	going to
wanna	want to
BRB	be right back
BTW	by the way
DND	do not disturb
LOL	laugh out loud
TTYL	talk to you later

Slang

Slang is only used in informal speech or, sometimes, in works of fiction. It is used in place of conventional words for things that are familiar, but possibly uncomfortable, to the speaker, and includes words that are considered taboo in most contexts. Slang words are labeled as "slang" in dictionaries. Different slang words are adopted by different groups of speakers—especially teenagers. They vary across small geographic areas and change frequently over time.

Sick! That was hardcore.

?

Slang term	Meaning
awesome	incredible, very good
bummed	depressed
chick	girl, woman
chillin'	being calm and relaxed
epic fail	a failure of huge proportions
wack	inferior
gross	repulsive
hardcore	intense
hater	an angry or jealous person
hissy fit	tantrum
hot	attractive
lame	unfashionable, of poor quality
my bad	it was my mistake
noob	someone unfashionable, a newcomer
sick	very good
sweet	excellent, very good
tool	someone stupid

Changing meanings

New slang words are invented all the time, and existing slang words often change their meanings from one generation to the next. For example, the slang term *busted* used to refer to something that was broken. The term then evolved to describe what happened when someone was caught doing something wrong. In modern slang, *busted* is sometimes used to refer to an unattractive person. Existing slang words are also often combined to form new ones.

chillin' + relaxin' ▸ **chillaxin'**

This means "taking a break."

friend + enemy ▸ **frenemy**

This is used to describe someone who is a friend, but who also acts in a hostile way.

Jargon

Jargon is a type of slang. It is the name for the technical vocabulary that is used by a particular profession. Jargon is usually unintelligible to those outside the profession, but enables those within it to refer to things concisely and without explanation.

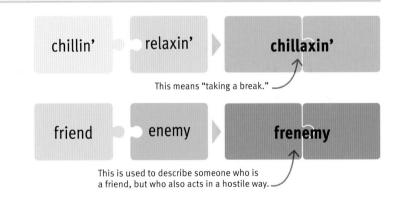

assistance from other officers

suspect vehicle

Call for **backup**! We have an **S/V** and the **perp** is **on the run**.

perpetrator (the person who has committed a crime)

trying to avoid being captured

Direct and indirect speech

THERE ARE TWO WAYS OF REPRESENTING SPEECH IN WRITING.

When a person's exact words are reproduced in writing within quotation marks, this is known as direct speech. When a person's speech is reported, using neither the exact words nor quotation marks, it is called indirect or reported speech.

Direct speech

Direct speech is always contained within quotation marks, indicating words that are spoken aloud by someone. Direct speech is usually written in the present tense (as it is spoken), and is accompanied by a simple clause in the past tense that tells the reader who is speaking.

What are your symptoms?

"What are your symptoms?" the doctor asked.

This direct speech gives the exact words of the doctor, so it is contained within quotation marks.

A comma is usually used to separate direct speech from its accompanying clause, but a question mark or exclamation point can be used instead.

This simple clause explains who is speaking.

Indirect speech

Indirect speech is also known as reported speech, because it is an account—or report—of what someone has said. Indirect speech does not require quotation marks. It is usually written in the past tense, because it is describing what someone has said. The present tense is occasionally used when reporting something that has always been—and remains—the case.

- **Be careful** when **converting speech** from direct to indirect. It must be clear from the **context** of the sentence or the **word order** which **pronoun** refers to which **person**.

- When writing **dialogue**, a **new line** should be started for **each new speaker**.

▷ **Reporting back**
These are not Peter's exact words, but they recount what he said, so this is an example of indirect speech.

Peter explained that **his** thumb kept twitching.

The third person is used because Peter is not the narrator.

▷ **Stating facts**
This indirect speech is reporting an unchanging fact, so the present tense is used.

He told the doctor that **he spends** all his time playing video games.

This means that he always has, does, and will spend his time playing video games.

Identifying characters

Alternating between different forms of speech makes a narrative more interesting to read. When converting direct speech (first person) to indirect speech (third person), it's important to take into account who is speaking, and to whom, and to change the relevant nouns and pronouns to match.

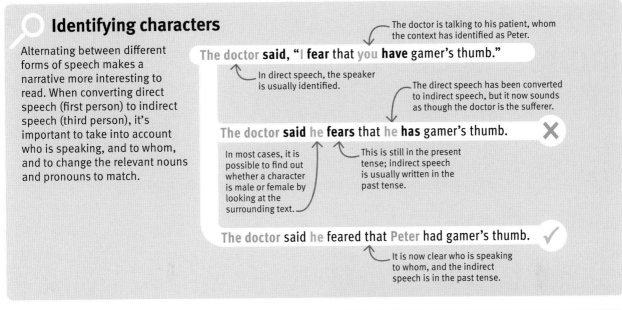

The doctor is talking to his patient, whom the context has identified as Peter.

The doctor said, "I fear that you have gamer's thumb."

In direct speech, the speaker is usually identified.

The direct speech has been converted to indirect speech, but it now sounds as though the doctor is the sufferer.

The doctor said he fears that he has gamer's thumb. ✗

In most cases, it is possible to find out whether a character is male or female by looking at the surrounding text.

This is still in the present tense; indirect speech is usually written in the past tense.

The doctor said he feared that Peter had gamer's thumb. ✓

It is now clear who is speaking to whom, and the indirect speech is in the past tense.

Time and space

If direct speech is being recounted (turned into indirect speech) in a different place and at a different time from where and when it happened, the adverbs and adverb phrases used must match the new situation. For example, the direct speech "Go to the hospital today!" would be recounted a week later in the following way: He was told to go to the hospital that day.

Direct speech	Indirect speech
now	then
here	there
this (morning)	that (morning)
next (week)	the following (week)
today	that day
tomorrow	the next day/the following day
yesterday	the previous day/the day before

Varying verbs

The most common verbs used to report speech are *said*, *told*, and *asked*. Indirect speech can be made more interesting if the writer uses a variety of reporting verbs. The verbs used in the simple clauses that indicate who said what in direct speech can be varied in the same way.

• **Indirect speech** often uses the words *said*, *asked*, or *told*, but don't **confuse** it with **direct speech**, which is always in **quotation marks**.

▷ **Descriptive direct speech**
The verb *sobbed* encourages the reader to sympathize with Peter. *Said* would not have this effect.

"I feel like a freak!" sobbed Peter.

▷ **Interesting indirect speech**
Use unusual verbs such as *promised* and *begged* to add emotion to indirect speech.

The doctor promised that Peter's symptoms were curable. Peter begged him to help.

Punctuation

What is punctuation?

PUNCTUATION REFERS TO THE MARKS USED IN WRITING THAT HELP READERS UNDERSTAND WHAT THEY ARE READING.

Sometimes words alone are not enough to convey a writer's message clearly. They need a little help from punctuation marks to illustrate relationships between words, pauses, or even emotions.

Several of the main **punctuation marks** also have **uses** in **mathematical** notation.

Punctuation marks

There are twelve commonly used punctuation marks. Using punctuation marks correctly and carefully makes it possible for a writer to convey his or her message clearly. Punctuation can also enable the writer to control whether text is read quickly or slowly.

Period

This marks the end of a sentence.

EXAMPLE
The dog slept.

Ellipsis

This represents an unfinished sentence or omitted text.

EXAMPLE
Everything seemed calm, but then...

Comma

This joins or separates elements in a sentence.

EXAMPLE
Hearing a cat, he jumped up.

Semicolon

This joins two main clauses or separates items in a list.

EXAMPLE
He ran after the cat; it ran up a tree.

Colon

This introduces text in a sentence.

EXAMPLE
He was interested in one thing: chasing the cat.

Apostrophe

This marks the possessive or omitted text.

EXAMPLE
The dog's owner couldn't see the cat.

Why we need punctuation

Some people might argue that writing would be simpler without punctuation. However, writers have something to say and want readers to understand exactly what they mean. Punctuation makes this possible.

	What punctuation does to writing
yes	This word has no punctuation marks. It is just a sequence of letters that together form a word. The reader can read this word in any way.
Yes.	This is a statement. It has a period (.), which marks the end of the sentence. This tells the reader to read the word calmly, as it states a fact.
Yes?	This is a question. It has a question mark (?) at the end of the sentence. It tells the reader to read the word as a question, with a slightly raised voice.
Yes!	This is an exclamation. It has an exclamation point (!) at the end of the sentence, which tells the reader to read it with emotion.
y-e-s	The letters of the word *yes* are separated here by hyphens (-). These tell the reader to read the individual letters slowly and carefully.

Hyphen

This joins or separates words or parts of words.

EXAMPLE
The single-minded dog barked at the cat.

Quotation marks

These enclose direct speech or quotations.

EXAMPLE
"Come on, Fido," his owner called.

Question mark

This marks the end of a direct question.

EXAMPLE
What are you doing?

Exclamation point

This marks the end of an exclamation.

EXAMPLE
Come here, now!

Parentheses

These surround additional information in a sentence.

EXAMPLE
The dog (tail between his legs) followed his owner.

Dash

This signals extra information in a sentence.

EXAMPLE
The cat—pleased with itself—leaped out of the tree.

Periods and ellipses

A PERIOD ENDS A SENTENCE, WHEREAS AN ELLIPSIS INDICATES THAT A SENTENCE IS UNFINISHED.

A period marks the end of a complete statement. It can also be used to show that a word has been abbreviated. An ellipsis represents text omitted from a sentence.

SEE ALSO
‹ 54–55 Voices and moods
‹ 68–69 Sentences
Exclamation points **112–113 ›**
Capital letters **158–159 ›**
Abbreviations **172–173 ›**

• If an **abbreviation** with a period comes at the end of a sentence, no additional period is needed. For example, "The undersea experiment commenced at 4:00 p.m."

Ending a statement

A period is used at the end of a statement. There is no space before a period, but a space is left after one. It is followed by a capital letter at the start of the next sentence.

The undersea experiment ended.

This period marks the end of the sentence.

The undersea experiment ended. said, "Swim to the surface.

REAL WORLD

Web and e-mail addresses

The period is used today in website and e-mail addresses. In these situations, it is known as a "dot" and functions as a separator between the parts of the address. Unlike in normal writing, the dot is stated when the address is read aloud, so the example here would read "w-w-w-dot-d-k-dot-com."

www.dk.com

Commands

Some commands, including orders and polite requests, end with a period. For commands that express greater emotion, such as anger or surprise, an exclamation point should be used.

Swim to the surface.

This period marks the end of this request.

Get out of the water!

This exclamation point expresses urgency.

• When using **abbreviations**, be consistent and either always use periods, or never use them.

• Most **acronyms**, such as **NASA** or **NATO**, should be written without periods.

In **telegrams**, the word *STOP* was used to mark the **end of a sentence** instead of a period, because it **cost less** than punctuation.

Abbreviations

A period can be used at the ends of certain abbreviations, representing letters that have been omitted. For example, *Dr.* stands for "Doctor." Some abbreviations, such as those for metric measurements and US states, are never spelled with a period.

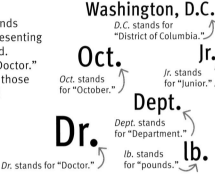

Washington, D.C.
D.C. stands for "District of Columbia."

Oct.
Oct. stands for "October."

Jr.
Jr. stands for "Junior."

Dept.
Dept. stands for "Department."

Dr.
Dr. stands for "Doctor."

lb.
lb. stands for "pounds."

GLOSSARY

Abbreviation A shortened form of a word, often with one or more periods to represent missing letters.

Acronym An abbreviation made up of the initial letters of a series of words and in which the letters are pronounced as they are spelled, rather than as separate letters.

Command A sentence that gives an instruction.

Statement A sentence that conveys a fact or piece of information.

Leading scientist Dr. Fisher Wait, I forgot to tell you..."

Ellipses

Three periods in a row are called an ellipsis. An ellipsis indicates that a sentence has been left unfinished, as when a speaker drifts into silence or is cut off abruptly. Ellipses can also represent omitted text within quotations.

I thought...
This ellipsis means that the speaker suddenly stopped speaking. No period is needed.

Could I...?
A question mark or exclamation point is kept after an ellipsis.

This ellipsis stands for the missing words from the start of the sentence in the quotation. The missing words could be "Today we heard that."

The report said that "...Dr. Fisher...is correct....The island is near..."

This ellipsis indicates missing text. Some style guides suggest placing spaces before and after the ellipsis.

If text is omitted after a complete sentence, the ellipsis is placed after the final punctuation mark.

Commas

COMMAS ARE USED TO SEPARATE ELEMENTS
IN A SENTENCE.

Commas clarify information by separating words, phrases,
or clauses. They are used to organize information into
groups, sorting it so a sentence is understood correctly.

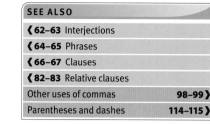

Introductions

Sometimes, a sentence begins with
a clause, phrase, or word that sets
the scene and leads the way to
where the main action begins in
the second half of the sentence.
A comma is placed after the
introduction to make the reader
pause and anticipate the main
information. An introduction to
a sentence could be a word such
as *However*, a phrase such as
Three years ago or a clause such
as *If this happens*.

This is an introductory phrase.

A comma is placed after the
introductory phrase, before the
main information is revealed.

**Once upon a time,
there was a garden.**

The main information
follows the comma.

This is an introductory clause.

**When Lisa visited the
garden, she saw a flower.**

The main
information comes
after the comma.

A comma is placed after
the introductory clause.

Working in pairs

If a sentence is interrupted by an additional phrase that is
not essential to the understanding of the sentence, a comma
is placed on either side of the phrase, like two parentheses.
Without the commas, the information is treated as essential.

Sometimes, the interruption is placed at the beginning
or end of a sentence. In these cases, only one comma
is used, since a comma is never placed at the start or
end of a sentence.

**A flower, like a sock,
can be striped.**

The interruption is placed within a pair of
commas to separate nonessential information.

**A flower like a sock
can be striped.**

Without the commas, the information becomes
part of the main sentence and changes its meaning.

**A flower can be
striped, like a sock.**

A comma is placed
before an interruption
at the end of a sentence.

A comma is placed after
an interruption at the
start of a sentence.

**Like a sock, a flower
can be striped.**

• Often, **quotations** are used without introductions, so no comma is needed. For example: **The guide says that this is "the best garden in France."**

• Don't use a comma if the first part of the quotation ends with an **exclamation point** or a **question mark**. For example: "Stop!" Tom cried. "The bridge is dangerous."

GLOSSARY

Adverb A word that describes the way something happens.

Clause A grammatical unit that contains a subject and a verb.

Conjunction A word used to connect phrases and sentences.

Direct speech Text that represents spoken words.

Interjection A word or phrase that occurs alone and expresses emotion.

Phrase A group of words that does not contain a verb.

Direct speech

In direct speech, a comma should be used between the introduction to the speech and the direct speech itself. The introduction can be at the start, end, or middle of the sentence. When in the middle, use a comma on either side of the introduction, between the first and second parts of the sentence.

A comma is placed before the quotation mark, after the introduction.

Grandma asked, "Can we find more of these flowers?"

A comma is placed before the quotation mark, before an introduction.

A comma is placed before the quotation mark after the introduction.

"The flowers," Lisa said, "are always in bloom in May."

Direct address

Commas are always used when someone is spoken to directly, by name. The placement of the comma depends on where the name appears in a sentence. The commas work in the same way as around an interruption: commas to either side of the name when it appears in the middle of a sentence, a comma after the name when it starts a sentence, and a comma before the name when it comes at the end of a sentence.

• If an **interruption** is taken out of a sentence, the sentence should still make sense.

• Commas with **interjections** such as *stop* or *help* work in the same way as those for direct address.

Let's eat Grandma.

In this example, the comma is missing, so Grandma is about to be eaten.

Let's eat, Grandma.

A comma is placed before the name when it appears at the end of a sentence.

Other uses of commas

COMMAS CAN BE USED TO JOIN MULTIPLE MAIN CLAUSES, REPRESENT OMITTED WORDS, AND SEPARATE ITEMS IN LISTS.

Sentences can be joined using a comma with a conjunction to create the right pace and variety in writing. A comma is also used to avoid repetition and to separate words or phrases in lists.

Commas to join clauses

Commas are used with conjunctions to join two or more main clauses to make a sentence. The comma before the last main clause is followed by one of these conjunctions: *and, or, but, nor, for, yet,* or *so.* If two clauses are short and closely linked, the comma can be omitted.

start of first main clause

A comma separates the first two main clauses in a set of three.

start of second main clause

Walkers turn left, joggers turn right, but cyclists go straight.

start of third main clause

A comma is placed before the conjunction *but.*

start of first main clause

start of second main clause

Sit here and enjoy the view.

No comma is needed before the conjunction because it joins two short, closely related main clauses.

Comma butterfly

A comma is also a type of butterfly with a small, white marking on the underside of each of its wings that resembles the punctuation mark.

• Use a **semicolon** to join two related sentences together without a conjunction.

• A **comma** can be used only with the **conjunctions** *and, or, but, for, nor, yet,* or *so* to **join clauses**.

• **Avoid** using **too many commas**. When a sentence contains a lot of pauses, it is difficult to read.

Commas and omitted words

When avoiding repetition that would make a sentence long and possibly boring, a comma can be used to represent the omitted words.

A comma is placed after the introductory phrase.

In the first month of the year, the flower was orange; in the second, red; and in the third, yellow.

Each of these commas represents the omitted word *month.*

Commas in lists

Commas are used to separate words or phrases in a list. A good way to test if the comma is in the correct position is to replace it with one of the conjunctions *and* or *or*. If the sentence doesn't make sense with *and* or *or*, don't add a comma.

The **comma** is one of the **most misused** punctuation marks.

Each interest is separated by a comma from another interest in the list.

The last word in the list is joined by a comma followed by the word *and*.

My interests are walking, flowers, birds, and gardening.

My interests are walking flowers, birds, and gardening.

Since there is no comma separating *walking* and *flowers*, the interest is *walking flowers*.

The comma before the conjunction is known as a "serial comma" and is useful for preventing ambiguity.

Commas with adjectives

A list of adjectives in front of a noun can be treated in two different ways. If each adjective modifies the noun, add a comma to separate them. However, if an adjective describes a combination of words that come after, no comma is needed. There are two ways to check if a comma should be used.

First, if *and* can be added between the adjectives, a comma should be placed between them. Second, swap the adjectives. If the meaning hasn't changed, it's correct to use a comma to separate the adjectives.

I saw a yellow, flying saucer.

When the comma is placed here, each adjective describes the noun separately: The saucer is flying and yellow.

I saw a blue flying saucer.

With no comma, the adjective *blue* describes the *flying saucer*.

GLOSSARY

Adjective A word that describes a noun.

Conjunction A word used to connect phrases and clauses.

Main clause A group of words that contains a subject and a verb and makes complete sense on its own.

Noun A word that refers to a person, place, or thing.

Verb A word that describes an action.

• The **serial comma**, set after the second-to-last item of the list, is especially useful when there are two instances of ***and*** in a sentence. For example, "The blue, pink, and black-and-white flowers have grown."

Semicolons

SEMICOLONS CONNECT SECTIONS OF TEXT THAT ARE
CLOSELY RELATED.

Semicolons can be used to indicate a close relationship
between main clauses or to separate complex items in
a list. They also precede certain adverbs when they are
used as conjunctions.

- **Never use** a semicolon to **connect a main clause to a subordinate clause**. A comma and a conjunction should be used. For example, "Sam had two red T-shirts, which were new."
- **Use** a semicolon to **connect two main clauses** that are not joined by a conjunction.

Connecting

A semicolon is used to join two main clauses and show
that they are of equal importance and closely related.
These clauses can stand alone as separate sentences,
or they can be connected by a comma and a conjunction.

May was warm; it was pleasant.

This clause is closely related to the
previous main clause because it provides
information as to why May was pleasant.

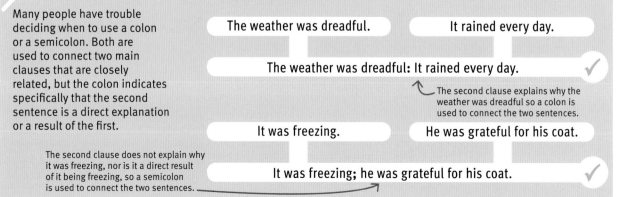

May was warm; it was pleasant.
cities were rainy: London; Paris

🔍 Identifying when to use a semicolon

Many people have trouble
deciding when to use a colon
or a semicolon. Both are
used to connect two main
clauses that are closely
related, but the colon indicates
specifically that the second
sentence is a direct explanation
or a result of the first.

| The weather was dreadful. | It rained every day. |

The weather was dreadful: It rained every day.   ✓

The second clause explains why the
weather was dreadful so a colon is
used to connect the two sentences.

| It was freezing. | He was grateful for his coat. |

The second clause does not explain why
it was freezing, nor is it a direct result
of it being freezing, so a semicolon
is used to connect the two sentences.

It was freezing; he was grateful for his coat.   ✓

Many **writers,** such as James **Joyce,** George **Orwell,** and Kurt **Vonnegut** have **refused** to use semicolons, deeming them pointless.

GLOSSARY

Clause A grammatical unit that contains a subject and a verb. Sentences are made up of one or more clauses.

Main clause A clause that makes complete sense on its own.

Subordinate clause A clause that provides additional information but depends on the main clause for it to make sense.

REAL WORLD

Ben Jonson's *English Grammar*

English dramatist Ben Jonson (1572–1637) is widely credited as the first person to set down rules on how to use semicolons in English. His book *English Grammar*, first published in 1640, systematically examined the period, comma, semicolon, and colon. Before this, there were no accepted standards on how to use these marks.

Before adverbs

A semicolon precedes certain adverbs, such as *however, therefore, consequently,* and *nevertheless,* when they are used as conjunctions to connect clauses.

However is used as a conjunction here, so it is preceded by a semicolon.

June was hot; however, some cities were rainy.

June was hot; however, some Texas; and Boston, England.

Lists

When a sentence includes a list in which some or all of the items already contain commas, semicolons are used to separate the list items. This makes the sentence easier to follow.

Without the semicolons, the reader might mistake *Texas* and *England* for cities.

Some cities were rainy: London; Paris, Texas; and Boston, England.

Commas separate cities from regions.

A region is needed to clarify which *Paris* the text is referring to.

A region is needed to clarify which *Boston* the text is referring to.

Colons

THE COLON SEPARATES PARTS OF A SENTENCE, WHILE ALSO INDICATING A CLOSE RELATIONSHIP BETWEEN THEM.

A colon connects a main clause with another clause, a phrase, or a word. It can be used to provide an explanation or for emphasis, or to introduce a list or quoted material.

SEE ALSO
〈 **70–71** Compound sentences
〈 **96–99** Commas
〈 **100–101** Semicolons
Quotation marks **108–109** 〉
Bullet points **116–117** 〉

Explanations

A colon shows that what follows a main clause is an explanation of it. The section following the colon can be a main clause, or just a word.

This main clause provides an explanation of what her secret is.

They know her secret: She is obsessed with socks.

Emphasis

A colon can be used to emphasize a point in a text, by causing the reader to pause before reading that point.

The single word emphasizes that she's interested in only one thing.

She thinks about one thing: socks.

Lists

A colon is also used to introduce a list. The section preceding the colon should be a complete statement, but the section following the colon can be just a simple list of things.

Her socks have the following patterns: striped, spotted, and paisley.

This is the introduction to the list.

The items in the list follow the colon.

The colon is also used in math for **ratios** or **scales**. For example, **3:1** means a ratio of **three to one**.

GLOSSARY

Clause A grammatical unit that contains a subject and a verb. Sentences are made up of one or more clauses.

Main clause A clause that makes complete sense on its own.

Subordinate clause A clause that provides additional information but depends on the main clause for it to make sense.

Emoticons

In the digital world, punctuation marks, especially the colon, are used to create informal graphic representations of emotions known as "emoticons." The most frequently used marks are the colon, semicolon, and parenthesis, but almost any punctuation mark can be used.

:-)   Basic smile

:-(Sad face

;-)   Winking smile

:-D   Smile with open mouth

:-$ Embarrassed face

:-O   Surprised face

Quotes

A colon is often used to introduce quoted text, especially literary quotations, where the author's exact words are repeated.

Quoted text follows the colon.

She was quoted in the newspaper: "I love socks!"

Titles

A colon is sometimes found in the titles of works of literature, film, art, and music. If the title is followed by a subtitle, a colon separates the two.

main title

The subtitle follows the colon.

Socks: The Sure-footed Life of a Collector

Bible references

When giving a Bible reference, the chapter and verse are separated by a colon.

book of the Bible

A colon separates the chapter and verse.

1 Corinthians 13:12 ← verse

chapter

- A colon never follows a **verb**.
- A **dash** can be used instead of a colon, but a **colon creates a greater pause** and a sense of anticipation for what follows it. Use a dash for emphasis and drama.
- A colon should be followed by **one space**.
- The **first word** following a colon should be **lowercase**, unless it begins a main clause.

Apostrophes

APOSTROPHES SHOW POSSESSION OR OMISSION.

The apostrophe is used to create the possessive form of nouns and represents letters that have been omitted in contractions. It can also be used to create a few unusual plural nouns.

SEE ALSO

❮ **32–33** Determiners
❮ **48–49** Auxiliary verbs
❮ **80–81** Negatives
Other confusing words   **170–171** ❯

Missing letters

An apostrophe represents missing letters in a contraction, which is when a word or words are shortened by omitting letters. There are about 100 common contractions. Only auxiliary verbs such as *be* and *have* can be used in this way.

Original form	Contracted form	Original form	Contracted form
it is	it's	he had; he would	he'd
she is	she's	I will	I'll
who is	who's	you will	you'll
I am	I'm	who will	who'll
you are	you're	is not	isn't
we are	we're	has not	hasn't
they are	they're	cannot	can't
I have	I've	could not	couldn't
we have	we've	will not	won't
would have	would've	did not	didn't

Rafael **wasn't** happy that the his name with two **f's** on

Apostrophe catastrophe

The use of apostrophes in plurals in commercial signs is widespread. This type of mistake is sometimes called a "greengrocer's apostrophe."

Plural forms

Occasionally, apostrophes are used to create plural forms where adding an *s* on its own would cause confusion, as when an abbreviation or a single letter is made plural. There are very few words that are pluralized in this way. Most plurals of regular nouns are formed by adding only an *s*.

with two **f's**

Without the apostrophe, it would be unclear that the phrase is talking about the letter *f*.

- Place an apostrophe where letters have been **omitted**. This is not always where the words have joined.
- Another way to form the **possessive of a noun** is to swap the position of the owner and the item it owns and connect them with the word *of*. For example, instead of writing "the Netherlands**'s** tulips," write "the tulips **of** the Netherlands."

Apostrophes frequently appear in non-English **surnames**, such as **O'Neill**, **N'Dor**, and **D'Agostino**.

Forming the possessive

An apostrophe marks a noun's possession (ownership) of something. There are two forms of possessive apostrophes. The first, an apostrophe followed by an *s* (-'s), shows possession of a singular noun. The second, an apostrophe after the *s* (-s'), shows possession of a plural noun ending in *s*.

When forming the possessive of a plural that ends in *s*, only an apostrophe is added.

grapes' seeds

The seeds belong to *grapes*, which is plural.

The new director belongs to the play, which is singular.

play's new director

To form the possessive of a singular noun, add an apostrophe, followed by the letter *s*.

women's story
people's faces

If a plural word ends in any letter other than *s*, such as *e*, *i* or *n*, an apostrophe is added, followed by the letter *s*.

play's new director had spelled Socrates's revised script.

Words ending in *s*

In the past, some grammar styles have recommended that the possessive of a proper noun ending in *s* be written with only an apostrophe, and no additional *s*. Today, an *s* is generally added in all cases.

The possessive of *Socrates* is *Socrates's* rather than *Socrates'*.

Socrates's revised script

The possessive of *Jess* is *Jess's* rather than *Jess'*.

Jess's disbelief

Hyphens

HYPHENS ARE USED TO EITHER JOIN OR
SEPARATE WORDS OR PARTS OF WORDS.

Sometimes two terms need to be shown to be connected, so that they
are treated as one. Alternatively, a separation between terms may need
to be emphasized. A hyphen can be used for both of these purposes.

Clarity

A hyphen is essential when the
meaning of a phrase might be
confused. When a hyphen is used
between two or more words, it is
a compound modifier indicating
that the words work together to
modify another word.

big-hair society

This hyphen indicates that the
society is interested in big hair.

big hair society

Without the hyphen,
the hair society is big.

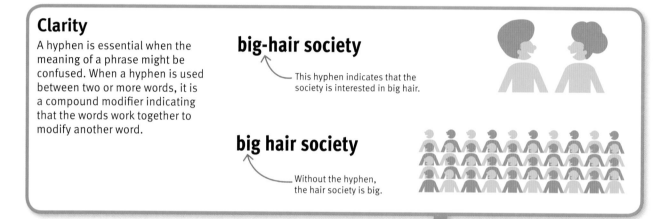

The celebrated big-hair society for a get-together about their

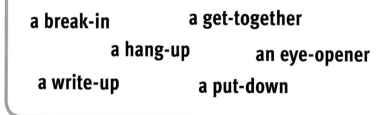

• **Compound modifiers** that
contain adverbs **ending in -ly,**
such as "extraordinarily hairy
experience," are **never hyphenated**.

• Names of **centuries** used as
modifiers should be **hyphenated**
before the noun, as in
"twentieth-century issues."

• A hyphen is used to **break a long
word** in two **between two syllables**
at the end of a line.

Verbs into nouns

When a phrasal verb is made into a noun, it is hyphenated. Phrasal
verbs themselves are never hyphenated. For example, the phrasal verb
get together in "Let's get together and talk about it" isn't hyphenated,
but a hyphen is used when it becomes a noun: "for a get-together."

a break-in   **a get-together**

a hang-up   **an eye-opener**

a write-up   **a put-down**

Prefixes

Hyphens are sometimes needed in words with prefixes. Many need to be hyphenated to avoid confusion with words spelled in a similar way. A hyphen is also often added when a prefix ending in a vowel is joined to a root word beginning with a vowel, in order to avoid having two vowels side-by-side. The prefix self- is always followed by a hyphen. Finally, a hyphen is needed when adding a prefix to a capitalized word or to a date.

re-formed ← The hyphen indicates that the society formed again. Without a hyphen, the word *reformed* means "changed for the better."

co-owner ← This hyphen is needed to divide the two *o*'s because *coowner* is hard to read.

self-service ← The prefix self- always has a hyphen following it.

pre-Roman ← A hyphen follows a prefix before a capital letter.

post-1500 ← A hyphen follows a prefix before a date.

GLOSSARY

Compound modifier A term used to describe a noun that combines two or more words.

Phrasal verb A verb composed of a verb followed by an adverb or a preposition that act together as a single unit.

Prefix A group of letters attached to the start of a word that can change the original word's meaning.

Root word A word to which prefixes and suffixes can be added.

Suffix A group of letters attached to the end of a word that can change the original word's meaning.

Writing numbers

Hyphens are needed when writing out fractions, or numbers from twenty-one (21) to ninety-nine (99).

twenty-four   three-quarters

re-formed after twenty-four years
beard- and hair-loss issues.

Suspended hyphens

Occasionally, a hyphen is found alone at the end of a word. This is called a suspended hyphen, and it occurs when two or more compound modifiers describing one noun and connected by *or*, *and*, or *to* use the same word. To avoid repetition, the first instance of the word is omitted and replaced with a hyphen.

beard- and hair-loss issues

This suspended hyphen followed by *and* indicates that there were both beard-loss and hair-loss issues.

Compound modifiers

When two or more words are used together to modify another word, a hyphen is often needed to show that these modifying words are acting as a single unit. These compound modifiers are almost always hyphenated when they precede the noun, but not when they follow the noun, unless a hyphen is needed for clarity.

hair-loss issues ← noun

A compound modifier before the noun is hyphenated.

A compound modifier after the noun is not hyphenated.

issues of hair loss

Quotation marks

QUOTATION MARKS INDICATE DIRECT SPEECH
OR QUOTED MATERIAL.

Quotation marks, sometimes simply called quotes, are always used in pairs. In addition to indicating speech or a quotation, they can also signal unusual words.

Direct speech

Quotation marks surround direct speech (text that represents spoken words). The material within quotation marks can be split into two sections at either end of the sentence, with text in the middle to explain who is speaking. Quoted material can also be placed at the beginning, in the middle, or at the end of a sentence.

GLOSSARY

Direct speech Text that represents spoken words.

Italics A style of type in which the letters are printed at an angle to resemble handwriting.

Quotation Text that reproduces another author's exact words.

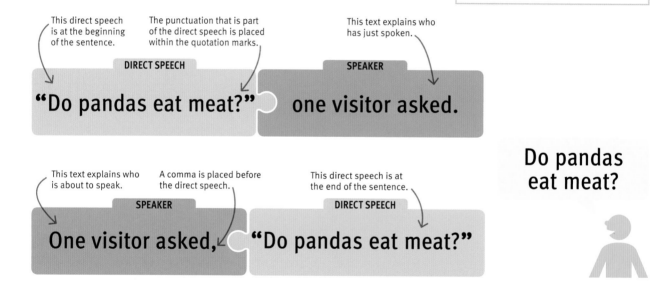

This direct speech is at the beginning of the sentence.

The punctuation that is part of the direct speech is placed within the quotation marks.

This text explains who has just spoken.

DIRECT SPEECH

"Do pandas eat meat?"

SPEAKER

one visitor asked.

Do pandas eat meat?

This text explains who is about to speak.

A comma is placed before the direct speech.

This direct speech is at the end of the sentence.

SPEAKER

One visitor asked,

DIRECT SPEECH

"Do pandas eat meat?"

Unusual words

Quotation marks can be used to separate particular words or phrases within text. These can indicate that another author's words are being used, that the words are unusual, or that the author does not take the expression seriously.

The zookeeper said that the panda show was "thrilling," but three pandas were asleep.

The writer has placed quotation marks around this word to suggest that he or she did not find the show as thrilling as expected, based on how it had been described.

Identifying where to place punctuation

In direct speech, a comma is used to separate the text that explains who is speaking from the spoken words. Periods and commas should always go within the quotation marks, while question marks and exclamation points should be left outside unless they are part of the quoted speech. If the end of the direct speech falls at the end of the sentence, only one punctuation mark is needed. When reproducing a quotation, the punctuation and capitalization of the text should be written exactly as it appears in the original text.

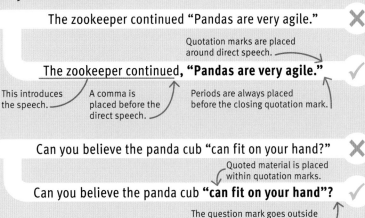

The zookeeper continued "Pandas are very agile." ✗

Quotation marks are placed around direct speech.

The zookeeper continued, **"Pandas are very agile."** ✓

This introduces the speech.

A comma is placed before the direct speech.

Periods are always placed before the closing quotation mark.

Can you believe the panda cub "can fit on your hand?" ✗

Quoted material is placed within quotation marks.

Can you believe the panda cub **"can fit on your hand"**? ✓

The question mark goes outside the quotation marks because it is not part of the quoted material.

Single quotation marks

Single quotation marks are used for quotations within quotations. Any double quotation marks within direct speech or a quotation are changed to single quotation marks to distinguish the words they surround from the rest of the speech or quotation.

• Quotation marks are used to **surround quotations** in the **same way** as they surround **direct speech**.

• In British English, **single quotation marks** are sometimes used in place of double quotation marks for **quoted speech**. Some **US newspapers** also use this style for headlines.

The direct speech is marked by double quotation marks.

SPEAKER

DIRECT SPEECH

The zookeeper said, **"I wouldn't call pandas 'cuddly.'"**

The zookeeper is quoting someone else's description of pandas, so the quoted word is within single quotation marks.

REAL WORLD

Air quotes

Air quotes are quotation mark shapes created with a person's hands when speaking. They serve to highlight unusual words, as quotation marks can in writing, and add a hint of sarcasm to the person's speech.

Titles of short works

Quotation marks are used for the titles of short works, such as short stories, articles, and song titles. The titles of longer works, such as books and movies, are italicized.

The name of the article is in quotation marks.

The article **"Panda Facts"** was an eye-opener.

Question marks

A QUESTION MARK SIGNALS THE END OF A SENTENCE THAT ASKS A QUESTION.

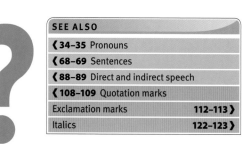

Usually, a period is used to indicate the end of a sentence. However, if the sentence is a question rather than a statement, it should end with a question mark.

Direct questions

A sentence that asks a question and expects an answer in response is a direct question, and requires a question mark. In direct questions, the subject (a noun or pronoun) follows the verb. This is in contrast to the word order of a statement, in which the verb follows the subject. Many direct questions start with question words, such as *when*, *who*, *where*, *why*, or *how*.

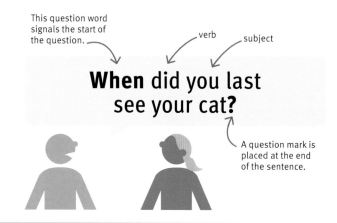

This question word signals the start of the question.

verb

subject

When did you last see your cat**?**

A question mark is placed at the end of the sentence.

Embedded questions

An embedded question is one that appears within a longer sentence, following an introductory phrase. The word order for an embedded question follows that of a statement, with the subject preceding the verb. This makes the question sound more polite. If the full sentence asks a question, it requires a question mark.

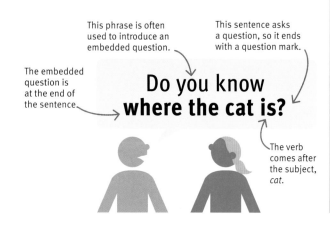

This phrase is often used to introduce an embedded question.

This sentence asks a question, so it ends with a question mark.

The embedded question is at the end of the sentence.

Do you know **where the cat is?**

The verb comes after the subject, *cat*.

Indirect questions

An indirect question always ends in a period. This type of question states what has been asked, rather than directly asking a question. It does not repeat the speaker's exact words, and usually does not require an answer. Indirect questions never end in a question mark.

He asked me if I knew **where the cat was.**

This is an indirect question because it does not require an answer, and it ends in a period.

- A question can be **just a word**, such as *Who?*, *What?*, *Where?*, *When?*, *Why?*, or *How?*
- A question mark **should not** normally **be used with another punctuation mark**. One **exception** is when a **period** is used with an abbreviation at the end of a sentence. For example, "Should we meet at 3:00 p.m.?"
- When a question mark appears within a title that is **italicized**, the question mark should also be italicized.

In **Spanish**, an **inverted question mark** (¿) is used to indicate the **beginning** of a question, in addition to the question mark at the end.

Tag questions

A tag question is one that can be added to the end of a statement. The speaker prompts the listener to respond in a certain way, and then adds the question to the end for confirmation. Tag questions follow a comma at the end of a statement.

This is a statement that makes sense on its own.

You don't think I'm responsible, **do you?**

This is the question, but it cannot appear on its own because it doesn't make sense without the rest of the sentence.

Rhetorical questions

A rhetorical question is a question that is asked only to stress a point. It often contains a note of emotion or sometimes exaggeration. No response is expected, since the answer to the question is either obvious or cannot be known. Rhetorical questions are punctuated with a question mark.

Do I look like a cat thief?

No response is expected, because the speaker does not think she looks like a cat thief.

Can we help you?

Occasionally, question marks are used to indicate tourist information points on signs. Signs like this exist in many places, but are particularly useful for tourists in countries where the spoken language is written in a different alphabet, such as in Japan.

GLOSSARY

Abbreviation A shortened form of a word, often with one or more periods to represent missing letters.

Italics A style of type in which the letters are printed at an angle to resemble handwriting.

Phrase A group of words that does not contain a verb.

Question A sentence that asks for information.

Statement A sentence that conveys a fact or piece of information.

Subject The person or thing that is performing the action of the verb.

Exclamation points

EXCLAMATION POINTS ARE USED AT THE END
OF EXCLAMATIONS.

An exclamation point indicates the end of an exclamation,
which is a sentence that expresses a writer's strong
emotions. It can also be used for emphasis.

SEE ALSO	
❰ **54–55** Voices and moods	
❰ **62–63** Interjections	
❰ **68–69** Sentences	
❰ **110–111** Question marks	
Parentheses and dashes	**114–115** ❱

Emotions

The exclamation point is used at the
end of an exclamation to express a
strong emotion, such as surprise,
excitement, or anger, or a raised voice.

This is so unexpected!

Surprise!

I love cheese!

Fear!

I'm allergic to cheese!

Stop nibbling on the cheese!

Anger!

Excitement!

• Use exclamation points **sparingly**
in **formal writing**. They rarely
improve a piece of writing.

• If it is unclear whether or not
an exclamation point is needed,
remember that it is **usually
preferable to end a statement
with a period.**

GLOSSARY

Exclamation A sentence expressing
a strong emotion, such as surprise,
or a raised voice.

Interjection A word or phrase that
occurs alone and expresses emotion.

Question A sentence that asks for
information.

REAL WORLD

Comics

Exclamation points are a feature
of comic books. Some comics use
them in almost every sentence.
An exclamation point can also
be part of an illustration, used
on its own next to a character's
head to indicate surprise, or with
interjections representing sounds,
such as *Pow!* or *Zap!* In the 1950s,
the exclamation point was called a
"bang." This may be because the
exclamation point often appeared
on its own in a speech bubble next
to the barrel of a gun to show that
it had just been fired.

Exclamations

Almost any type of sentence can be made into an exclamation. The most common types of exclamations are emotional statements, commands, and interjections.

Exclamation points are **rarely** used in **names,** but the name of the Canadian town of **Saint-Louis-du-Ha! Ha!** officially has two.

Statements

A statement, which normally ends in a period, can be made into an exclamation if it conveys an emotion. An emotional statement ends with an exclamation point instead of a period.

There's a mouse in the kitchen!

Commands

Exclamation points are often used in commands, especially when they are direct orders rather than polite requests.

Be quiet and don't move suddenly!

Interjections

Interjections—words usually exclaimed in urgency or surprise—are some of the most common types of exclamations. Interjections are often single words rather than sentences.

Help!

Emphasis

Exclamation points are often placed next to interruptions within parentheses or dashes to add emphasis to an interruption. Never use an exclamation point alongside a question mark.

The interruption uses an exclamation point to emphasize how grateful the speaker was.

Our hero (thankfully!) arrived just in time.

• **One exclamation point** has a greater impact than several, so using **more than one** exclamation point **should be avoided.**

Identifying exclamations

Sentences beginning with *what* and *how* can either ask or state something, so the only way to know which punctuation mark to use is to understand what the sentence is saying and how it is being said.

What a nightmare this is? ✗

What a nightmare this is! ✓

This sentence is stating something, not asking something. It is an exclamation, so it requires an exclamation point rather than a question mark.

What is a nightmare! ✗

What is a nightmare? ✓

This sentence is asking something, not exclaiming something. It is a question, so it requires a question mark rather than an exclamation point.

Parentheses and dashes

( ) —

PARENTHESES AND DASHES INDICATE A STRONG INTERRUPTION WITHIN A SENTENCE.

Parentheses and dashes allow writers to interrupt the normal run of a sentence and insert additional information. Parentheses are always used in pairs around the extra text, while dashes can be used alone or in pairs.

SEE ALSO

❰ 88–89 Direct and indirect speech
❰ 96–99 Commas
❰ 106–107 Hyphens
Numbers, dates, and time 118–119 ❱
Abbreviations 172–173 ❱

• **Parentheses** can be used around an *s* to show that there may be **one or more** of something: for example, "boy(s)."

Parentheses for interruptions

Parentheses surround extra information that is added to a sentence. The extra text disrupts the normal run of the sentence but can easily be removed without changing the meaning. Parentheses can also be used to enclose an entire sentence, which is punctuated in the same way as any other sentence.

(which was late)

This gives extra information, which could be removed without affecting the overall meaning of the sentence.

The driver bought a new watch. (His old one had stopped working.)

This sentence gives more information, but can be removed without spoiling the story.

The period is contained within the parentheses.

The freight train (which was late [with] lychees (exotic fruit)." Afte

Brackets

Brackets clarify text within a quotation or provide additional information. The information in brackets is not part of the original quotation.

"laden [with] lychees"

This is part of a quotation.

Brackets show that a word has been changed from or added to the original quote.

Parentheses for clarification

Parentheses are used around information providing clarification, such as an alternative name or spelling, a translation, or a definition.

lychees (exotic fruit)

The information inside these parentheses defines what lychees are.

• **Brackets** are used within a quotation with the italicized Latin word *sic*, which is used to show that words within a **quotation** have been **reproduced exactly** as they were written. For example, "I heard that the farmer, Mr. Cwpat [*sic*], is alive."

• If using a keyboard that doesn't have a dash, typing **two hyphens (--)** is an acceptable substitute. **Never use a dash** in place of a hyphen, though.

A dash is **longer than a hyphen**. On old-fashioned **typewriters**, **two hyphens** typed one after the other were used instead of a **dash**.

Dashes for interruptions

Dashes perform the same function as parentheses, surrounding additional information in a sentence. While parentheses must always be used in pairs, only one dash is required if the interruption comes at the beginning or end of a sentence.

—by all accounts—

The sentence would still make sense without the part within the dashes, so this part could be removed.

It was a long wait—the longest I'd ever had.

No spaces should be left between the dash and the surrounding words.

This part of the sentence gives additional information about how long the wait was.

was—by all accounts—"laden 5–6 hours, it finally arrived.

Dashes for ranges

A dash can be used to express ranges of numbers, as in the case of dates or page references. In these situations, only the first and last numbers are written. Technically, ranges require the use of a shorter dash called an "en dash," as opposed to the longer "em dash." A dash also expresses ranges of months or days of the week, and it can be used to indicate the direction of travel.

5–6 hours

This means "5 to 6 hours." If the word *from* is written before the number, use *to*, not a dash.

Monday–Friday

This includes Tuesday, Wednesday, and Thursday.

the Trys–Qysto route

This means that the route goes from Trys to Qysto.

Bullet points

BULLET POINTS DRAW THE READER'S ATTENTION TO
THE KEY POINTS IN A DOCUMENT.

Bullet points are used to create lists. Bulleted items appear
in technical documents, websites, or presentations as a way of
condensing important information into brief phrases or sentences.

SEE ALSO	
❰ **98–99** Other uses of commas	
❰ **100–101** Semicolons	
❰ **102–103** Colons	
Layout and presentational features	**194–195** ❱
Writing to inform	**196–197** ❱
Writing to explain and advise	**204–205** ❱
Presentation skills	**228–229** ❱

Key points

Bulleted items are used to emphasize
important points in a document by
separating them from the main
text and presenting them as a list.
This enables the reader to process
essential information right away.
The bulleted text can be written
as complete sentences, phrases,
or single words.

We'll need to be fully prepared for the mission briefing. We'll have to make sure the jet pack is tuned up. We should also get the sewing kit out to finish off the penguin costumes we started last week. Finally, we'll need to dismantle the kite and pack it up as kit.

This running text
provides a lot of detail.

SLIDE 1

Only the most important
information from the
text is given here.

**Before the mission briefing, we'll
need to complete several tasks:**
- **tune up the jet pack**
- **finish the penguin costumes**
- **pack up the kite kit**

Writing bulleted items

Bulleted information has a greater
impact if the items are of similar
lengths and written in the same way.
If the first item starts with a verb, for
example, the remaining items should
do the same. This creates a balanced
list that is easy to follow and gives
the items equal importance.

The bulleted items are
all of a similar length.

SLIDE 2

**On the mission, we'll have
to do the following activities:**
- **go undercover**
- **impersonate penguins**
- **follow people**
- **jump out of helicopters**

All of the bulleted items
begin with verbs.

- **Use bullet points sparingly**: A few bulleted sections have a greater impact than many.
- **Numbered lists** are an alternative to bulleted lists. These are usually indented and punctuated in the same way as bulleted lists.

Although the most common style of **bullet point** is •, there are many other options, such as º, −, or ◊.

Presentations

Speakers often use bulleted lists as visual aids when giving presentations. When addressing a large audience within a short time frame, it's important to get the message across clearly and effectively. Bulleted lists are ideal for this purpose.

Punctuating bulleted text

Bulleted information should be indented from the main text. The text introducing the bullet points should be followed by a colon. Different rules apply depending on whether or not the bulleted items are full sentences.

The bulleted information is indented from the main text.

A colon is placed after the introductory sentence.

SLIDE 4

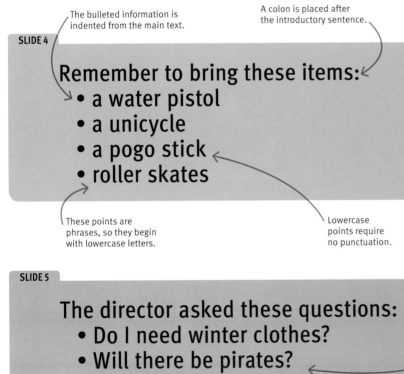

Remember to bring these items:
- a water pistol
- a unicycle
- a pogo stick
- roller skates

These points are phrases, so they begin with lowercase letters.

Lowercase points require no punctuation.

◁ **Lowercase bullets**
If the bulleted items are not full sentences, they can begin with a lowercase letter. In general, no punctuation is required at the end of lowercase bullet points.

◁ **Complete sentences**
If the bulleted items are complete sentences, each one needs to begin with a capital letter and end with a period, question mark, or exclamation point.

SLIDE 5

The director asked these questions:
- Do I need winter clothes?
- Will there be pirates?
- Can I bring my pig?
- Will we receive any gadgets?

Each of these points is a complete sentence, beginning with a capital letter and ending with a question mark.

Numbers, dates, and time

NUMBERS ARE REPRESENTED IN WRITING AS BOTH NUMERALS AND WORDS.

In addition to mathematical calculations, numerals are sometimes used in writing. They are especially useful for writing dates and time, and decimals and numbers over one hundred.

- When writing a **range of numerals**, as in page references, write the first and last page of the reference and **separate the numerals** with a dash: for example, 14–17 (which includes pages 15 and 16).
- When writing informally, **years can be abbreviated** using an apostrophe followed by the last two numerals, as in "the summer of '97."

Writing out numbers

Fractions and numbers up to one hundred should be written out as words, unless the text uses numbers frequently, as in scientific or mathematical works.

eight spaceships

↳ The numeral 8 is written out.

The **Arabic numbering system** is more accurate than the **Roman system** because it includes the **number zero**.

GLOSSARY

Arabic numerals Everyday numerals such as 1, 2, and 3.
Roman numerals Numbers represented by certain letters of the alphabet, such as *i*, *v*, and *x*.

Flying on board **eight** spaceships, discovered **325** comets on April **10**,

Arabic numerals

Everyday numerals are called Arabic numerals because Arabs introduced them to Europe from India. The ten characters are 0, 1, 2, 3, 4, 5, 6, 7, 8, and 9. These are combined to represent every possible number.

325 comets

↳ Use Arabic numerals for numbers over one hundred.

Dates

Numerals are always used for the day and year of a date. When writing years of more than four digits, as in 10,000 BCE, a comma is used. If the month comes first, a comma is needed between the date and year, and after the year when the date appears in the middle of the sentence.

Date format	Example
day-month-year	The discovery on 10 April 2099 was exciting.
month-day-year	The discovery on April 10, 2099, was exciting.
year-month-day	The discovery on 2099 April 10 was exciting.

Identifying when to use words or numerals

If a sentence begins with a number—even a very high number—the number should be written out in words, or the sentence should be rewritten to avoid starting with a number.

325 comets were discovered. ✗

Sentences should never start with numerals.

Three hundred twenty-five comets were discovered. ✓

This number has been written out because it is at the start of the sentence. This option is not ideal with longer numbers.

This sentence has been reworded and is the more succesful version.

The aliens discovered **325** comets. ✓

Roman numerals

Roman numerals use the letters *i* (one), *v* (five), *x* (10), *l* (50), *c* (100), *d* (500), and *m* (1,000) from the alphabet to represent numbers. Numbers over ten are a combination of these letters. Both upper- and lowercase Roman numerals are used to refer to acts and scenes in plays—for example, "Act IV, scene i." Uppercase Roman numerals are sometimes used in names of royalty, such as "King Henry VIII." Lowercase Roman numerals can be used for page references—for example, "xiv–xvii."

If a lower Roman numeral is placed before a larger one, subtract it from the larger number, so *ix* is 10 (x) minus 1 (i) = 9.

Roman	Number	Roman	Number
I, i	1	XX, xx	20
II, ii	2	L, l	50
III, iii	3	C, c	100
IV, iv	4	CD, cd	400
V, v	5	CDX, cdx	410
VI, vi	6	D, d	500
VII, vii	7	CM, cm	900
VIII, viii	8	M, m	1,000
IX, ix	9	MCMXC	1,990
X, x	10	MMXIII	2,013

the aliens from planet Squark IV 2099, between 1:30 and 11:00 p.m.

Time

Numerals are usually used to write the time of day, with a colon separating the hour from the minutes. If expressing time in quarters or halves, or when using the phrase *o'clock*, the time should be written in words.

Between **1:30** and **11:00 p.m.**

This abbreviation stands for "post meridiem" and refers to the afternoon.

time in numerals ↗   ↖ time in words

Between **half past one** and **eleven o'clock.**

• In numbers over a thousand, a **comma** is placed before every group of **three digits, except within addresses** – for example, **20,000** and **300,000**.

• When writing the time of day using the phrase *o'clock*, **spell out** the number—for example, "eleven o'clock."

Other punctuation

SLASHES, AT SIGNS, AMPERSANDS, AND ASTERISKS ARE
A FEW OF THE LESS COMMONLY USED PUNCTUATION MARKS.

SEE ALSO

❰ 86–87 Colloquialisms and slang
❰ 118–119 Numbers, dates, and time
Abbreviations　　　　　　　172–173 ❱
Writing for the Web　　　　214–215 ❱

Slashes are used in web addresses, to show alternatives,
to represent a period of time, and in units of measurement.
"At" signs (@), ampersands (&), asterisks (*), and pound
signs (#) usually represent omitted words or letters.

The **at sign** was
originally used to
represent a **Spanish
unit of weight** called
an *arroba*.

Slashes in Internet addresses

Slashes are used to write Internet addresses. In this
situation, they are called "forward slashes" and link
the address of a minor page to that of a main site.

Style Skunks' main website   linked "news" page

www.styleskunks.com/news

Slashes for alternatives

Slashes are used to show alternatives such as *and/or* and
he/she. These are found in technical documents, such as
forms, or where space is limited, as in newspaper articles.
It is usually better to write the alternatives out.

This means that she looked
for shoes or hats, or both.

She looked for shoes and/or hats.

At signs

The at sign is used to write e-mail addresses. It separates
the unique user name from the name of the host domain.

host domain

user name

questions@styleskunks.com

Ampersands

The ampersand represents the word *and*. It is found in the names
of businesses and organizations, and is used in academic references.

This could also be written
"Squirrels and Swirls."

She loved the fashion label Squirrels **&** Swirls.

Asterisks

Asterisks are used to show that there is extra information at the bottom of the page. The extra information is known as a footnote. They are also used in newspaper articles when a direct quotation includes a word that is too offensive to be written in full. An asterisk represents each letter that has been omitted from the work. This reduces the word's impact, but it remains recognizable to readers who are familiar with it.

The asterisk leads the reader to a footnote explaining that the socks are low quality.

Free socks* will be included with all shoe orders.

- To mark the **omission of** one or more **words** from a passage, never use an asterisk; an **ellipsis (...)** should be used instead.

- If there is a need for **more than one footnote** on a page, use one **asterisk (*)** for the first footnote reference, and **two asterisks (**)** for the second, but do not use more than three in a sequence. In this case, numbering the footnotes would be a better option.

- When writing a **long Internet address** that breaks at the end of a line, break it after a slash—after ".com/" for example.

Pound signs

Found on every telephone keypad, the pound sign, also known as the number sign or hash, represents the word *number* in informal writing. It is usually preferable to write the word *number* instead.

It was the #1 fashion website in the world.

This means "number one."

Twitter

The social networking service Twitter has adopted some of the less commonly used punctuation marks and given them a new significance. The at sign, for example, is used before someone's user name to mention or reply to that user, while the pound sign is used to add "tags" to words, making them searchable by other users.

- **Slashes** are found in certain abbreviations. For example, *c/o* appears in addresses and means "care of," while *miles/hour* means "miles per hour."

- The **ampersand (&)** should never be used in place of the word *and* in formal writing, nor should the **at sign** be used in place of the word *at*.

Italics

ITALICS ARE LETTERS THAT ARE PRINTED AT AN ANGLE TO
RESEMBLE HANDWRITING.

Words or phrases are styled in italic letters to distinguish them
from the surrounding text. Italics may indicate a title, a foreign
word or phrase, or emphasis.

Foreign words

Foreign words or phrases that have
not been adopted into the English
language should be written in italics.
These are sometimes followed by a
translation, either in parentheses or
quotation marks. Genus and species
names of living things are Latin words
and should always be italicized.
The genus starts with a capital letter,
while the species is written in
lowercase letters.

The foreign word
is italicized.

The translation is placed
in parentheses.

oma (grandma)

The genus is
capitalized.

The species is written with
lowercase letters.

Bombus terrestris (bumblebee)

The scientific name
is italicized.

The common name
is placed in parentheses.

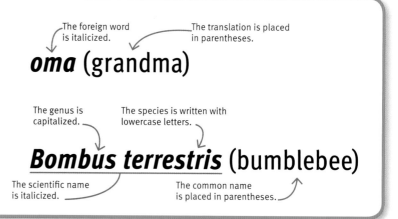

My *oma* (grandma) loves the
I think *Big Beach Splash!*, a film

- If it is unclear whether a **foreign word** should be
italicized or not, look it up in a **dictionary**. If the word
is not in an English dictionary, it should be italicized.
- **Proper names** are **not italicized** even if they are
in a different language—for example, Londres
(French for London).

Punctuation

Do not italicize punctuation
following words in italics
unless it is part of the title
or phrase being italicized.

The exclamation
point is in italics
because it is part
of the movie title.

Big Beach Splash!,

The comma is not
italicized because it is
not part of the movie title.

Titles

Italic type is used to write the titles of long works, such as books, journals, movies, or musical compositions. Shorter works, such as poems or short stories, are written in quotation marks. The names of ships should also be italicized.

Big Beach Splash! — movie title

Surfing is Simple — book title

Italicize	Do not italicize
• titles of printed matter such as books, newspapers, journals, magazines, very long poems, and plays	• the name of a holy book such as the Bible or the Koran • chapters within a book, articles in a newspaper or magazine, titles of short stories or poems—put these in quotation marks
• titles of movies, and radio and television programs	• individual episodes of a radio or television program—put these in quotation marks
• names of specific ships, submarines, aircraft, spacecraft, and artificial satellites	• the abbreviations before a ship's name: RMS *Titanic*, USS *Arizona* • a brand of vehicle: Rolls-Royce, Boeing 747 • names of trains
• long musical compositions such as albums and operas	• titles of songs and short compositions—put these in quotation marks
• works of art, such as paintings and sculptures	• buildings and monuments: the Empire State Building, the Statue of Liberty

book ***Surfing is Simple***, but about surfing, is ***much*** better.

Emphasis

Italics can be used when a writer wants to emphasize certain words or draw attention to a contrast between two terms. They may also indicate that the word or phrase should be given greater emphasis when spoken.

The movie is ***much*** better.

This word has been italicized to emphasize how much better the speaker thinks the movie about surfing is, compared to the book.

This style is called **italic** because it was first used in **Italy** in **1501**.

• When **writing by hand** or typing with a device that does not have italics, underline the word or phrase instead.

Why learn to spell?

SPELLING IS IMPORTANT FOR BOTH READING AND WRITING.

Rules can help with spelling; however, there are many exceptions to these rules, which can sometimes make spelling difficult. Learning to spell well is worth the effort, since it helps a writer convey meaning clearly.

Letters

There are twenty-six letters in the English alphabet, which can be written as lowercase or capital letters. These letters also make specific sounds, with some making more than one sound. In special cases, two letters—such as *c* and *h*—combine to produce one unique sound different from any individual letter sound, such as *ch* in *change*. Understanding when to use lowercase and capital letters helps improve spelling, and better spelling increases the overall quality of writing.

The word *alphabet* comes from the **first two letters** of the **Greek** alphabet: *alpha* and *beta.*

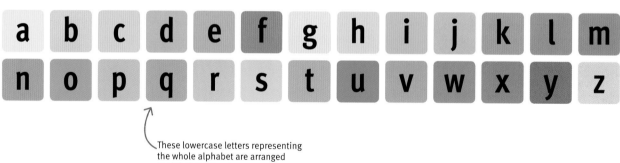

These lowercase letters representing the whole alphabet are arranged in alphabetical order.

The QWERTY keyboard—named after the first six letters and arranged in capital letters—was put in this order so that the most common letters were not close together, thereby avoiding mistakes that caused jams in early typewriters.

Meanings

Many English words come from Latin or Greek, and learning to recognize these roots and understand what they mean can help with spelling. For example, *mar* is the Latin word for "sea," and it is used in the English words *marine* and *maritime*. A common Greek example is *dec*, which means "ten," and this is used in the English words *decade* and *decathlon*. Some root words, such as *build,* which comes from the Old English word *byldan*, are instantly recognizable and form the basis for other related words, including *building*, *builder*, and *rebuild*.

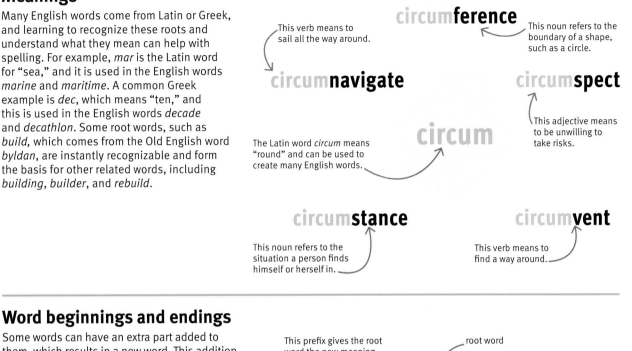

circum**ference**

This verb means to sail all the way around.

This noun refers to the boundary of a shape, such as a circle.

circum**navigate**

circum**spect**

This adjective means to be unwilling to take risks.

circum

The Latin word *circum* means "round" and can be used to create many English words.

circum**stance**

This noun refers to the situation a person finds himself or herself in.

circum**vent**

This verb means to find a way around.

Word beginnings and endings

Some words can have an extra part added to them, which results in a new word. This addition is called a prefix (word beginning) or a suffix (word ending) and can change the meaning of the word. For example, *social* acquires the opposite meaning when the prefix anti- is added, resulting in *antisocial*. However, when the suffix -ite is added to the same root word, the result is *socialite*, which refers to a person who enjoys social activities.

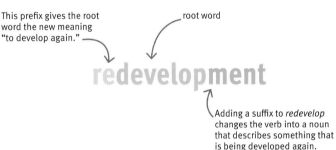

This prefix gives the root word the new meaning "to develop again."

root word

re**develop**ment

Adding a suffix to *redevelop* changes the verb into a noun that describes something that is being developed again.

Choose the right words

In some cases, spelling errors can produce a different meaning from the one expected. This is especially true when words that are spelled differently but pronounced the same (homophones) create unintentional, but sometimes amusing, results.

Replace with *mousse* for a type of dessert.

Replace with *yew* for a species of tree.

Replace with *current* for a body of moving water.

Mike ate a lemon **moose** under the **ewe** tree, then went for a swim. The **currant** caught him, and he let out a **whale**. Suddenly it was a scary **plaice**. If he didn't **dye**, he'd have an epic **tail**.

Replace with *wail* for a high-pitched cry.

Replace with *place* for a specific point or location.

Replace with *die* to describe the end of living.

Replace with *tale* for a type of story.

Alphabetical order

ALPHABETICAL ORDER IS A SIMPLE WAY OF ORGANIZING GROUPS OF WORDS.

From a short list of students in a classroom to a long index in a book, alphabetical order makes information easy to store and find.

Sorting a list

Alphabetical order is the arranging of words based on where their initial letters are in the alphabet. Using this system, words are sorted by their first letters, then by their second letters, and so on. For example, the words *buy* and *biscuit* both begin with the letter *b*, but the second letter in each word is different: The letter *i* in *biscuit* comes before the letter *u* in *buy*, so *biscuit* would come before *buy* in an alphabetical list.

- If a long word has the same letters as a short word, but then goes further—such as *cave* and *caveman*—the **short word (e.g. *cave*) will always come first** in a dictionary.

- The alphabet is **useful for locating a seat** in a theater or a book in a library, as rows are usually labeled in alphabetical order.

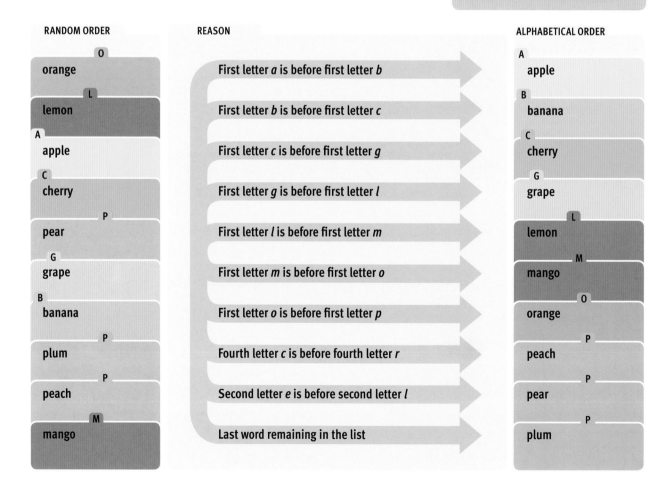

RANDOM ORDER	REASON	ALPHABETICAL ORDER
O orange	First letter *a* is before first letter *b*	**A** apple
L lemon	First letter *b* is before first letter *c*	**B** banana
A apple	First letter *c* is before first letter *g*	**C** cherry
C cherry	First letter *g* is before first letter *l*	**G** grape
P pear	First letter *l* is before first letter *m*	**L** lemon
G grape	First letter *m* is before first letter *o*	**M** mango
B banana	First letter *o* is before first letter *p*	**O** orange
P plum	Fourth letter *c* is before fourth letter *r*	**P** peach
P peach	Second letter *e* is before second letter *l*	**P** pear
M mango	Last word remaining in the list	**P** plum

Special cases

Organizing words according to their initial letters does not always work. For example, abbreviations, capital letters, and numerals need to be treated in special ways. In all cases, however, it is important to be consistent.

The English **alphabet** is based on the **Latin** alphabet of the **Romans**.

king cobra
kingfisher
king penguin

Treat capitalized words in exactly the same way as lowercase words.

Hague, The
Hamburg
High Wycombe

Sacramento
St. (Saint) Helier
Salzburg

Arrange any abbreviated terms as if they were spelled out.

Names of people are arranged by surnames, so the first name comes after the comma.

∏ (Pi)
101 Dalmations
Toy Story

If terms consist of more than one word, treat them as if they were written without the space. In this example, the list is arranged by looking at the fifth letter.

blueberry
Coconut Island
date

If a phrase contains an article, such as *the*, ignore it and sort by the second word.

Dahl, Roald
Meyer, Stephenie
Twain, Mark

Collect terms with symbols or numerals at the beginning.

The dictionary

A dictionary is a collection of words and their definitions in alphabetical order. The words are arranged this way to make it easier for somebody to find a word and check its spelling or definition.

handwriting
writing done by hand, not typed or printed

The first three letters begin with the letters *han*, but the fourth letter *d* in *handwriting* comes before the letter *g* in *hang*.

hang
to support something from above

This word appears after the four-letter word *hang* because it has a fifth letter, *a*.

hangar
a very large building where aircraft are stored

Ignore the hyphen (-) and arrange the word by the fifth letter, *g*.

hang-glider
a huge kite that a person can hang from

The third letter *p* comes after the third letter *n* in *hang-glider*.

happen
to take place

The fifth letter *y* comes after the fifth letter *e* in *happen*, so this is the last word.

happy
pleased and content

REAL WORLD

Indexes

An index is a list of important topics in a reference book that is arranged in alphabetical order. Next to each key topic, a page number (or several page numbers) refers to the location of that key topic in the book. This makes it quicker and easier for the reader to find specific information.

Vowel sounds

THE ENGLISH ALPHABET CONTAINS FIVE VOWELS: *A, E, I, O,* AND *U.*

Each vowel has a short or long phoneme, or sound. Each sound made by a vowel can be written down as a grapheme—one or more letters that represent a sound.

SEE ALSO

❮ **120–121** Other punctuation
❮ **126–127** Why learn to spell?
❮ **128–129** Alphabetical order
Consonant sounds **132–133** ❯
Syllables **134–135** ❯
Silent letters **160–161** ❯
Irregular word spellings **164–165** ❯

Short vowel sounds

A vowel can sound short, or abrupt. For example, the word *rat* has a short "a" sound and the grapheme that represents this sound is *a*. A more complex word, such as *tread*, has a short "e" sound and the grapheme is *ea*. The letter *y* sometimes takes the place of a vowel. For example, the word *gym* has a short "i" sound but the grapheme is *y*.

The **Taa language,** spoken mainly in Botswana, has **112 different sounds**.

▷ **Short "a"**
This sound is represented only by the grapheme *a*.

cat

▷ **Short "e"**
This sound is represented by the graphemes *a, ai, e, ea, eo,* and *ie*.

many   said   reptile
head   leopard   friend

▷ **Short "i"**
This sound is represented by the graphemes *e, i, o, u,* and *y*.

pretty   insect   women
busy   rhythm

▷ **Short "o"**
This sound is represented by the graphemes *a* and *o*.

salt   octopus

▷ **Short "u"**
This sound is represented by the graphemes *o, ou,* and *u*.

dove   young   buffalo

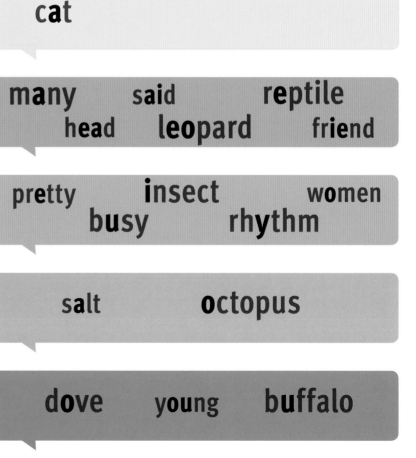

Long vowel sounds

A vowel can sound long, or stretched. For example, the word *alien* has a long "a" sound at the beginning of the word and the grapheme that represents this sound is *a*. A more complex word, such as *monkey*, has a long "e" sound in its second syllable and the grapheme is *ey*.

• The letter *y* is a consonant when it is the first letter of a syllable that has more than one letter, such as *yellow*. If *y* is anywhere else in the syllable, it acts like a vowel: In the word *trendy*, it sounds like an "e."

a

▷ **Long "a"**
This sound is represented by the graphemes *a, ai, aigh, ay, a–e, ei, eigh,* and *ey*.

apron   snail   straight   ray
snake   reindeer   sleigh   they

e

▷ **Long "e"**
This sound is represented by the graphemes *e, ea, ee, ei, ey, e–e, ie,* and *y*.

he   beaver   cheetah   ceiling
donkey   these   thief   smelly

i

▷ **Long "i"**
This sound is represented by the graphemes *i, eigh, I, ie, igh, i–e, y, ye,* and *y–e*.

bison   height   I   pie   night
pike   fly   eye   type

o

▷ **Long "o"**
This sound is represented by the graphemes *o, oa, oe, ol, ou, ough, ow,* and *o–e*.

cobra   goat   toe   folk
soul   dough   crow   antelope

u

▷ **Long "u"**
This sound is represented by the graphemes *u, ew, ue,* and *u–e*.

unicorn   chew
barbecue   use

Complex vowel sounds

In addition to short and long vowel sounds, there are also complex vowel sounds in English. For example, the grapheme *oo* makes two different sounds depending on the word: a short vowel sound, as in the word *hook*, or a long vowel sound, as in the word *loot*.

Complex vowel sound	Examples
aw	awful, author
oi	toil, annoy
ow	house, cow
oo (short)	look, put
oo (long)	moot, suit

Consonant sounds

THERE ARE 21 CONSONANTS IN THE ENGLISH LANGUAGE:
THE WHOLE ALPHABET MINUS THE FIVE VOWELS.

Most consonants have one phoneme, or sound, but some
have multiple sounds. Like vowels, consonants are written
down as graphemes—letters that represent sounds.

Single consonant sounds

Single consonant sounds are sounds
that are represented by consonants.
For example, the single consonant
sound "f" is heard in the word *fan*,
and this is represented by the
grapheme *f*. However, the single
consonant sound "f" can also be
heard in the word *phase*; here, it
is represented by the grapheme *ph*.
The letters *c*, *q*, and *x* do not have
single consonant sounds, but are
often paired with other letters to
form digraphs or blends.

▽ **The "b" sound**
This consonant is represented
by the graphemes *b* and *bb*.

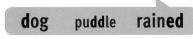
bat   rabbit

▽ **The "d" sound**
This consonant is represented
by the graphemes *d*, *dd*, and *ed*.

dog   puddle   rained

▽ **The "f" sound**
This consonant is represented
by the graphemes *f*, *ff*, *gh*,
and *ph*.

flamingo   puff
laugh   dolphin

▽ **The "g" sound**
This consonant is represented
by the graphemes *g*, *gh*, *gg*,
and *gu*.

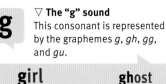
girl   ghost
haggle   guinea

▽ **The "h" sound**
This consonant is represented
by the graphemes *h* and *wh*.

hen   who

▽ **The "j" sound**
This consonant is represented
by the graphemes *ge*, *gg*, *gi*,
gy, *j*, and *dge*.

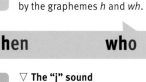
gerbil   suggest   giraffe
gymnast   jaguar   badger

▽ **The "k" sound**
This consonant is represented
by the graphemes *c*, *cc*, *ch*, *ck*, *k*,
and *que*.

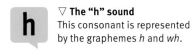
cat   raccoon   chameleon
duck   kitten   mosque

▽ **The "l" sound**
This consonant is represented
by the graphemes *l* and *ll*.

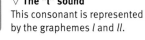
lion   bull

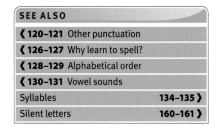
▽ **The "m" sound**
This consonant is represented
by the graphemes *m*, *mb*, *mm*,
and *mn*.

mouse   lamb
hummingbird   column

▽ **The "n" sound**
This consonant is represented by
the graphemes *gn*, *kn*, *n*, and *nn*.

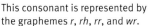
gnome   knot   newt   sunny

▽ **The "p" sound**
This consonant is represented
by the graphemes *p* and *pp*.

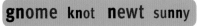
pig   puppy

▽ **The "r" sound**
This consonant is represented by
the graphemes *r*, *rh*, *rr*, and *wr*.

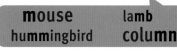
rat   rhinoceros
parrot   wren

▽ **The "s" sound**
This consonant is represented
by the graphemes *c*, *s*, *sc*, *ss*,
and *st*.

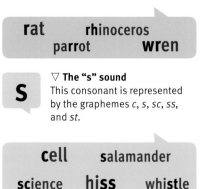
cell   salamander
science   hiss   whistle

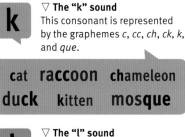

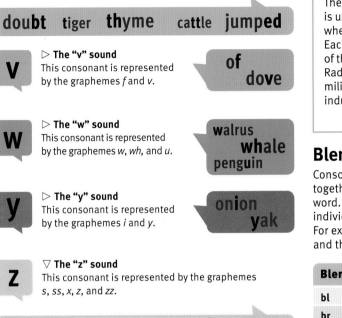

t ▽ The "t" sound
This consonant is represented by the graphemes *bt, t, th, tt,* and *ed.*

dou**bt** **tiger** **thyme** ca**ttle** jump**ed**

v ▷ The "v" sound
This consonant is represented by the graphemes *f* and *v.*

o**f**
do**v**e

w ▷ The "w" sound
This consonant is represented by the graphemes *w, wh,* and *u.*

walrus
whale
peng**u**in

y ▷ The "y" sound
This consonant is represented by the graphemes *i* and *y.*

on**i**on
yak

z ▽ The "z" sound
This consonant is represented by the graphemes *s, ss, x, z,* and *zz.*

plea**s**e **sci**ssor**s** **x**ylophone **z**ebra bu**zz**

Digraphs

A digraph is a single sound that is made by combining two letters. For example, the word *shining* begins with the digraph "sh" and is represented by the grapheme *sh.* This digraph can appear in other words, such as *action,* but in this case it is written as *ti.*

Digraph	Grapheme	Examples
ch	ch, t, tch	**ch**icken, na**t**ure, ha**tch**
ng	n (before k), ng	mo**n**key, hatchli**ng**
sh	ce, ch, ci, sh, ss, ti	o**ce**an, **ch**ef, spe**ci**al, **sh**eep, mi**ss**ion, mo**ti**on
th (voiceless)	th	slo**th**
th (voiced)	th	fea**th**er
zh	ge, s	bei**ge**, vi**s**ion

NATO phonetic alphabet

The NATO phonetic alphabet is used to avoid confusion when spelling words verbally. Each word is spoken in place of the name of the letter. Radio broadcasters in the military and aviation industries use this alphabet.

A	Alpha	N	November
B	Bravo	O	Oscar
C	Charlie	P	Papa
D	Delta	Q	Quebec
E	Echo	R	Romeo
F	Foxtrot	S	Sierra
G	Golf	T	Tango
H	Hotel	U	Uniform
I	India	V	Victor
J	Juliet	W	Whiskey
K	Kilo	X	X-ray
L	Lima	Y	Yankee
M	Mike	Z	Zulu

Blends

Consonant blends are two or more consonants that join together. They can appear at the beginning or end of a word. Like digraphs, they are never separated, but the individual sound that is represented by each letter is heard. For example, the word *bright* begins with the blend *br,* and the individual letters—*b* and *r*—are clearly heard.

Blend	Examples
bl	**bl**ock
br	**br**ead
cl	**cl**am
cr	**cr**acker
ct	perfe**ct**
dr	**dr**ink
fl	**fl**oor
fr	**fr**uit
ft	si**ft**
gl	**gl**aze
gr	**gr**apefruit
lb	bu**lb**
ld	mi**ld**
lf	se**lf**
lk	mi**lk**
lm	e**lm**
ln	ki**ln**
lp	pu**lp**
lt	ma**lt**
mp	cho**mp**
nd	gri**nd**
nk	dri**nk**
nt	mi**nt**

Blend	Examples
pl	**pl**um
pr	**pr**etzel
pt	ada**pt**
sc	**sc**allop
sch	**sch**ool
scr	**scr**ape
sk	**sk**eleton
sk	whi**sk**
sl	**sl**ither
sm	**sm**oke
sn	**sn**ack
sp	**sp**aghetti
sp	cri**sp**
sph	**sph**ere
spl	**spl**atter
spr	**spr**inkle
squ	**squ**id
st	**st**eak
st	toa**st**
str	**str**awberry
sw	**sw**eet
tr	**tr**out
tw	**tw**in

Syllables

BREAKING UP WORDS INTO SYLLABLES CAN HELP WITH PRONUNCIATION AND SPELLING.

Every English word consists of one or more syllables. Separating words into syllables helps split complex words into simple, easy-to-remember parts.

Sounding out syllables

One way to determine the correct pronunciation of a word is to break it up into syllables and say each part aloud. For example, the word *melody* can be broken up into three syllables: *me*, *lo*, and *dy*. Single syllable words, such as *cook* and *shop*, are never divided. There are certain rules about how to break up a word.

▷ **Long vowel sounds and consonants**
If the first part of the word makes a long vowel sound and a consonant comes between two vowels, the word is usually divided before the consonant.

Sa makes a long vowel sound.

sa-ving

The consonant *v* is between two vowels, *a* and *i*.

▷ **Single-letter syllables and special sounds**
Never separate two or more letters that together make a single sound. A long vowel sounded alone forms a syllable by itself.

Ph sounds like an *f*.

O makes a long vowel sound.

phys-i-o-ther-a-py

Th makes a unique sound.

▷ **Short vowel sounds and consonants**
If the first part of the word makes a short vowel sound and a consonant comes between two vowels, the word is usually divided after the consonant.

Mod makes a short vowel sound.

mod-est

The consonant *d* is between two vowels, *o* and *e*.

▷ **Prefixes and suffixes**
A prefix is divided from the root word. If the word ends in the suffix -le and this is preceded by a consonant, the word is divided before the consonant.

The prefix re- is separated from *handle*.

re-han-dle

The suffix -le is preceded by the consonant *d*.

▷ **Identical consonants and different vowel sounds**
Two identical consonants next to each other are separated. The word is also divided where two different vowel sounds meet. Most suffixes are separated from the root word.

Identical consonants are separated.

Here, *di* and *ate* make different vowel sounds.

im-me-di-ate-ly

The suffix -ly is separated from *immediate*.

GLOSSARY

Consonant A letter of the alphabet that is not a vowel.

Prefix A group of letters attached to the start of a word that can change the original word's meaning.

Suffix A group of letters attached to the end of a word that can change the original word's meaning.

Vowel One of the five letters *a*, *e*, *i*, *o*, and *u*.

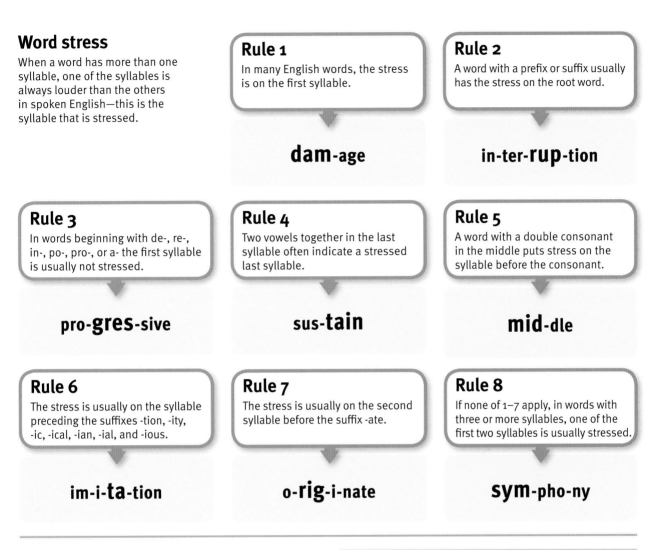

Word stress

When a word has more than one syllable, one of the syllables is always louder than the others in spoken English—this is the syllable that is stressed.

Rule 1
In many English words, the stress is on the first syllable.

dam-age

Rule 2
A word with a prefix or suffix usually has the stress on the root word.

in-ter-**rup**-tion

Rule 3
In words beginning with de-, re-, in-, po-, pro-, or a- the first syllable is usually not stressed.

pro-**gres**-sive

Rule 4
Two vowels together in the last syllable often indicate a stressed last syllable.

sus-**tain**

Rule 5
A word with a double consonant in the middle puts stress on the syllable before the consonant.

mid-dle

Rule 6
The stress is usually on the syllable preceding the suffixes -tion, -ity, -ic, -ical, -ian, -ial, and -ious.

im-i-**ta**-tion

Rule 7
The stress is usually on the second syllable before the suffix -ate.

o-**rig**-i-nate

Rule 8
If none of 1–7 apply, in words with three or more syllables, one of the first two syllables is usually stressed.

sym-pho-ny

Iambic pentameter

Syllables are often used in literature to give sentences a lilting rhythm and to emphasize certain parts of a word. A poetic form called iambic pentameter consists of ten syllables in each line. The ten syllables are divided into five pairs of alternating unstressed and stressed syllables. The rhythm in each line resembles the "da-DUM" sound of a heartbeat.

The only English letter whose name has more than one syllable is **w,** which is pronounced **"duh-bull-you."**

▷ **Shakespearean syllables**
Many people have used this technique, including the English playwright William Shakespeare (1564–1616). This famous line is taken from his tragedy *Macbeth*.

Is **this** - a **dag** - ger **I** - see **be** - fore **me**

The first syllable in a pair is unstressed and represents the quieter "da" in the heartbeat rhythm.

The second syllable in the pair is stressed and represents the louder "DUM" in the heartbeat rhythm.

Morphemes

A MORPHEME IS THE SMALLEST MEANINGFUL PART OF A WORD.

All words are made up of at least one morpheme. An understanding of morphemes can help with spelling, since a morpheme in one word can apply to other similar words.

Free and bound morphemes

There are two types of morphemes: free and bound. Free morphemes are separate words, and can form the root of a longer word. Bound morphemes are parts of words—usually prefixes or suffixes—that attach to a free morpheme. For example, the word *cats* has two morphemes: The noun *cat* is the free morpheme and the suffix -s is the bound morpheme.

fortunate

This free morpheme is an adjective that refers to good luck or success.

fortunate**ly**

This suffix is a bound morpheme and changes the free morpheme into an adverb.

unfortunate**ly**

This prefix is another bound morpheme and gives the adverb the opposite meaning.

Adding information

A bound morpheme can add information to a free morpheme without changing the basic meaning of the word. For example, adding the bound morpheme -est to the end of the free morpheme *fast* results in the word *fastest*. The meaning has become more specific.

GLOSSARY

Adjective A word that describes a noun.

Adverb A word that modifies the meaning of an adjective, verb, or other adverb.

Noun A word that refers to a person, place, or thing.

Prefix A group of letters attached to the start of a word that can change the original word's meaning.

Suffix A group of letters attached to the end of a word that can change the original word's meaning.

Verb A word that describes an action.

Rule 1
Adding the bound morpheme -s to the end of a free morpheme results in a plural word.

cup / cup**s**

The cup**s** are very large.

Rule 2
To show possession, add the bound morpheme -s and an apostrophe to the end of a free morpheme.

swimmer / swimmer**'s**

The swimmer**'s** goggles were too small.

Rule 3
The comparative form occurs when the bound morpheme -ier is added to the end of a free morpheme.

hungry / hungr**ier**

He was hungr**ier** than his friends.

Rule 4
The superlative form occurs when the bound morpheme -est is added to the end of a free morpheme.

long / long**est**

It was the long**est** day ever.

Acting in a different way

Some words add more than just detail. For example, the free morpheme and adjective *kind* can combine with the bound morpheme ending -ness, which forms the noun *kindness*. The meaning of a word can also change. For example, the word *helpful* can acquire the opposite meaning when the bound morpheme un- is added, which results in the word *unhelpful*.

• Understanding morphemes can help with unfamiliar words. Take **demagnetize**: the morpheme is the noun **magnet**, but the **suffix -ize** changes it to a verb. However, the newly created word **magnetize** acquires the opposite meaning when the **prefix de-** is added, and refers to the act of making something **less magnetic**.

Rule 1
The bound morpheme ending -ness changes an adjective into a noun.

bright / bright**ness**

It is very bright in this room.

This room's bright**ness** is overwhelming.

Rule 2
The bound morpheme ending -ion changes a verb into a noun.

act / act**ion**

She wanted to act in the play.

The play contained many action scenes.

Rule 3
The bound morpheme -ful attaches to the end of a noun and changes it into an adjective.

spite / spite**ful**

The annoyed boy ignored his sister out of spite.

The spiteful boy became very annoyed.

Rule 4
The bound morpheme un- attaches to the start of a word to give it the opposite meaning.

helpful / **un**helpful

The helpful boy carried the bags.

The unhelpful boy did not carry the bags.

In the field of linguistics, **morphology** is the identification, analysis, and description of words that **form a language,** including root words and parts of speech.

Understanding English irregularities

THE ENGLISH LANGUAGE HAS BEEN SHAPED BY MANY LANGUAGES.

SEE ALSO

❮ 86–87 Colloquialisms and slang

Roots	140–141 ❯
Hard and soft letter sounds	144–145 ❯
Irregular word spellings	164–165 ❯

English has its foundations in Latin and Greek and continues to evolve as foreign words are adopted. With so many influences, it is understandable that English has so many spelling irregularities.

Latin influences

Latin is more than 2,000 years old and originated in the Roman Empire. English has adopted Latin at different times in history. In the years of the Roman Empire (27 BCE–476 CE), contact with Rome introduced new vocabulary. During the Middle Ages (fifth–fifteenth centuries CE), Latin was the language of the Church, which exerted an enormous influence on language—in fact, the first printed books were religious texts. In subsequent centuries, people invented words for new things by combining existing Latin words.

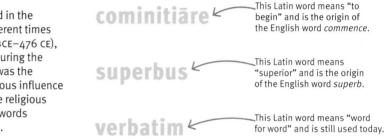

cominitiāre
This Latin word means "to begin" and is the origin of the English word *commence*.

superbus
This Latin word means "superior" and is the origin of the English word *superb*.

verbatim
This Latin word means "word for word" and is still used today.

Greek influences

Ancient Greek literature and myths have greatly influenced the English language. Most Greek terms in English were created by combining Greek roots to describe things named in modern times, such as *dinosaur*. For this reason, Greek words are usually technical words used in medicine and science.

skeleton
This Greek word means "dried up" and is the same as the English word *skeleton*.

pharmakon
This Greek word refers to a place that dispenses medicine and is the origin of the English word *pharmacy*.

deinos and **saurus**
In Greek, the word *deinos* means "terrible" and *saurus* means "lizard." When combined, they form the origin of the English word *dinosaur*.

REAL WORLD

The Domesday Book

The Domesday Book was written in Latin and compiled in 1085–1086 CE. It is Britain's earliest public record, and was drawn up on the orders of King William I to describe the resources of late eleventh-century England. Latin was the language used for government documents and by the Church, and continued to be used for important documents up to Victorian times.

Old English influences

A more familiar-sounding form of English began when the Anglo-Saxons came from continental Europe to England in about the fifth century CE. English from this time is now referred to as Old English and it was related to German. Modern English words that derive from Old English usually have one or two syllables, and refer to everyday things, such as food, animals, parts of the body and family relationships. Old English words are usually spelled differently from the modern equivalent, but they are often pronounced in a similar way.

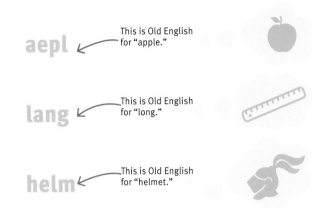

aepl ← This is Old English for "apple."

lang ← This is Old English for "long."

helm ← This is Old English for "helmet."

French influences

One of the languages that has influenced English the most is French—a Latin-based language. This is because for about 300 years after the Norman Conquest in 1066, the most powerful people in England spoke a form of French called Norman. For this reason, many English words relating to government, law, money, and warfare come from the French language.

parler ← This French word means "to speak" and is the origin of the English word *parliament*.

recrue ← This French word refers to untrained soldiers and is the origin of the English word *recruit*.

saudier ← This French word refers to a person who is paid for military service and is the origin of the English word *soldier*.

Other influences

There are many other languages that have influenced English over time. For example, the English words *bangle* and *shampoo* derive from Hindi words, and *alligator* and *canoe* derive from Spanish words.

The most famous remnant of **Old English** is *Beowulf*. This epic poem survives in a **single manuscript** dating to sometime between the **eighth and eleventh centuries** CE. The author's identity remains a mystery.

Language of origin	Examples
French	ballet, cuisine
German	hamburger, kindergarten
Italian	fresco, graffiti
Spanish	anchovy, bonanza
Dutch	cookie, tulip
Arabic	algebra, giraffe
Sanskrit	guru, karma
Hindi	bandanna, cheetah
Persian	balcony, lilac
Russian	gulag, mammoth
Czech	pistol, robot
Norwegian	fjord, ski
Dravidian (Indian subcontinent)	mango, peacock
African languages	jumbo, zombie
American Indian languages	chocolate, igloo
Chinese	ketchup, tea
Japanese	origami, tsunami

Roots

THE ROOT IS THE PART OF A WORD THAT CONTAINS
MEANING, EVEN WITHOUT A PREFIX OR SUFFIX.

SEE ALSO

❰ **136–137** Morphemes

❰ **138–139** Understanding
English irregularities

Prefixes and suffixes   **142–143** ❱

A root can be an existing English word or part of a word,
and it usually originates from Latin or Greek. Learning to
identify roots can help with spelling and building vocabulary.

Whole root words

English includes many whole root
words, which often stem from Greek
or Latin. These words cannot be
separated into smaller words, since
they are already in their simplest form.
However, a whole root word can be
made longer by adding a prefix or
suffix. For example, the word *build*
can become *building*, *builder* and
rebuild. Each new word has a different
meaning, but they are all related to
the whole root word.

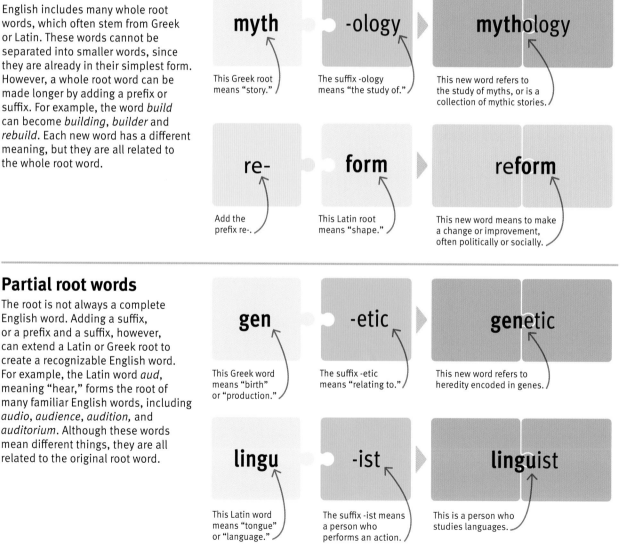

myth

This Greek root
means "story."

-ology

The suffix -ology
means "the study of."

mythology

This new word refers to
the study of myths, or is a
collection of mythic stories.

re-

Add the
prefix re-.

form

This Latin root
means "shape."

reform

This new word means to make
a change or improvement,
often politically or socially.

Partial root words

The root is not always a complete
English word. Adding a suffix,
or a prefix and a suffix, however,
can extend a Latin or Greek root to
create a recognizable English word.
For example, the Latin word *aud*,
meaning "hear," forms the root of
many familiar English words, including
audio, *audience*, *audition*, and
auditorium. Although these words
mean different things, they are all
related to the original root word.

gen

This Greek word
means "birth"
or "production."

-etic

The suffix -etic
means "relating to."

genetic

This new word refers to
heredity encoded in genes.

lingu

This Latin word
means "tongue"
or "language."

-ist

The suffix -ist means
a person who
performs an action.

linguist

This is a person who
studies languages.

Latin root words

There are nearly 1,000 Latin root words used in English. Many of these words were introduced through French, which stems from Latin, after the Norman conquest of England in 1066.

Latin root	Meaning	Examples
aqua, aque	water	**aqua**rium, **aqua**tic, **aque**duct
bi	two	**bi**annual, **bi**cycle, **bi**nary
cent	one hundred	**cent**ipede, **cent**ury, per**cent**
circum	round	**circum**ference, **circum**navigate, **circum**stance
form	shape	con**form**, **form**ation, trans**form**
jud	judgment	ad**jud**icate, **jud**ge, **jud**icial
liber, liver	free	**liber**ation, **liber**ty, de**liver**
liter	letter (alphabet)	**liter**al, **liter**ate, **liter**ature
mater, matr	mother	**mater**nity, **matr**iarch, **matr**only
min	small	**min**iature, **min**imum, **min**ority
pater, patr	father	**pater**nal, **patr**iotic, **patr**on
quad	four	**quad**rant, **quad**ratic, **quad**rilateral
terr	earth	extra**terr**estrial, **terr**ain, **terr**itorial
tri	three	**tri**angle, **tri**cycle, **tri**nity
uni	one	**uni**corn, **uni**form, **uni**versal

When words **share** the same root—such as *employ* in the words *employee, employer,* and *employment*— they are known as a **word family**.

Greek root words

There are hundreds of Greek roots used in English, especially relating to science. For example, *scope* in Greek means "to examine," and is seen in many English words, such as *microscope* and *telescope*.

Greek roots	Meanings	Examples
aero	air	**aero**bics, **aero**sol, **aero**space
bibl, biblio	book	**Bibl**e, **biblio**graphy, **biblio**phile
bio	life	anti**bio**tic, **bio**graphy, **bio**logy
cycl, cyclo	circle	bi**cycl**e, **cycl**ical, **cyclo**ne
dec	ten	**dec**ade, **dec**agon, **dec**athlon
dem, demo	people	epi**dem**ic, **demo**cracy, **demo**graphy
mega	great	**mega**lomania, **mega**phone, **mega**ton
pan	all	**pan**demic, **pan**orama, **pan**theism
path	feeling	**path**ology, sym**path**y, tele**path**y
phobia	fearing	agora**phobia**, arachno**phobia**, claustro**phobia**
phos, photo	light	**phos**phorus, **photo**graph, **photo**synthesis
poly	many	**poly**gon, **poly**math, **poly**technic
psych	spirit	**psych**iatry, **psych**ic, **psych**ology
tele	far off	**tele**kinetic, **tele**phone, **tele**vision
therm	heat	exo**therm**ic, **therm**al, **therm**ometer

• There's **no easy way** to **recognize** whether a root is **Latin** or **Greek**. The best way to find out is to look the word up in a **dictionary**. The origin of the root will be mentioned in the entry.

GLOSSARY

Prefix A group of letters attached to the start of a word that can change the original word's meaning.

Suffix A group of letters attached to the end of a word that can change the original word's meaning.

Prefixes and suffixes

PREFIXES AND SUFFIXES ARE COLLECTIVELY CALLED AFFIXES.

Prefixes are added to the start of a word and suffixes are added to the end of a word. They can change a word's meaning or its part of speech, or—combined with a partial root word—create a new word.

Prefixes

A prefix is added to the start of a root to change the meaning of that root or create a new word. For example, the root word *do* acquires the opposite meaning when the prefix un- (meaning "not") is added, resulting in the word *undo*. When the prefix demo- (meaning "common people" in Greek) is added to the partial root *crat* (meaning "rule" in Greek), it results in the whole English word *democrat*. Other prefixes can be added to the root *crat* to form the English words *aristocrat*, *autocrat*, and *bureaucrat*.

• Most **prefixes** are not separated from the root by a **hyphen**. However, **ex-** (as in "former") and **self-** are **always** followed by a **hyphen**.

Prefixes	Meaning	Examples
a-, an-	not	**a**typical, **an**onymous
ab-	away from	**ab**normal
ad-	toward	**ad**vance
al-	all	**al**most
all-	all	**all**-knowing
ante-	before	**ante**room
anti-	against	**anti**social
be-	make	**be**friend
co-, col-, com-, con-	together	**co**operate, **col**laborate, **com**munity, **con**fidence
de-	opposite	**de**tach
de-	down	**de**cline
dis-	not	**dis**embark
em-, en-	cause to	**em**battle, **en**amor
ex-	out of, from	**ex**port
ex-	former	**ex**-husband
extra-	beyond	**extra**ordinary
fore-	before	**fore**arm
im-, in-	in	**im**port, **in**come
im-, in-, ir-	not	**im**mature, **in**credible, **ir**rational
inter-	among	**inter**national
intra-	within	**intra**mural

Prefixes	Meaning	Examples
intro-	in	**intro**duction
mid-	middle	**mid**way
mis-	wrongly	**mis**conception
non-	not	**non**sense
out-	more than others	**out**standing
out-	separate	**out**house
over-	too much	**over**do
para-	beyond, beside	**para**normal
per-	through	**per**form
post-	after	**post**war
pre-	before	**pre**mature
pro-	for	**pro**active
re-	again	**re**apply
retro-	back	**retro**spective
se-	away from	**se**gregate
self-	oneself	**self**-confidence
sub-	under	**sub**marine
super-, sur-	over, above	**super**natural, **sur**vive
sus-	under	**sus**pect
trans-	across	**trans**mit
ultra-	beyond	**ultra**sound
un-	not	**un**cover
under-	beneath, below	**under**mine

Suffixes

A suffix is added to the end of a root—which is either a whole word or part of a word—and changes its meaning or its part of speech. For example, adding the suffix -ant (meaning a person who performs an action) to the end of the word *account* results in a new word with a new meaning: *accountant*. On the other hand, the verb *exist* becomes the noun *existence* when the suffix -ence ("state of") is added.

Suffixes	Meaning	Examples
-able, -ible	able to	sustain**able**, sens**ible**
-acy	state or quality	conspir**acy**
-age	action of	advant**age**
-age	collection	assembl**age**
-al	act of	deni**al**
-al, -ial	having characteristics of	season**al**, controvers**ial**
-ance, -ence	state of	defi**ance**, compet**ence**
-ant, -ent	person who performs an action	account**ant**, stud**ent**
-ate	become	infl**ate**
-cian	profession of	techni**cian**
-cy	state of being	accura**cy**
-dom	place or state of being	free**dom**
-ed	past tense	stopp**ed**
-en	made of	gold**en**
-en	become	bright**en**
-ent	state of being	differ**ent**
-er, -or	person who performs an action	drumm**er**, investigat**or**
-er	more	short**er**
-ery	action of	robb**ery**
-ery	place of	bak**ery**
-esque	reminiscent of	pictur**esque**
-est	the most	short**est**
-ette	small	maison**ette**
-ful	full of	cheer**ful**
-hood	state of	child**hood**
-ia, -y	state of	amnes**ia**, monarch**y**

Suffixes	Meaning	Examples
-ic, -tic, -ical	having characteristics of	histor**ic**, poet**ic**, rad**ical**
-ice	state or quality	just**ice**
-ify	make	magn**ify**
-ing	present participle	hopp**ing**
-ish	having the quality of	child**ish**
-ism	the belief in	modern**ism**
-ist	one who	art**ist**
-ite	one connected with	social**ite**
-ity, -ty	quality of	real**ity**, socie**ty**
-ive, -ative, -itive	tending to	pass**ive**, superl**ative**, sens**itive**
-less	without	use**less**
-like	resembling	child**like**
-ling	small	half**ling**
-ly	how something is	friend**ly**
-ment	condition of, act of	entertain**ment**
-ness	state of	happi**ness**
-ous, -eous, -ious	having qualities of	ridicul**ous**, nause**ous**, cur**ious**
-s, -es	more than one	otter**s**, fox**es**
-ship	state of	friend**ship**
-sion, -ssion, -tion	state of being	intru**sion**, permi**ssion**, classifica**tion**
-some	tending to	cumber**some**
-ward	in a direction	back**ward**
-y	characterized by	storm**y**

Hard and soft letter sounds

THE LETTERS *C* AND *G* CAN MAKE HARD AND SOFT SOUNDS.

SEE ALSO	
❰ 130–131 Vowel sounds	
❰ 132–133 Consonant sounds	
Silent letters	160–161 ❱
Irregular word spellings	164–165 ❱

The letter that follows *c* or *g* determines if a word has a hard or soft sound. This sound can occur in any part of the word, not just at the beginning.

The hard and soft *c*

The letter *c* makes a hard sound when it appears before any letter other than *e*, *i*, or *y*. A soft *c* sounds like an *s*—as in *silly*—and can be heard in words where *c* occurs before the letters *e*, *i*, or *y*.

> • Sometimes, **a word** has a **hard "c" sound** that is followed by the letter *e* or *i*. In these cases, the letter *h* is added to make the *c* hard. Some example words include **chemist** (the letter *e*) and **chiropractic** (the letter *i*).

▷ **Hard "c" sounds**
There are many words in English with a hard "c" sound. A word like *cartoon* has a hard "c" sound because *c* precedes the letter *a*.

cartoon   **cow**   **crack**
re**c**all   un**c**le   por**c**upine

▷ **Soft "c" sounds**
These words all have a soft "c" sound. The word *cereal* has a soft "c" sound because *c* precedes the letter *e*.

cereal   **circus**   **cyan**
de**c**ent   pen**c**il   fan**c**y

Words with both "c" sounds

Sometimes, one word includes a hard and a soft "c" sound. These are unusual in English; however, they do follow the same rules.

circulate   bicycle
soft "c" sound / hard "c" sound   soft "c" sound / hard "c" sound

Most words with a **soft c** or **g** come from **Latin**.

clearance   vacancy
hard "c" sound / soft "c" sound   hard "c" sound / soft "c" sound

The hard and soft *g*

The letter *g* makes a hard sound when it appears before any letter other than *e*, *i*, or *y*. The soft *g* sounds like a *j*—as in *jelly*—and usually comes before the letters *e*, *i*, or *y*.

> • Some words have a **hard "g" sound** that is followed by an "e" or "i" sound. In such cases, the **letter *u*** is added to make a hard "g" sound, as seen in ***guess*** (the letter *e*) and ***guide*** (the letter *i*).

▷ **Hard "g" sounds**
The hard "g" sound is common in English. The word *glue* has a hard "g" sound because *g* precedes the letter *l*.

galaxy   green   gullible

igloo   lagoon   fragrant

▷ **Soft "g" sounds**
These words have a soft "g" sound. The word *gene* has a soft "g" sound because *g* precedes the letter *e*.

gene   ginger   gymnast

angel   legible   allergy

Words with both "g" sounds

There are some words that include a hard and a soft "g" sound. There are not many words in English that have both sounds.

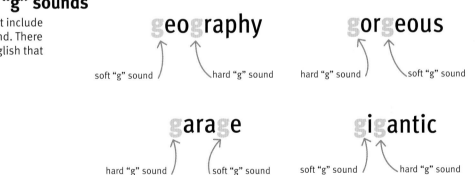

geography

soft "g" sound   hard "g" sound

gorgeous

hard "g" sound   soft "g" sound

garage

hard "g" sound   soft "g" sound

gigantic

soft "g" sound   hard "g" sound

Hard *g* exceptions

Some words make a hard sound even if *g* precedes the letters *e*, *i*, or *y*. These exceptions to the rule just have to be learned, so, if uncertain, check the correct spelling in a dictionary.

These are some common exceptions to the hard *g* rule.

geese   baggy

giggle   gear   girl   get

craggy   geyser

gill   giddy

gift

Words ending in -e or -y

WORDS ENDING IN -E OR -Y OFTEN CHANGE
THEIR SPELLINGS WHEN A SUFFIX IS ADDED.

The final -e in words is usually silent. If a suffix
is added, the -e is sometimes dropped. A final -y
sometimes changes to an *i* when a suffix is added.

SEE ALSO

❮ **130–131** Vowel sounds
❮ **132–133** Consonant sounds
❮ **140–141** Roots
❮ **142–143** Prefixes and suffixes
Silent letters   **160–161** ❯

Words ending in -e
The silent -e serves an important function by changing the
vowel sound of the previous syllable. For example, the words
plan and *plane* are distinguished in spelling only by the
silent -e, and this difference is reflected in the way they
are pronounced. When adding a suffix, the spelling of words
ending in a silent -e follows certain rules.

Root word	Suffix	New word
argue	-ment	argument
awe	-ful	awful
due	-ly	duly
nine	-th	ninth
true	-ly	truly
whole	-ly	wholly
wise	-dom	wisdom

△ **Exceptions**
There are many exceptions to the rules,
some of which are listed in this table.

▷ **Rule 1**
If a word ends
in a silent -e, the
silent -e is dropped
when a suffix
beginning with
a vowel is added.

▷ **Rule 2**
If a word ends in a
silent -e, the silent
-e is kept when a
suffix beginning
with a consonant
is added.

▷ **Rule 3**
If a word ends
in -ce or -ge,
the silent -e must
be retained with
the suffixes -able
and -ous.

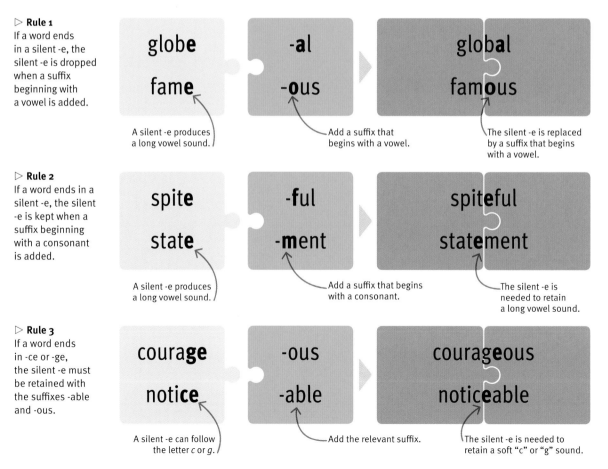

Rule 1
globe   fame   →   -al   -ous   →   global   famous
A silent -e produces a long vowel sound.   Add a suffix that begins with a vowel.   The silent -e is replaced by a suffix that begins with a vowel.

Rule 2
spite   state   →   -ful   -ment   →   spiteful   statement
A silent -e produces a long vowel sound.   Add a suffix that begins with a consonant.   The silent -e is needed to retain a long vowel sound.

Rule 3
courage   notice   →   -ous   -able   →   courageous   noticeable
A silent -e can follow the letter *c* or *g*.   Add the relevant suffix.   The silent -e is needed to retain a soft "c" or "g" sound.

• The **suffix -y acts as a vowel**, so, if adding it to words ending in a silent -e, drop the silent -e. For example, *ice* becomes *icy* and *spice* becomes *spicy*.

Words ending in -y

Words that end in -y can also change spelling when a suffix is added. The main factor that determines this spelling change is whether the final -y is preceded by a consonant or a vowel.

Root word	Suffix	New word
day	-ly	daily
dry	-ness	dryness
shy	-ly	shyly
shy	-ness	shyness
sly	-ly	slyly
sly	-ness	slyness

▷ **Exceptions**
Like words ending in -e, there are exceptions to the rules for words ending in -y.

▷ **Rule 1**
If a word ends in a consonant and -y, the -y is replaced by *i* when any suffix except for -ing is added.

▷ **Rule 2**
If a word ends in a -y preceded by a vowel, the -y is kept when a suffix is added.

▷ **Rule 3**
If a word ends in a -y, the -y is kept when the suffix -ing is added.

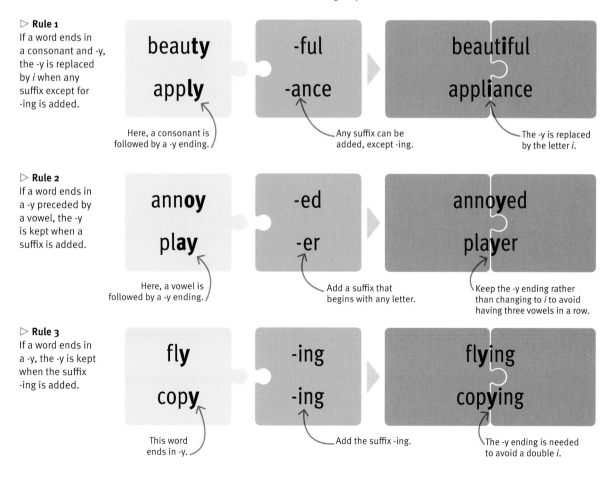

Rule 1

beau**ty** + -ful → beaut**i**ful

app**ly** + -ance → appl**i**ance

Here, a consonant is followed by a -y ending.

Any suffix can be added, except -ing.

The -y is replaced by the letter *i*.

Rule 2

ann**oy** + -ed → annoy**ed**

pl**ay** + -er → play**er**

Here, a vowel is followed by a -y ending.

Add a suffix that begins with any letter.

Keep the -y ending rather than changing to *i* to avoid having three vowels in a row.

Rule 3

fl**y** + -ing → fl**y**ing

cop**y** + -ing → cop**y**ing

This word ends in -y.

Add the suffix -ing.

The -y ending is needed to avoid a double *i*.

Words ending in -tion, -sion, or -ssion

THREE DIFFERENT SUFFIXES CAN REPRESENT THE "SHUN" SOUND AT THE END OF A WORD.

The suffixes -tion, -sion, and -ssion make a "shun" sound. Certain rules are helpful when choosing the correct ending to put at the end of a word.

GLOSSARY

Consonant A letter of the alphabet that is not a vowel.

Noun A word that refers to a person, place, or thing.

Suffix A group of letters attached to the end of a word that can change the original word's meaning.

Verb A word that describes an action.

Vowel One of the five letters *a, e, i, o,* and *u.*

Words ending in -tion

The suffix -tion means "the act of." For instance, *digestion* means "the act of digesting." Most verbs that take the -tion ending already end in -t, so only -ion needs to be added. This suffix is the most common ending.

▷ **Rule 1**
If a verb ends in -t, then add -ion to avoid a double *t* before the suffix.

▷ **Rule 2**
If a verb ends in -te, then remove the e and add -ion.

▷ **Rule 3**
Some verbs drop the last letter and add an extra vowel before the suffix. To find out which vowel to add, always check a dictionary.

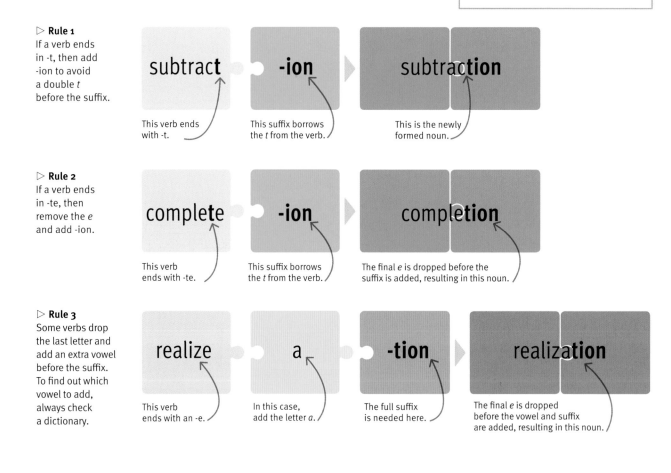

subtract → **-ion** ▷ **subtraction**

This verb ends with -t.

This suffix borrows the *t* from the verb.

This is the newly formed noun.

complete → **-ion** ▷ **completion**

This verb ends with -te.

This suffix borrows the *t* from the verb.

The final *e* is dropped before the suffix is added, resulting in this noun.

realize → **a** → **-tion** ▷ **realization**

This verb ends with an -e.

In this case, add the letter *a.*

The full suffix is needed here.

The final *e* is dropped before the vowel and suffix are added, resulting in this noun.

Words ending in -sion

The suffix -sion means "the state of." For example, *conclusion* means "the state of concluding." There are about 50 words in common use that end in -sion. Most verbs change their endings in order to add the suffix.

▷ **Rule 1**
If the verb ends in -se, then remove the e and add -ion because s is already present.

▷ **Rule 2**
This suffix is used when the verb ends in -d, -l, -r, -s, or -t. Usually, the last letter of the verb is dropped in order to add -sion and turn the verb into a noun.

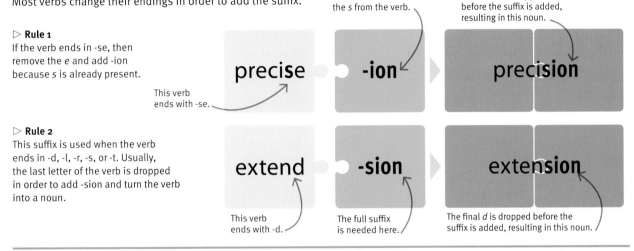

This suffix borrows the s from the verb.

The final e is dropped before the suffix is added, resulting in this noun.

This verb ends with -se.

This verb ends with -d.

The full suffix is needed here.

The final d is dropped before the suffix is added, resulting in this noun.

Words ending in -ssion

This suffix -ssion means "the result of." For example, *impression* means "the result of impressing." Usually, a verb needs to change its ending before the suffix is added.

▷ **Rule 1**
If a verb ends in -ss, then just add -ion.

▷ **Rule 2**
If the verb ends with a -t, then remove it and add -ssion.

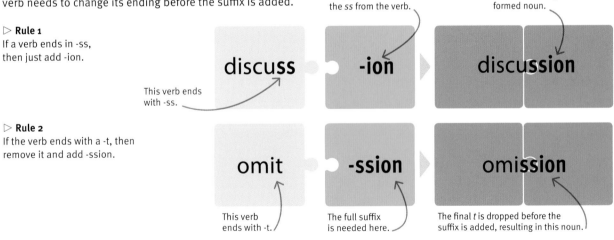

This suffix borrows the ss from the verb.

This is the newly formed noun.

This verb ends with -ss.

This verb ends with -t.

The full suffix is needed here.

The final t is dropped before the suffix is added, resulting in this noun.

Unusual spellings

Some words that end with a "shun" sound do not follow the rules and just need to be learned. If unsure about the correct spelling, always check a dictionary.

Ending	Examples
-sian	A**sian**, Rus**sian**
-xion	comple**xion**, crucifi**xion**
-cion	coer**cion**, suspi**cion**
-cean	crusta**cean**, o**cean**

The only words in which the **"sh" sound** at the start of the last syllable is spelled with the letters *sh* are *cushion* and *fashion*.

Words ending in -able or -ible

SPELLING WORDS WITH SIMILAR-SOUNDING SUFFIXES CAN BE CONFUSING.

The suffixes -able and -ible both mean "able to." For example, *adaptable* means "able to adapt." However, it can be difficult to decide which suffix to use, as they are not interchangeable.

Words ending in -able

The suffix -able is usually added to complete words to turn them into adjectives. Learning a few simple rules makes it easier to decide which suffix to use. More words end in -able than -ible, so, if in doubt, choose -able. Best of all, check the correct spelling in a dictionary.

SEE ALSO

❰ 26–27 Adjectives
❰ 136–137 Morphemes
❰ 140–141 Roots
❰ 142–143 Prefixes and suffixes
❰ 144–145 Hard and soft letter sounds
Single and double consonant words 154–155 ❱

GLOSSARY

Adjective A word that describes a noun.

Suffix A group of letters attached to the end of a word that can change the original word's meaning.

Syllable A unit of pronunciation that has one vowel sound.

Verb A word that describes an action.

Vowel One of the five letters *a*, *e*, *i*, *o*, and *u*.

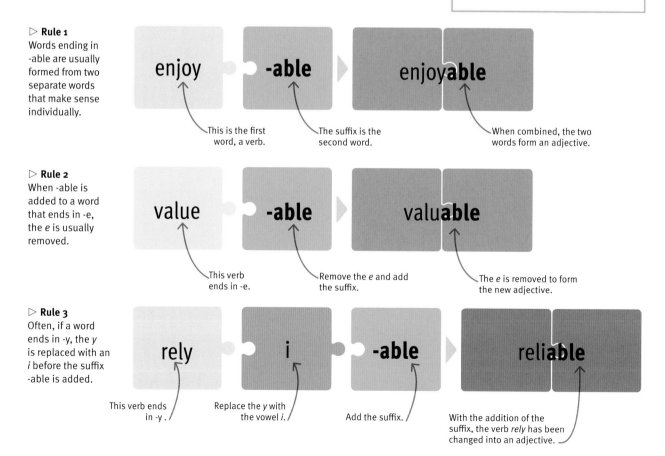

▷ **Rule 1**
Words ending in -able are usually formed from two separate words that make sense individually.

enjoy + -able ▷ enjoy**able**

This is the first word, a verb. — The suffix is the second word. — When combined, the two words form an adjective.

▷ **Rule 2**
When -able is added to a word that ends in -e, the e is usually removed.

value + -able ▷ valu**able**

This verb ends in -e. — Remove the e and add the suffix. — The e is removed to form the new adjective.

▷ **Rule 3**
Often, if a word ends in -y, the y is replaced with an i before the suffix -able is added.

rely + i + -able ▷ reli**able**

This verb ends in -y. — Replace the y with the vowel i. — Add the suffix. — With the addition of the suffix, the verb *rely* has been changed into an adjective.

Words ending in -ible

The suffix -ible is usually added to partial root words, many of which have Latin or Greek origins, but it can also be added to complete words. Several rules help to distinguish words that end in -ible from those that end in -able.

▷ **Rule 1**
Most words ending in -ible cannot be divided into two English words that make sense on their own. The suffix is needed in order to make a whole word.

▷ **Rule 2**
Words with *s* or *ss* before the ending usually take -ible. If they end in a vowel, the vowel is dropped.

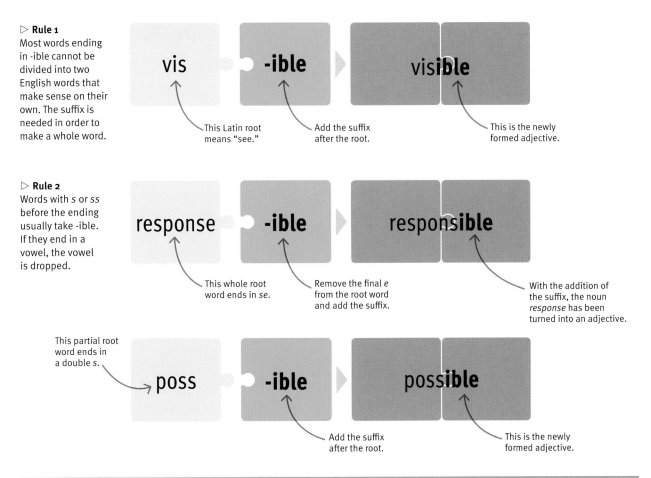

vis **-ible** ▷ **visible**

This Latin root means "see."

Add the suffix after the root.

This is the newly formed adjective.

response **-ible** ▷ **responsible**

This whole root word ends in *se*.

Remove the final *e* from the root word and add the suffix.

With the addition of the suffix, the noun *response* has been turned into an adjective.

This partial root word ends in a double *s*.

poss **-ible** ▷ **possible**

Add the suffix after the root.

This is the newly formed adjective.

Soft and hard "c" and "g" sounds

Words that end in -able usually have a hard "c" or "g" sound. In contrast, words that end in -ible usually have a soft "c" or "g" sound.

Hard "c" or "g" sounds	Soft "c" or "g" sounds
ami**cable**	for**cible**
communi**cable**	invin**cible**
despi**cable**	redu**cible**
indefati**gable**	le**gible**
navi**gable**	tan**gible**

The word ***uncopyrightable*** is the **longest** English **word** in normal use that contains no letter more than **once.**

• Many words that **begin with *a*** use the **suffix** that also begins with *a*: **-able.** Some common examples include ***adorable***, ***advisable***, and ***available***.

Words ending in -le, -el, -al, or -ol

THESE WORD ENDINGS ARE NOT USUALLY SUFFIXES.

Similar-sounding word endings like -le, -el, -al, and -ol can cause spelling difficulties. However, there are some guidelines that can help with using them. As with all tricky spellings, a dictionary is a valuable checking tool.

Words ending in -le

The most common of these word endings is -le. This word ending is not a suffix because it does not change the meaning or part of speech of a root word. The -le word ending is usually found in nouns (such as *table*), verbs (such as *tickle*), and adjectives (such as *vile*).

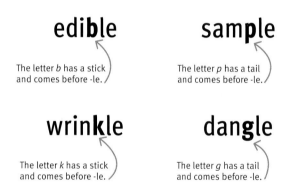

edible

The letter *b* has a stick and comes before -le.

sample

The letter *p* has a tail and comes before -le.

wrinkle

The letter *k* has a stick and comes before -le.

dangle

The letter *g* has a tail and comes before -le.

△ **The rule**
Words ending in -le are often preceded by a letter with a stick or tail—part of the letter reaching high, as in *b*, or low, as in *p*.

Some other **common words** that end with **-ol** use **oo** to create a long vowel sound, as in the words *cool*, *pool*, *school*, and *tool*.

article
missile regale role
textile bale
bicycle capsule
chronicle axle debacle
docile hostile revile
aisle

Of course, a number of words that end with -le do not follow this rule. Some commonly used ones are listed here.

GLOSSARY

Adjective A word that describes a noun.

Noun A word that refers to a person, place, or thing.

Root The smallest part of a word without a prefix or suffix attached.

Suffix A group of letters attached to the end of a word that can change the word's meaning.

Verb A word that describes an action.

Vowel One of the five letters *a*, *e*, *i*, *o*, and *u*.

Words ending in -el and -al

As is the case with -le, the word endings -el and -al generally do not act as suffixes because they are not changing a root word's meaning or part of speech.

travel

The letter *v* does not have a tail or stick.

camel

The letter *m* does not have a tail or stick.

central

The letter *r* does not have a tail or stick.

local

The letter *c* does not have a tail or stick.

△ **The rule**
Words ending in -el and -al are often preceded by a letter without a stick or tail (part of the letter reaching high or low).

-el exceptions	-al exceptions
ang**el**	acquitt**al**
bag**el**	betray**al**
chap**el**	capit**al**
comp**el**	coast**al**
decib**el**	frug**al**
g**el**	fundament**al**
gosp**el**	homicid**al**
host**el**	hospit**al**
hot**el**	judgment**al**
mod**el**	ment**al**
nick**el**	municip**al**
parall**el**	orbit**al**
prop**el**	pet**al**
scalp**el**	port**al**
snork**el**	verb**al**

△ **Exceptions to the rule**
As with words ending in -le, there are a number of exceptions, which end in -el or -al but do not follow this rule.

The -al ending as a suffix

The word ending -al can also be used as a suffix because it can sometimes change the meaning of a root word. Words that end with this suffix are usually nouns or adjectives.

▽ **The rule**
The -al ending can act as a suffix that attaches to a root word, which can be a whole word or part of a word.

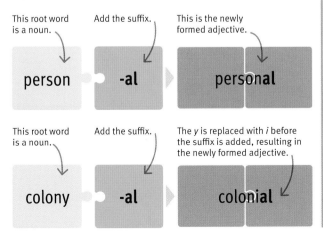

This root word is a noun.

Add the suffix.

This is the newly formed adjective.

person → -al ▷ person**al**

This root word is a noun.

Add the suffix.

The *y* is replaced with *i* before the suffix is added, resulting in the newly formed adjective.

colony → -al ▷ colon**ial**

Words ending in -ol

On rare occasions, -ol is also used as a word ending. This ending is usually found in nouns and verbs. If in doubt, always check the spelling in a dictionary before using it.

Here are ten nouns and verbs that end with -ol.

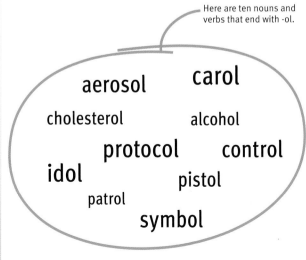

aerosol   carol
cholesterol   alcohol
protocol   control
idol   pistol
patrol
symbol

Single and double consonant words

SINGLE AND DOUBLE CONSONANTS USUALLY SOUND THE SAME.

It is not always obvious if a word contains a single or a double consonant—some spellings just have to be learned. However, there are a few rules that can help.

Consonants and short vowel sounds

In words with more than one syllable, if the first syllable is stressed and has a short vowel sound, then the following consonant is doubled. For example, the word *letter* has a double *t* because the first syllable, *let*, is stressed and has a short vowel sound. Compare this to *retire*, which does not have a double *t*. This is because the stress is on the second syllable, *tire*, which has a long vowel sound.

• The letters *h*, *w*, *x*, and *y* are **never** doubled, even when a suffix beginning with a **vowel** is added. For example, the consonant is not doubled in the words **washed**, **drawer**, **fixable**, and **flying**.

depart

The letter *p* is not doubled because the stress is on the second syllable, *part*.

hammer

The letter *m* is doubled because the stress is on the first syllable, *ham*.

prepare

The letter *p* is not doubled because the stress is on the second syllable, *pare*.

valley

The letter *l* is doubled because the stress is on the first syllable, *val*.

Exceptions to the rule

Many words do not follow the rule above. In most cases, these are root words and are therefore not attached to a prefix or suffix. Some of these words, such as *melon*, have a single consonant after a short vowel sound. Double consonants can also occur after unstressed syllables, as in *correct*. These exceptions can make spelling difficult, so check a dictionary if uncertain.

Single consonant	Double consonant
comet	accept
domino	accumulate
epic	correct
galaxy	effect
lizard	necessary
melon	occur
palace	recommend
radish	sufficient
valid	terrific

Double consonants and suffixes

Consonants that come at the end of a word are often doubled when a suffix is added. This mostly applies to verbs. For example, the final consonant of the verb *sit* is doubled after adding the suffix -ing, which results in the word *sitting*.

> • Consonants are **doubled** when adding a **prefix** or **another word** that ends with the same letter as the first letter of the root. For example, the prefix **mis-** and root *spell* combine to make *misspell*.

▷ **Rule 1**
When adding a suffix that begins with a vowel, such as -er, to a verb that has one syllable and ends with a short vowel sound and a consonant, the final consonant is often doubled.

▷ **Rule 2**
When adding a suffix that begins with a vowel, such as -ing, to a verb with more than one syllable, which ends with a short vowel sound and a consonant, the final consonant is usually doubled.

▷ **Rule 3**
When adding a suffix that begins with e, i, or y to a verb that ends in c, the final consonant is not doubled. Instead, the letter k is added after c in order to keep the hard "c" sound.

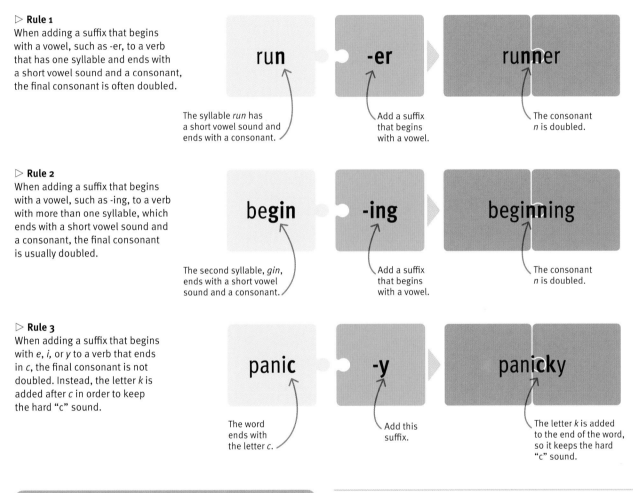

Rule 1
run → -er → runner

The syllable *run* has a short vowel sound and ends with a consonant.
Add a suffix that begins with a vowel.
The consonant n is doubled.

Rule 2
begin → -ing → beginning

The second syllable, *gin*, ends with a short vowel sound and a consonant.
Add a suffix that begins with a vowel.
The consonant n is doubled.

Rule 3
panic → -y → panicky

The word ends with the letter c.
Add this suffix.
The letter k is added to the end of the word, so it keeps the hard "c" sound.

GLOSSARY

Consonant A letter of the alphabet that is not a vowel.

Prefix A group of letters attached to the start of a word that can change the original word's meaning.

Suffix A group of letters attached to the end of a word that can change the original word's meaning.

Syllable A unit of pronunciation that has one vowel sound.

Vowel One of the five letters a, e, i, o, and u.

In English, *bookkeeper* and *bookkeeping* are the only words with **three** consecutive **double letters**.

The "*i* before *e* except after *c*" rule

THE "*I* BEFORE *E* EXCEPT AFTER *C*" RULE IS USED TO REMEMBER SPELLINGS CONTAINING *IE* OR *EI*.

This rule has been used for more than 150 years, and it works in the majority of cases. There are, however, many exceptions to the rule, and it's best to learn these and to be aware of them.

SEE ALSO

❮ **130–131** Vowel sounds

❮ **138–139** Understanding English irregularities

Irregular word spellings **164–165** ❯

• There are **no *cein*** words in the English language. If a *c* is followed by an *ie/ei* combination then an *n*, the spelling should **always be *ie***, as in ***science***.

The rhyme

A useful rhyme was created to help people remember the "*i* before *e*" rule. Originally, it consisted of only two lines, but it has been expanded over the years to include some exceptions to the rule.

The start of the rhyme means that *i* usually comes before *e* in words that contain an "ee" sound, such as *thief*.

The *e* also goes first when the sound in the word is "ay," as in *eight*.

I before e,
Except after c
When the sound is "ee"
Or when sounded as "ay,"
As in neighbor and weigh,
But leisure and seize
Do as they please.

However, when the "ee" sound comes after the letter *c*, the *e* goes before the *i*, as in *receive*.

The end of the rhyme notes that there are some words that don't follow any particular rule.

REAL WORLD

Loan words

A word that has been borrowed from another language is called a loan word. Many loan words use an *e* before *i* spelling. These words include *geisha* from Japanese, *sheikh* from Arabic, and *rottweiler* from German. Many names borrowed from foreign languages are also spelled with the *e* first, such as *Keith*, *Heidi*, *Neil*, and *Sheila*.

• If in **doubt**, always use a **dictionary** to confirm whether a word uses *ie* or *ei*.

Single syllable sounds

As mentioned in the rhyme, the sound of the *ie* or *ei* can be used to figure out which letter combination is right. There are four main rules to remember if the *ie/ei* is pronounced as one syllable. However, most of the rules have exceptions, which have to be learned.

Rule 1

If the sound is "ee," the *i* goes before the *e*.

niece, belief, achieve, field

There are numerous exceptions to this rule that have to be learned.

protein, seize, either, leisure, caffeine

Rule 2

If the "ee" sound follows the letter *c*, the *e* goes first.

receive, receipt, deceit, ceiling

One exception to this rule is when the *ci* sounds like "sh."

ancient, conscience, species

The rule also doesn't apply to words ending in *y* that have been modified.

fancied, policies, bouncier

Rule 3

The *e* goes before the *i* if the sound is "ay" or "eye."

eight, height, feisty

Sometimes, the "eye" sound can also be heard when the *i* goes before *e*.

die, pie, lie, cried

Rule 4

The *e* goes before the *i* if the sound is "eh," as in *met*.

heifer, their, heir

exceptions to this rule

friend, unfriendly

Double syllable sounds

If the *i* and *e* are pronounced as two different sounds, it's easy to figure out which letter comes first. If the "i" sound is pronounced first, then the *i* comes first in the spelling, and vice versa.

di-et, a-li-en, sci-ence, so-ci-e-ty

Pronounced *i* then *e*
In these words, the *i* syllable is said first, so the *i* comes first in the spelling.

de-i-ty, see-ing, be-ing, re-ig-nite, here-in

Pronounced *e* then *i*
In these words, the *e* syllable is said first, so the *e* comes first in the spelling.

Capital letters

THE MOST COMMON USE OF A CAPITAL LETTER
IS AT THE BEGINNING OF A SENTENCE.

In addition to starting sentences, capital letters are used
for the names of people and places, and expressions
of time, such as days of the week.

Starting a sentence

The first word of a sentence
begins with a capital letter. This
draws the reader's attention and
emphasizes the beginning of the
new sentence. A capital letter
follows a period, an exclamation
point, or a question mark at the
end of the previous sentence.

On that

The first word in a sentence
begins with a capital letter.

Expressions of time

Days of the week, months
of the year, and national and
religious holidays, such as
Christmas, are all written with
capital letters. However, the
names of the seasons, such
as winter, are never capitalized.
Historical periods and events,
such as the Industrial Revolution
and the Olympic Games, are
always capitalized.

Saturday

The days of the week
are always capitalized.

Bronze **A**ge

Both letters are
capitalized for this
historical period.

Halloween

Celebrations are
always capitalized.

On that **S**aturday afternoon in
Olivia as she hurried to meet her

• Remember to begin every
quotation with a capital letter.

A, H, I, M, O, T, U, V, W, X,
and Y are all **symmetrical**
capital letters.

REAL WORLD

Capital letters and titles

The titles of books, plays, songs,
newspapers, movies, and poems
require capital letters. Smaller words
within a title, such as the articles *a*
and *the*, or the prepositions *of* and
in, are not usually capitalized unless
they are at the start of a title. For
example, *The New York Times* spells
The with a capital *T* because it is the
first word of the newspaper's title.

• Unlike other pronouns, such as *you*, *he*, *she*, *it*, and *them*, *I* is **always spelled** with a **capital letter**.

The English alphabet **originally only had capital letters**. Lowercase letters were introduced in the **eighth century CE**.

Identifying when to use capital letters

It's important to use capital letters correctly so it's clear where one sentence ends and another begins. Proper nouns must also be capitalized, so that the names of people or places, or expressions of time, can be easily distinguished from other common things.

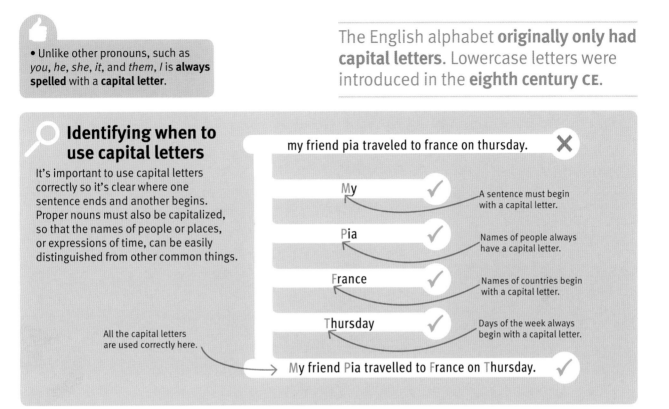

my friend pia traveled to france on thursday. ✗

My ✓ — A sentence must begin with a capital letter.

Pia ✓ — Names of people always have a capital letter.

France ✓ — Names of countries begin with a capital letter.

Thursday ✓ — Days of the week always begin with a capital letter.

All the capital letters are used correctly here. → My friend Pia travelled to France on Thursday. ✓

San Francisco, the rain drenched friends at the Katwalk Café.

People and places

Proper nouns, such as the names of people or places, always begin with a capital letter. A capital letter is also required when describing a specific place, such as "the South," which may refer to the southern region of a country. However, capital letters are not required when indicating a general direction, as in "north of the shopping center."

San Francisco — A city requires a capital letter. For cities with two parts, both words are capitalized.

Olivia — The name of a person must be capitalized.

River Nile — Both parts of this specific river name are capitalized.

Katwalk Café — Both parts are capitalized as they form the name of a place of business.

Disneyland — This is the name of a place, so it is capitalized.

Africa — Names of continents are capitalized.

Silent letters

A SILENT LETTER IS WRITTEN BUT NOT PRONOUNCED.

English includes many words with silent letters. This can sometimes make spelling difficult; however, learning to recognize certain patterns can help with spelling these words.

SEE ALSO

❮ 130–131 Vowel sounds
❮ 132–133 Consonant sounds
❮ 134–135 Syllables
❮ 136–137 Morphemes
❮ 156–157 The "*i* before *e* except after *c*" rule
Irregular word spellings 164–165 ❯

Silent letters

Letters that do not affect the sound of a word are called silent letters. In many cases, these letters were once clearly heard, but over time the pronunciation of the words has changed, even though the spelling has stayed the same.

condemn — If the silent *n* is removed, it does not change the sound of this word—but it would be misspelled.

Letter	When it can be silent	Examples
a	before or after another vowel	aisle, cocoa, head
b	after *m*	crumb, limb, thumb
	before *t*	debt, doubt, subtle
c	after *s*	muscle, scent, scissors
d	before or after *n*	Wednesday, handsome, landscape
e	at the end of a word	giraffe, humble, love
g	before *h*	daughter, though, weigh
	before *n*	campaign, foreign, gnome
h	at the beginning of a word	heir, honest, hour
	after *ex*	exhausting, exhibition, exhilarate
	after *g*	ghastly, ghost, ghoul
	after *r*	rhapsody, rhinoceros, rhyme
	after *w*	whale, wheel, whirlpool
k	before *n*	knee, knight, know
l	before *d*	could, should, would
	before *f*	behalf, calf, half
	before *m*	almond, calm, palm
n	after *m*	autumn, hymn, solemn
p	before *n*	pneumatic, pneumonia, pneumonic
	before *s*	psalm, psychiatry, psychic
	before *t*	pteranodon, pterodactyl, receipt
t	before *ch*	catch, stretch, witch
	after *s*	castle, Christmas, listen
u	with other vowels	building, court, guess
w	before r	wreck, write, wrong
	with *s* or *t*	answer, sword, two

Auxiliary letters

An auxiliary letter is a type of silent letter that can change the pronunciation of a word. For example, if the letter *a* in *coat* is removed, this would spell another word, *cot*, which sounds different and has a different meaning from *coat*.

Here, the silent *e* is an auxiliary letter because, if it is removed, the sound changes. It would also be confused with the existing word *kit*.

Letter	When it can be silent	Examples
a	after *o*	b**o**at, c**o**at, g**o**at
b	after *m*	clim**b**, com**b**, tom**b**
c	before *t*	indi**c**t
d	before *g*	ba**d**ge, do**d**ge, ju**d**ge
e	at the end of a word	hop**e**, kit**e**, sit**e**
g	after *i* and before *n*	beni**g**n, desi**g**n, si**g**n
	after *i* and before *m*	paradi**g**m
h	after *c*	ac**h**e
i	only in one word	bus**i**ness
l	before *k*	fo**l**k, ta**l**k, wa**l**k
	before *m*	ca**l**m, pa**l**m
s	after *i*	ai**s**le, i**s**land
w	before *h*	**w**ho, **w**hom, **w**hose

Regional variations

One aspect that varies from one accent to the next is the silencing and sounding of particular letters. The English language includes a range of regional accents, each with its own peculiarities. Even so, two people raised in the same region might pronounce the same word differently.

Some speakers don't pronounce the final *r* in this word.

Letter	When it can be either silent or heard	Examples
h	before *e*	**h**erb
	after *w*	w**h**ich, w**h**ip, w**h**iskey
r	after a vowel	bo**r**n, ca**r**, sta**r**
t	before or after another consonant	of**t**en, fas**t**en, **t**sunami

About **60 percent** of English words contain a **silent letter**.

• Some words that contain silent letters stem from **other languages**. The words *knife*, *knock* and *know*, which all have a **silent k**, are **Old Norse** words. The words *bright*, *daughter* and *night*, which all contain the **silent gh**, are **Anglo-Saxon** words.

Compound words

A NEW WORD FORMED FROM THE UNION OF
TWO WORDS IS CALLED A COMPOUND WORD.

SEE ALSO

❮ 20–21 Parts of speech
❮ 22–23 Nouns
❮ 38–39 Verbs
❮ 140–141 Roots
Irregular word spellings 164–165 ❯

A compound word is made up of two smaller words that
have been joined together. There are many compound
words in the English language.

Adding detail

Some words are joined to other
words to add detail, making the
resulting compound word more
specific. For example, the word
house can modify the word
boat to create the new compound
word *houseboat*. The word *boat*
can be modified again with other
words, such as *motor* and *steam*,
to create new compound words
that describe other types of
boats: For example, *motorboat*
and *steamboat*.

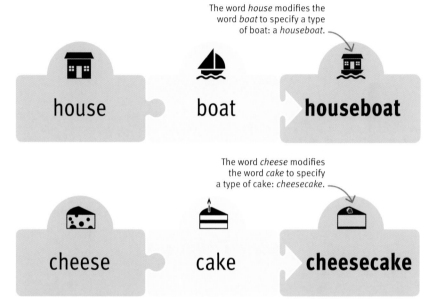

The word *house* modifies the
word *boat* to specify a type
of boat: a *houseboat*.

house + boat → **houseboat**

The word *cheese* modifies
the word *cake* to specify
a type of cake: *cheesecake*.

cheese + cake → **cheesecake**

• Most compound words are nouns.
Verbs formed from two words tend
to stay as two words: For example,
the verb *turn around* **can be
distinguished from the compound
word** *turnaround*—a noun that
usually refers to the act of processing
or completing something.

GLOSSARY

Noun A part of speech that refers
to a person, place, or thing.

Verb A part of speech that describes
an action.

Word 1	Word 2	Compound word
air	craft	aircraft
baby	sitter	babysitter
book	keeper	bookkeeper
card	board	cardboard
dish	washer	dishwasher
fire	place	fireplace
ginger	bread	gingerbread
horse	shoe	horseshoe
key	hole	keyhole
news	paper	newspaper
river	side	riverside
snow	flake	snowflake
sun	rise	sunrise
tax	payer	taxpayer
wall	paper	wallpaper

New meaning

This type of compound word is formed when two smaller words are combined to form a new word that is unrelated to the original words. For example, *hogwash* is made up of two words, *hog* (a type of swine) and *wash* (to cleanse). When combined, these words form the compound word *hogwash*—a noun that describes something as nonsense.

Some languages, such as German and Finnish, **can combine three words.** For example, *Farbfernsehgerät* means **"color television set"** in German.

• Two words can be joined together to form a compound word if the combination creates **one idea or item**, such as *afterlife* or *backbone*. If two words do not create one idea or item, they should stay separate.

The word *glove* combines with the word *fox*, resulting in a type of plant: *foxglove*.

The word *tail* combines with the word *pony*, resulting in a type of hairstyle: a *ponytail*.

fox + glove > **foxglove**

pony + tail > **ponytail**

Word 1	Word 2	Compound word
block	buster	blockbuster
cart	wheel	cartwheel
heart	beat	heartbeat
honey	moon	honeymoon
in	come	income
life	style	lifestyle
lime	light	limelight
master	piece	masterpiece
off	shoot	offshoot
over	come	overcome
scare	crow	scarecrow
show	case	showcase
sleep	walk	sleepwalk
type	writer	typewriter
wind	shield	windshield

REAL WORLD

Evolving compound words

Some words go together so often that they might at first seem to be compound words, such as *post office*, *half moon*, and *ice cream*. Many words begin as two separate words (*wild life*), then become hyphenated (*wild-life*), and then, eventually, become a compound word (*wildlife*).

SLOW DOWN FOR WILDLIFE

Irregular word spellings

SOME SPELLINGS DON'T FOLLOW ANY RULES.

SEE ALSO

❰ **134–135** Syllables
❰ **138–139** Understanding English irregularities
❰ **156–157** The "*i* before *e* except after *c*" rule

The only way to remember irregular spellings is to learn them. However, there are ways to do this that are more fun than just staring at the words.

Weird words

Some words are difficult to spell because they are not spelled like they sound. For example, *said* rhymes with *led* and *fed* but is spelled very differently. Other irregular spellings are tricky because they go against common rules. For example, the word *foreign* does not follow the "*i* before *e* except after *c*" rule.

• One way to learn a spelling is to put up **reminders** everywhere. Write the **troublesome word** in **large letters,** and then put it on the **wall** or anywhere around the house where it will be seen **throughout the day**.

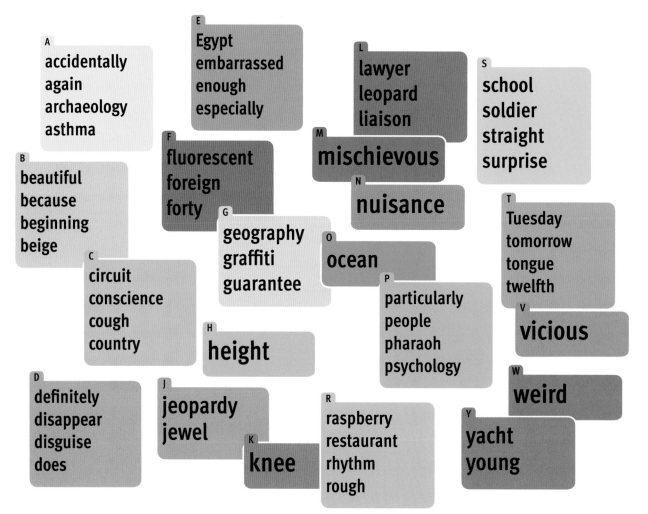

A
accidentally
again
archaeology
asthma

B
beautiful
because
beginning
beige

C
circuit
conscience
cough
country

D
definitely
disappear
disguise
does

E
Egypt
embarrassed
enough
especially

F
fluorescent
foreign
forty

G
geography
graffiti
guarantee

H
height

J
jeopardy
jewel

K
knee

L
lawyer
leopard
liaison

M
mischievous

N
nuisance

O
ocean

P
particularly
people
pharaoh
psychology

R
raspberry
restaurant
rhythm
rough

S
school
soldier
straight
surprise

T
Tuesday
tomorrow
tongue
twelfth

V
vicious

W
weird

Y
yacht
young

Write it out

One technique to learn a spelling is to look at the word, cover it up, write it out from memory, then check it. Do this as many times as necessary until the word is right.

LOOK

tongue

COVER

tong

WRITE

tongue

CHECK

tongue

tongue

What's the problem?

Another way to learn an irregular spelling is to investigate what makes it so difficult. Look at the word and underline the part that is strange or hard to remember. Highlighting the problem will make it easier to recall.

It's strange that this word uses an *f* and *th* to make the final sound.

leopard

The *o* is silent.

restaurant

The *aur* sounds like it should be spelled *er*.

twel**fth**

Speak differently

If a word isn't written how it sounds, say it out loud, pronouncing it so that it does match the spelling.

defin**IT**ely

Try stressing *it* to remember that it isn't spelled *at*.

WED NES DAY

Say this word in its separate parts to make it easier to spell.

particul**ARLY**

Start to stress the *arly* to remember that it isn't spelled *erly*.

Words within words

Another trick is to look for smaller words in longer ones. This will associate the longer word with the smaller word. Visualizing these small words with pictures will make spelling the longer word much easier.

Draw images like this to visualize the words within words.

There is a rat in separate

Silly sayings

Making up ridiculous phrases can help people to remember spellings. These are called mnemonic devices. One method is to think of a phrase whose words begin with each letter in the tricky word. Other sayings can remind people of the number of particular letters in a word.

RHYTHM — Rhythm Helps Your Two Hips Move

Each word in the saying starts with a letter from the spelling.

BECAUSE — Big Elephants Can't Always Use Small Exits

This saying reminds people that the word has one *c* and two *s*'s.

NECESSARY — One coffee with two sugars

Homonyms, homophones, and homographs

SOME WORDS HAVE THE SAME PRONUNCIATION OR SPELLING BUT MEAN DIFFERENT THINGS.

SEE ALSO

❮ **78–79** Commonly misused words
❮ **140–141** Roots
❮ **142–143** Prefixes and suffixes
❮ **160–161** Silent letters
❮ **164–165** Irregular word spellings
Writing to describe **208–209** ❯

Variations in pronunciation or spelling are what distinguish homonyms, homophones, and homographs. Using the correct word is important for both spoken and written English.

Homonyms

Words with the same spelling and pronunciation, but different meanings, are called homonyms. For example, the word *fair* can refer to an event with games and rides or to the idea of treating somebody in a reasonable way.

The word **homonym** come from the Greek **homos**, which means **"same,"** and **onyma**, which means **"name."**

Crossword puzzles

Crossword puzzles can be difficult without a good understanding of homonyms, homophones, and homographs. The clues in cryptic crosswords take advantage of the confusion caused by these words in order to mislead the reader.

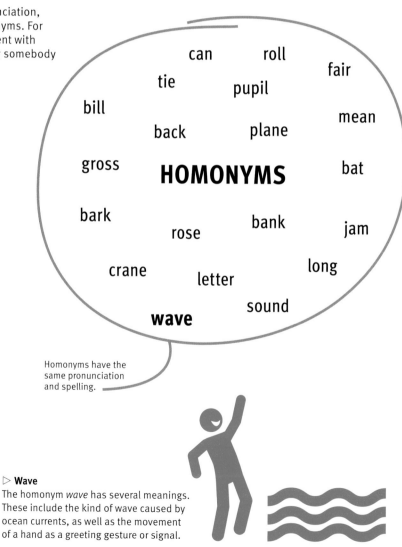

can   roll   fair
tie   pupil
bill   mean
back   plane
gross   **HOMONYMS**   bat
bark   bank   jam
rose
crane   long
letter
sound
wave

Homonyms have the same pronunciation and spelling.

▷ **Wave**
The homonym *wave* has several meanings. These include the kind of wave caused by ocean currents, as well as the movement of a hand as a greeting gesture or signal.

Homophones

Words with identical pronunciation but different spellings and meanings are called homophones, which means "same sound" in Greek. Most homophones come in pairs, such as *reed* and *read*; however, there are also some groups of three words, as in *to*, *too*, and *two*.

Homophones have the same pronunciation but different spellings.

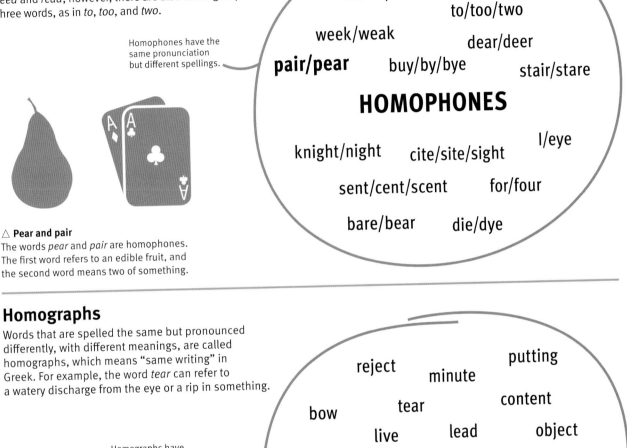

HOMOPHONES

which/witch
read/reed
to/too/two
week/weak
dear/deer
pair/pear
buy/by/bye
stair/stare
knight/night
cite/site/sight
I/eye
sent/cent/scent
for/four
bare/bear
die/dye

△ **Pear and pair**
The words *pear* and *pair* are homophones. The first word refers to an edible fruit, and the second word means two of something.

Homographs

Words that are spelled the same but pronounced differently, with different meanings, are called homographs, which means "same writing" in Greek. For example, the word *tear* can refer to a watery discharge from the eye or a rip in something.

Homographs have different pronunciations but the same spelling.

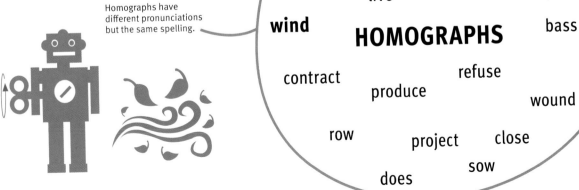

HOMOGRAPHS

reject
minute
putting
bow
tear
content
live
lead
object
wind
bass
contract
refuse
produce
wound
row
project
close
does
sow

△ **Wind**
The homograph *wind* has two meanings. One relates to a turning or twisting action, and the other refers to a strong breeze.

Confusing words

SIMILAR-SOUNDING WORDS CAN BE DIFFICULT TO SPELL.

English includes many words that look and sound the same, or nearly the same. Recognizing small differences in pronunciation can help with spelling.

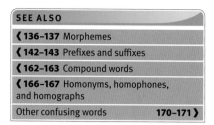
Noun and verb confusion

Some nouns and verbs are often confused because of their similar or identical pronunciation. In some cases, a small change in the sound of a word can indicate a different part of speech, as in the noun *advice* and verb *advise*. More often, however, words have the same pronunciation but a different spelling and meaning, as in *effect* and *affect*.

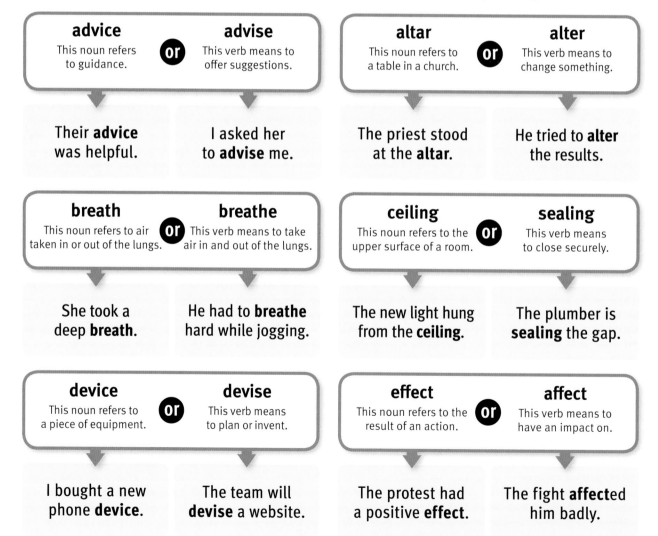

advice
This noun refers to guidance.

or

advise
This verb means to offer suggestions.

Their **advice** was helpful.

I asked her to **advise** me.

altar
This noun refers to a table in a church.

or

alter
This verb means to change something.

The priest stood at the **altar**.

He tried to **alter** the results.

breath
This noun refers to air taken in or out of the lungs.

or

breathe
This verb means to take air in and out of the lungs.

She took a deep **breath**.

He had to **breathe** hard while jogging.

ceiling
This noun refers to the upper surface of a room.

or

sealing
This verb means to close securely.

The new light hung from the **ceiling**.

The plumber is **sealing** the gap.

device
This noun refers to a piece of equipment.

or

devise
This verb means to plan or invent.

I bought a new phone **device**.

The team will **devise** a website.

effect
This noun refers to the result of an action.

or

affect
This verb means to have an impact on.

The protest had a positive **effect**.

The fight **affect**ed him badly.

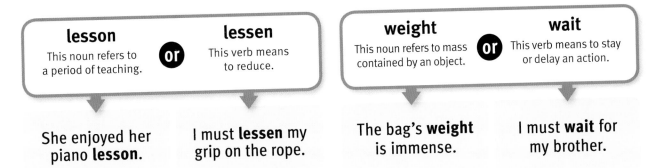

lesson
This noun refers to a period of teaching.

or

lessen
This verb means to reduce.

weight
This noun refers to mass contained by an object.

or

wait
This verb means to stay or delay an action.

She enjoyed her piano **lesson**.

I must **lessen** my grip on the rope.

The bag's **weight** is immense.

I must **wait** for my brother.

Commonly misspelled words

There are many other words that sound the same or similar to each other, but have different spellings and meanings. In all cases, it's important to use the correct word in order to be understood, particularly in written form. If uncertain which is the correct word to use, check a dictionary.

Word	Example sentence
are	Those boys **are** always getting into trouble.
hear	I could **hear** the plane flying overhead.
know	The taxi driver didn't **know** the way to my house.
lose	There was no way she could **lose** in the finals.
passed	He **passed** the present to his friend.
weather	The **weather** report predicted snowfall.

Word	Example sentence
our	**Our** team was invited to the national championships.
here	**Here** is the latest photo of my family.
now	There is **now** a café where my house used to be.
loose	My friend's **loose** change fell out of his pocket.
past	She drove **past** the park on the way home.
whether	I am not sure **whether** to wear my coat today or not.

One or two words?

Some phrases have different meanings according to whether they are spelled as one word or two. For example, the single word *everyday* means routine or commonplace, whereas *every day* means each day.

Word	Example sentence
anyone	**Anyone** caught smoking will be punished.
already	Our passports have **already** been inspected.
altogether	The song was **altogether** inappropriate.
everyday	I was wearing **everyday** clothes around the house.
maybe	**Maybe** one day they will uncover the truth.

Phrase	Example sentence
any one	**Any one** of those people could be to blame.
all ready	We are **all ready** to board the plane.
all together	The paintings were exhibited **all together** for the first time.
every day	I need to use a hairdryer **every day** after my shower.
may be	There **may be** more than one culprit.

• Learning the meanings of commonly used **roots**, **prefixes**, and **suffixes** can help with confusing words.

Other confusing words

MISSPELLED WORDS OFTEN ARISE FROM CONFUSED MEANINGS.

SEE ALSO
❰ 104–105 Apostrophes
❰ 166–167 Homonyms, homophones, and homographs
❰ 168–169 Confusing words

Some words are misunderstood and therefore spelled incorrectly. Choosing the wrong word can alter the meaning of a sentence, which may confuse the reader.

Confused meanings

Some words are incorrectly spelled because their meanings are not properly understood. In some cases, two words may sound similar, which only adds to the confusion.

With such words, the difference in meaning and spelling has to be learned; there is no trick or rule to remember. Consult a dictionary if in doubt about which word to use.

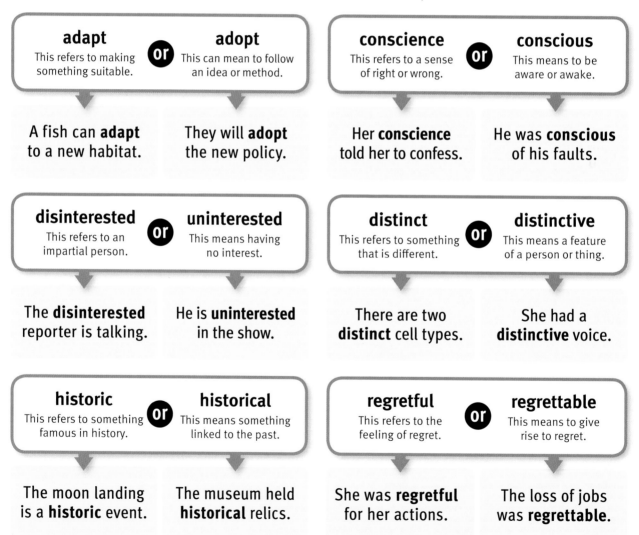

adapt or **adopt**
This refers to making something suitable. This can mean to follow an idea or method.

A fish can **adapt** to a new habitat.
They will **adopt** the new policy.

conscience or **conscious**
This refers to a sense of right or wrong. This means to be aware or awake.

Her **conscience** told her to confess.
He was **conscious** of his faults.

disinterested or **uninterested**
This refers to an impartial person. This means having no interest.

The **disinterested** reporter is talking.
He is **uninterested** in the show.

distinct or **distinctive**
This refers to something that is different. This means a feature of a person or thing.

There are two **distinct** cell types.
She had a **distinctive** voice.

historic or **historical**
This refers to something famous in history. This means something linked to the past.

The moon landing is a **historic** event.
The museum held **historical** relics.

regretful or **regrettable**
This refers to the feeling of regret. This means to give rise to regret.

She was **regretful** for her actions.
The loss of jobs was **regrettable**.

Triple trouble

Sometimes, three words sound very similar but mean different things. In such cases, be extra careful to understand the differences between the three words and learn the spellings.

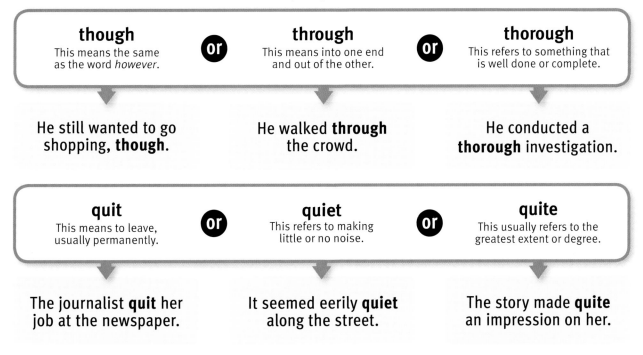

though	or	**through**	or	**thorough**
This means the same as the word *however*.		This means into one end and out of the other.		This refers to something that is well done or complete.

He still wanted to go shopping, **though**.

He walked **through** the crowd.

He conducted a **thorough** investigation.

quit	or	**quiet**	or	**quite**
This means to leave, usually permanently.		This refers to making little or no noise.		This usually refers to the greatest extent or degree.

The journalist **quit** her job at the newspaper.

It seemed eerily **quiet** along the street.

The story made **quite** an impression on her.

More confused meanings

There are many examples of words that are widely and repeatedly misspelled because their meanings are not clearly understood. Always reread the sentence to make sure the correct word is used.

Word	Example
accident	The bicycle **accident** left her with a large bruise.
angel	The religious text mentioned an **angel**.
desert	It was very hot in the middle of the **desert**.
elicit	The father tried to **elicit** a response from his son.
envelop	The fog was about to **envelop** the town.
lightening	The hairdresser was **lightening** my hair.
rational	There was no **rational** reason for her behavior.

Word	Example
incident	There was an **incident** of bullying on the team.
angle	Every **angle** in a square is the same size.
dessert	My favorite **dessert** is key lime pie.
illicit	The airport confiscated **illicit** food from the man.
envelope	He put the letter in an **envelope**.
lightning	The **lightning** storm caused havoc.
rationale	She explained the **rationale** for her decision.

Funny puns

Tabloid newspapers are renowned for their use of puns in headlines. Puns take advantage of the potential confusion between words that sound the same to create jokes or wry commentary.

Abbreviations

A WORD OR PHRASE THAT IS WRITTEN IN A
SHORTENED FORM IS CALLED AN ABBREVIATION.

SEE ALSO

❮ **94–95** Periods and ellipses

❮ **158–159** Capital letters

❮ **164–165** Irregular word spellings

Picking the right words **182–183** ❯

The English language contains many abbreviations, which are used to represent longer words or phrases in speech, or where space is limited. In some cases, the abbreviation is better known than the full name.

The symbol @ is an abbreviation for "at" and is used in **e-mail addresses** and **text messsages**.

Common abbreviations

The way an abbreviation is written usually depends on the category to which it belongs. Often, a period is used to represent missing text. For abbreviated Latin phrases, periods are used after each letter. Abbreviations that are formed from the initial letters of a group of words usually don't use periods.

REAL WORLD

NASA

One of the world's most recognized abbreviations is the name of the American government agency NASA, which stands for the National Aeronautics and Space Administration. The first letter from each word forms this acronym—an abbreviation that is pronounced as a word, not as separate letters. The NASA logo shown here is on the side of a space shuttle.

Abbreviation	Words in full
3-D	three-dimensional
a.m.	*ante meridiem* (Latin); before noon (English)
b.	born (indicating birth date)
BCE	before the Common Era
Brit.	British
C	Centigrade or Celsius
CE	Common Era
dept.	department
DIY	do-it-yourself
ed.	edition or editor
e.g.	*exempli gratia* (Latin); for example (English)
est.	established or estimated
EST	Eastern Standard Time
etc.	*et cetera* (Latin); and the rest (English)
EU	European Union
F	Fahrenheit
FAQ	frequently asked questions
GMT	Greenwich Mean Time
HTML	HyperText Markup Language

Abbreviation	Words in full
i.e.	*id est* (Latin); that is (English)
IOU	I owe you
LED	light-emitting diode
long.	longitude
MD	medical doctor
Mr.	Mister
Mrs.	Mistress (referring to wife)
PDF	Portable Document Format
percent	*per centum* (Latin); in each hundred (English)
p.m.	*post meridiem* (Latin); after noon (English)
PM	Prime Minister
Pres.	President
P.S.	*post scriptum* (Latin); written after (English)
PTO	please turn over
SMS	Short Message Service
UK	United Kingdom
US	United States
USB	Universal Serial Bus
www	World Wide Web

Shortenings

A shortening is a representation of a single word, typically in lowercase letters. Usually, the beginning or the end of a word is dropped; in rare cases, both the beginning and end of a word are omitted. The use of a period depends on whether the abbreviation is formal or informal. Occasionally, shortening results in spelling changes, as when *bicycle* is changed to *bike*.

advertisement ▷ **ad**
The first two letters produce this informal word.

in**flu**enza ▷ **flu**
The three middle letters make this informal word.

latitude ▷ **lat.**
The first three letters create this formal abbreviation, which requires a period.

we**blog** ▷ **blog**
The last four letters create this informal word.

Contracted abbreviations

A contracted abbreviation occurs when letters from the middle of a word are removed. These words are usually related to a position or qualification. This type of abbreviation usually begins with a capital letter. A period is normally used at the end of a contracted abbreviation.

Docto**r** ▷ **Dr.**
Take out the middle four letters to get this abbreviation.

Junio**r** ▷ **Jr.**
Remove the middle four letters to form this abbreviation.

Limit**e**d ▷ **Ltd.**
Remove the letters *imi* and *e* to make this abbreviation.

Se**rg**ean**t** ▷ **Sgt.**
Remove the letters *er* and *ean* to create this abbreviation.

Initialisms

An initialism is created from the first letter of each word. Each letter is pronounced separately and written in capital letters. Initialisms generally don't require periods between the letters.

United **S**tates of **A**merica ▷ **USA**

British **B**roadcasting **C**orporation ▷ **BBC**

Digital **V**ideo **D**isc ▷ **DVD**

Acronyms

An acronym is a word formed from the initial letters of a group of words. It is different from an initialism because it is pronounced as it is spelled, not as separate letters. Acronyms are written in capital letters and without periods.

Acquired **I**mmuno**D**eficiency **S**yndrome ▷ **AIDS**

North **A**tlantic **T**reaty **O**rganization ▷ **NATO**

Personal **I**dentification **N**umber ▷ **PIN**

British and American spellings

BRITISH AND AMERICAN WORDS ARE OFTEN SPELLED
USING DIFFERENT ENDINGS.

In British English, the *l* is often doubled before a suffix, but not
in American English. Words that end in -ise, -yse, -ce, -re, and -our
in British English may also be spelled differently in American English.

SEE ALSO
❮ 142–143 Prefixes and suffixes
❮ 154–155 Single and double consonant words

English-language
spelling was first
standardized by the
English writer **Samuel
Johnson** in 1755.

Doubling the letter *l*

Words that are written with a double *l*
in British English are often written
with only a single *l* in American English.
This usually occurs when a suffix,
such as -or, -ed, -er, or -ing, is added
to a word ending in a single *l*.

British English	American English
cancelled	canceled
counsellor	counselor
fuelled	fueled
jeweller	jeweler
marvelled	marveled
modelling	modeling
quarrelled	quarreled
traveller	traveler

Words ending in -ise or -ize and -yse or -yze

Most words that end with -ise or -yse in British
English end with -ize or -yze in American
English. However, the -ize and -yze spellings
are also widely used in Britain.

British English	American English
analyse	analyze
criticise	criticize
hypnotise	hypnotize
mobilise	mobilize
modernise	modernize
organise	organize
recognise	recognize
visualise	visualize

Words ending in -ce or -se

Certain words that end with -ce in British
English end with -se in American English.
Depending on the part of speech, some words,
such as *practice* and *licence*, are spelled in two
different ways in British English, whereas
this distinction is ignored in American English.

British	American
defence	defense
licence (noun); license (verb)	license (noun and verb)
offence	offense
pretence	pretense
practice (noun); practise (verb)	practice (noun and verb)

Words ending in -re or -er

Many British words that end with -re are spelled with -er in American English. This difference is commonly seen in the spelling of metric measurements, such as *metre* and *litre* in British English, compared to *meter* and *liter* in American English.

British English	American English
calibre	caliber
centre	center
fibre	fiber
lustre	luster
meagre	meager
sombre	somber
spectre	specter
theatre	theater

Words ending in -our or -or

Words that end with -our in British English often end with -or in American English. However, in British English, when one of the endings -ous, -ious, -ary, -ation, -ific, -ize, or -ise is added to a noun that ends in -our, the -our is usually changed to -or. For example, *humour* becomes *humorous*, and *glamour* becomes *glamorise*.

British English	American English
behaviour	behavior
colour	color
flavour	flavor
humour	humor
labour	labor
neighbour	neighbor
rumour	rumor
vigour	vigor

Same spelling

Many British and American words are spelled the same, regardless of the rules. In most cases, there is no reason for this and the words just have to be learned. If uncertain, check how words are spelled in a dictionary.

rebelled   **endurance**   **feather**

mediocre

advertise   **exercise**

fooling   **actor**

Webster's Dictionary

Noah Webster (1758–1843) is frequently credited with introducing American spelling. Webster wanted to emphasize a unique American cultural identity by showing that Americans spoke a different language from the British. He also advocated spelling words phonetically. In 1828, he published *An American Dictionary of the English Language*, which forms the basis of American spelling to this day.

• American and British spellings are both **correct**, as long as one or the other is used **consistently**.

• Occasionally, American English uses the British spelling for **names**, as in the case of the space shuttle *Endeavour* or **Ford's Theatre** in Washington, D.C.

More British and American spellings

SPELLING DIFFERENCES BETWEEN BRITISH AND AMERICAN ENGLISH CAN SOMETIMES AFFECT A WORD'S PRONUNCIATION.

Small differences between British and American spellings do not usually change the meaning of a word. However, British English may use two words to indicate two meanings, whereas American English uses the same word for both meanings.

Different sounds or words

A minor change in the spelling of a word can affect its sound, even if the meaning is the same. Occasionally, British and American English use different words to mean the same thing.

British English	American English
aeroplane	airplane
aluminium	aluminum
disorientated	disoriented
pavement	sidewalk
sledge	sleigh or sled

Different meanings

Sometimes, British English uses two words that sound the same but with different spellings to indicate different meanings. American English uses the same word for both meanings.

The *Oxford English Dictionary* is widely thought to be the **authority** on the English language and includes both **British** and **American** spellings.

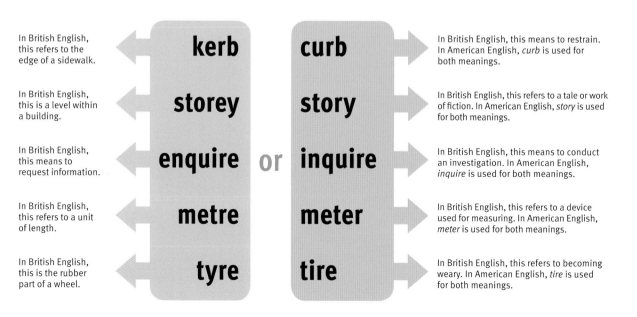

In British English, this refers to the edge of a sidewalk.

kerb

curb

In British English, this means to restrain. In American English, *curb* is used for both meanings.

In British English, this is a level within a building.

storey

story

In British English, this refers to a tale or work of fiction. In American English, *story* is used for both meanings.

In British English, this means to request information.

enquire or **inquire**

In British English, this means to conduct an investigation. In American English, *inquire* is used for both meanings.

In British English, this refers to a unit of length.

metre

meter

In British English, this refers to a device used for measuring. In American English, *meter* is used for both meanings.

In British English, this is the rubber part of a wheel.

tyre

tire

In British English, this refers to becoming weary. In American English, *tire* is used for both meanings.

Silent vowels

In British English, some words have two vowels in a row, one of which is silent. In American English, this silent vowel is usually dropped.

British English	American English
anaemia	anemia
foetus	fetus
manoeuvre	maneuver
paediatric	pediatric
palaeontology	paleontology

Past tenses ending in -ed or -t

When verbs are written in the past tense, their spellings can differ between British and American English. This is mainly the case with verbs in which the last letter is *l*, *m*, or *n*. American English uses the regular ending -ed, whereas British English often uses the irregular ending -t.

British English	American English
burnt or burned	burned
dreamt or dreamed	dreamed
learnt or learned	learned
smelt or smelled	smelled
spelt or spelled	spelled

Retaining or dropping the silent -e

Certain words in American English do not have a silent -e ending, while British spelling usually retains the silent -e. This pattern occurs most commonly when a suffix, such as -ment, has been added to a word that ends in a silent -e.

British English	American English
acknowledgement	acknowledgment
ageing or aging	aging
axe	ax
judgement	judgment
useable or usable	usable

• Some words that are **hyphenated** in British English are **compound words** in American English. For example, British English uses *ear-splitting* and *kind-hearted*, while American English uses *earsplitting* and *kindhearted*.

REAL WORLD
Mid-Atlantic English

In the early part of the twentieth century, many American actors, such as Katharine Hepburn, tried to cultivate an accent that was neither obviously American nor British. This was sometimes called "mid-Atlantic English." The fashion for this accent has disappeared, and today the term is used to refer to written English that avoids obvious "Britishisms" or "Americanisms."

Communication skills

Effective communication

GOOD COMMUNICATION SENDS THE RIGHT MESSAGE.

To communicate means to exchange ideas and information with others. Communicating effectively means exchanging ideas and information with others in such a way that they understand precisely what is meant.

Everyday communication

Communicating effectively isn't just about writing an A-grade essay. People need to pass on information in many different scenarios every day. Most communication has a desired effect: for example, to give the recipient information or to persuade them to do something.

Good communication skills can help in many different situations.

Sending an invitation
Giving a friend advice
Making a complaint
Giving travel directions
Selling an item on the Internet
Auditioning for a play

Getting the message

Bad communication will not have the desired effect. For example, an unclear recipe will produce an inedible cake, a lackluster political speech will lose votes, and an incomplete party invitation will confuse the intended guests, who may fail to show up.

This version gives precise details about the time and location.

This invitation does not specify what time or where the party is taking place.

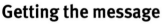

I'm having a party next Saturday. It would be great to see you there. Remember to dress up.

The term *dress up* is vague and could refer to costumes or formal attire.

Please join me to celebrate my birthday on

Saturday, July 14, at 7:00 p.m.

My address is
44 Culver Street, Eureka, CA 95501.

The dress code is formal.

The exact dress code is specified.

Sending the right message

In order to send clear and effective messages, it's important to consider various factors.

LET'S PARTY!

Don't miss the
celebration of the year on

Saturday, July 14, at 7:00 p.m.

There will be **food, dancing, fireworks, magic,** and **much, much more.**

My address is
44 Culver Street, Eureka, CA 95501.

X

HOW TO GET HERE

Tone

Picking the right tone is important. Tone refers to the mood or feeling of a text. For example, a party invitation should be enthusiastic, an advice column should be sympathetic, and a business letter should be formal and serious.

Language

Effective communication should be written using appropriate language. The choice of vocabulary and sentence structures will help to communicate the right message.

Layout

The font size and color, the arrangement of text on the page, and the use of images can simplify a message or draw attention to pieces information. The layout of some forms of communication, such as newspaper articles and letters, follows specific conventions.

Method

It's important to pick the right method of communication, such as an e-mail, newspaper article, or leaflet. People also communicate verbally in a debate or by giving a speech. Nonverbal methods of communication, such as body language and eye contact, should also be considered.

This sounds fun...

Audience

A message needs to be tailored to its audience. For example, a piece of writing for young children may use simple and fun language, while an adult audience will understand more complicated vocabulary.

Purpose

All communication has a purpose. This is the effect that the message should have on the audience. For example, it may be to encourage them to go to a party, to give them advice, or to pass on news.

Picking the right words

EFFECTIVE COMMUNICATION USES VARIED AND
APPROPRIATE VOCABULARY.

It's important to pick words that are clear and suit the purpose
and audience of the text. Using the same words all the time can
be boring, so try to use a varied range of vocabulary.

SEE ALSO	
❮ 26–27 Adjectives	
❮ 84–85 Idioms, analogies, and figures of speech	
❮ 86–87 Colloquialisms and slang	
Genre, purpose, and audience	190–191 ❯
Writing to inform	196–197 ❯
Newspaper articles	198–199 ❯
Writing to describe	208–209 ❯
Writing for the Web	214–215 ❯

Avoid overused words

Using a wide range of vocabulary makes a piece of
writing more entertaining and original. Here are some
overused words to avoid, such as *got* and *great*, and
some alternatives, known as synonyms.

very

pleasant

agreeable

charming

delightful

incredibly **truly**

unusually

extremely

nice

countless

numerous

many

myriad

acquired

obtained

received

thrilling

entertaining

amusing

enjoyable

lots of

wonderful

fabulous   incredible

fantastic

got

great

finally   **next**

later

then

fun

• **Look up** any **new** words and find out what they mean.
Then, write them down and try to use them in the **future**.

Less is more

It's important not to use several words when
one will do. Overly long phrases might seem
impressive, but they are often unclear. Most long
phrases can be replaced with shorter versions.

Military jargon

Members of the armed forces
use jargon to communicate
with one another for speed
and secrecy. Many of these
terms are abbreviations of
longer phrases. For example,
DPV is an abbreviation for
"Desert Patrol Vehicle."

Unclear version	Concise version
she is of the opinion that	she thinks that
concerning the matter of	about
in the event that	if
regardless of the fact that	although
due to the fact that	because
in all cases	always
he is a man who	he
a small number of	a few

How formal

The words people use depend on the situation they're in and the person they're talking to. In informal situations, people tend to use colloquial words, but when writing to someone they don't know, or someone in authority, they use formal vocabulary.

> Hey man. This homework sucks. I just don't get it.

A text message to a friend can include slang, such as "Hey man" and "sucks."

Dear Mrs. Jones,

Jake experienced some difficulties in completing last night's homework. Although he tried very hard, he could not understand the excercise. He may need some extra help so that he can finish the work.

Your truly,
Sheila Jessop

A letter to a teacher should be written in formal language.

Word play

Writers also choose words to entertain readers. By using particular combinations of words, they can create humor and sound patterns. There are three main types of word play: puns, alliteration, and assonance.

Puns
A pun is a play on words. It exploits the multiple meanings of a word, or similar sounding words, to create humor.

Once **a pun** a time...

Alliteration
Alliteration is the effect created when words next to or close to each other begin with the same letter or sound. It is often used in newspaper headlines.

Thomas Turner tripped over the **table.**

Assonance
Assonance is the effect created by the repetition of vowel sounds. It is often used in poetry.

Is it **true you** like **blue**?

Getting technical

Jargon is the term for words or phrases that are only used and understood by members of a particular group or profession. For example, doctors, lawyers, and sports professionals use certain terms to communicate quickly and effectively. However, it's best to avoid using jargon outside of these circles, since it can be meaningless to other people.

Get me his **vitals.**

Doctors use this term to refer to patients' vital statistics, such as their pulse, body temperature, and breathing rate.

Making sentences interesting

THE BEST PIECES OF WRITING USE SENTENCES THAT ARE CLEAR BUT ALSO INTERESTING TO READ.

A text containing very similar sentences will be boring to read. Using a variety of sentence types with plenty of detail will make a piece of writing more engaging.

Pick and mix

Good writers vary the types of sentences that they use in their work. Lots of short sentences can make a piece of writing monotonous and disjointed. Using some longer sentences instead helps the writing flow and links ideas together. There are three main types of sentences to choose from.

> This simple sentence contains the subject *monster* and the main verb *was*.

> This compound sentence has two main clauses linked by the conjunction *and*.

A monster was on the loose. It came out at night and its howls filled the air. People said that the monster had green fur and red eyes, although no one had ever seen it.

> This complex sentence contains a main clause and a subordinate clause.

Change of pace

Rather than using a random mixture of sentences, it's possible to select a particular type of sentence for effect—for example, to change the pace or add tension or excitement.

> A long sentence in a speech can reinforce the seriousness of a problem.

She began to run. The monster followed. Her heart was racing. The monster wasn't far behind. She had to make a decision. She jumped into the lake.

> A string of short sentences in a story can create excitement.

Pulling herself out of the water, she could see light from the cottage in the distance. She scrambled up the riverbank, and ran through the mud, under the oak trees, around the bend in the road, and up the path. She was home.

> Using a short sentence after a very long one can relieve tension.

"If we don't all gather together and track down the bloodthirsty monster, our children will not be safe on the streets and we will not be able to sleep soundly in our beds. We need to act now."

> Following the long sentence with a short sentence can make a powerful final point.

A fresh start

Good writers avoid starting all the sentences in a paragraph in the same way because it sounds monotonous. Sentences can easily be rewritten to stop this from happening.

> All these sentences start with the same word, *there*.

There was a chill in the air as Jessica walked through the woods. **There** was nobody around. **There** was a sudden growl in the distance.

> This passage gives exactly the same information, but in a more interesting way.

There was a chill in the air as Jessica walked through the woods. Nobody was around. Suddenly, she heard a growl in the distance.

Add detail

Adding extra detail using adjectives and adverbs will make a sentence more informative and interesting. The position of an adverb can also be changed to vary the sentence structure.

> This sentence isn't very interesting.

Jessica backed away from the monster.

> Adding an adverb tells the reader about the way the girl is moving. The adjective describes the mood of the monster.

Jessica **nervously** backed away from the **angry** monster.

> Moving the adverb changes the structure of the sentence.

Nervously, Jessica backed away from the angry monster.

GLOSSARY

Main clause A group of words that contains a subject and a verb and makes complete sense on its own.

Subordinate clause A group of words that contains a subject and a verb but depends on a main clause for its meaning.

- Add more detail to a sentence by using **prepositions**, which tell the reader **where** something is or **when** something is happening. Prepositions include *about, across, after, at,* and *under.*
- Use a variety of **conjunctions** to link clauses and make sentences **flow** from one to another. These are **connecting words**, such as *so, because, until, whereas,* and *but.*

REAL WORLD
Exciting commentary

Sports commentators often describe the events of a game or race with very short sentences. This makes the commentary as fast-paced and exciting as the event itself. It's particularly effective for radio commentaries when listeners can't see the action, but are relying on the commentary to create the mood.

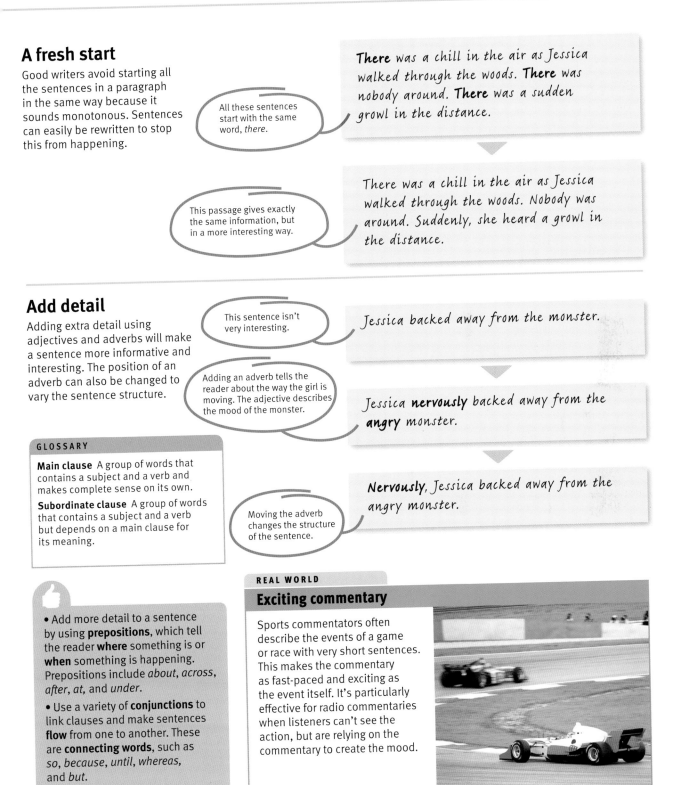

Planning and research

IT IS ESSENTIAL TO PLAN A PIECE OF WRITING.

Good writers always plan their work—on paper rather than in their heads. Planning helps a writer generate ideas, organize them into a clear structure, and avoid leaving anything out.

First scribbles

The best way to start planning a project is to jot down any relevant ideas, words, and phrases. One method is to use a mind map. At this stage in the planning process, it is useful to think of as many relevant ideas as possible—they can be cut down later.

▷ **Map out ideas**
A mind map is a visual method of writing down notes. The free structure of a mind map can make it a very effective way to generate ideas. However, a simple list is also fine.

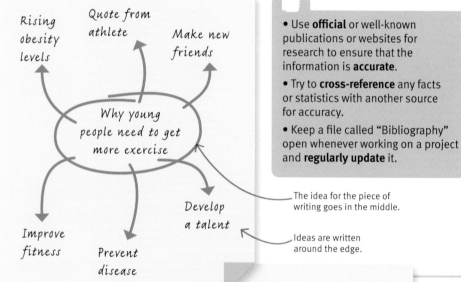

Rising obesity levels

Quote from athlete

Make new friends

Why young people need to get more exercise

Develop a talent

Improve fitness

Prevent disease

- Use **official** or well-known publications or websites for research to ensure that the information is **accurate**.

- Try to **cross-reference** any facts or statistics with another source for accuracy.

- Keep a file called "Bibliography" open whenever working on a project and **regularly update** it.

The idea for the piece of writing goes in the middle.

Ideas are written around the edge.

Research

It's important to research a piece of writing in order to gain a good overall understanding of a topic, and to gather specific examples, quotations, or statistics. Sources for research include books, websites, and newspapers. To avoid plagiarism (copying someone else's work), always rephrase the sentences.

▷ **Neat notes**
Notes should be neat, organized, and as detailed as possible. Disorganized or incomplete notes will hinder the writing process, and the information may have to be found again.

Write down the source for each statistic, quotation, and fact.

At a later stage, color code each note to show which paragraph it will be used in.

Put quotation marks around quotations now to avoid plagiarism later.

Worldwide obesity has more than doubled since 1980. (World Health Organization Report, 2012)

"Physical inactivity is an independent risk factor for coronary heart disease—in other words, if you don't exercise, you dramatically increase your risk of dying from a heart attack when you're older."
Dr. John Hobbs

Bibliography

When doing research, it's essential to keep a running list of sources to create a document called a bibliography. This should include all books, magazines, websites, and television programs used for the project. Each source should go on a single line, with periods or commas between details, and a period at the end.

Put the author's last name first.

The book title should be in italics or underlined.

Find the publisher and the publication date on one of the first few pages of the book.

Roberts, Alice. *The Complete Human Body Book.* New York: DK Publishing, 2010.

John Hobbs, Doctor, interviewed on 3/3/2013.

http://www.who.int/dietphysicalactivity/childhood/en/

Include the full addresses of any websites.

Include the details of any people who were interviewed.

The plan

The next stage is to organize the ideas and research into a clear structure using paragraphs. A piece of writing needs to start with an introduction that states what the work is about. Each new idea forms a new paragraph. Finally, a conclusion sums everything up. Paragraphs need to follow a clear progression: for example, in order of importance or chronology (date order).

A plan should include the main points that will be made in each paragraph.

It isn't necessary to use full sentences in a plan, but always use complete sentences when writing the final piece.

It's useful to give each paragraph a color and go back to the notes and color each note according to which paragraph it relates to. This will make it easier to find the right notes during writing.

▷ **Going according to plan**
Using a plan will keep a piece of writing focused. However, it's common to add, take out, or move ideas around during writing.

Introduction
Background information. How young people today get less exercise than ever. This is linked to bad health and delinquency. Include shocking statistics.

1. It's easy to change
Exercise like running, starting a soccer team, and walking is cheap and doesn't require equipment. It doesn't take up much time—give figures.

2. Health benefits
Exercise makes you happier, helps you lose weight, improves fitness levels. Include some statistics.

3. Social benefits
Team sports are sociable—young people will mix with others and make more friends. Keeps young people out of trouble. Encourages healthy competitive and team spirit.

4. Long-term benefits
A generation with fewer health problems. More success in professional sports.

Conclusion
How the worrying situation discussed in the introduction could change. Vision for the future. Quote from Olympic champion.

Paragraphing

PARAGRAPHS ARE USED TO ORGANIZE A PIECE OF WRITING.

It's important to structure a long piece of writing, such as an essay, article, or letter, into paragraphs. This will break the text up into separate points, which will make it easier to read.

SEE ALSO

❮ 58–59 Conjunctions
❮ 184–185 Making sentences interesting
❮ 186–187 Planning and research
Reading and commenting
on texts   192–193 ❯

Starting an introduction with a question will catch the reader's attention.

One way of starting a new paragraph is to indent the first line.

This paragraph is about the health benefits of exercise.

> What's your excuse? Perhaps you don't like getting sweaty, you have no time, or you're just plain lazy. Whatever the reason, you're not alone; fewer and fewer young people are getting enough exercise. However, sports offer numerous health and social benefits, so it's time to stop complaining and get moving.

> ...Thus, regular exercise will not only improve your long-term health, but also make you feel happier and less stressed out.
> In addition to the health benefits, playing sports can improve your social life. It is an opportunity to see your friends on a regular basis and to meet new people by joining a team.

The next sentences are about social benefits, so they start a new paragraph.

A good start

The opening paragraph should state what a piece of writing is about. It also needs to grab the reader's attention so that he or she wants to read on. The first line should be something strong and original, such as a quotation, a rhetorical question, or a statistic.

The great American basketball player Michael Jordan once said, "I can accept failure, but I can't accept not trying."

Start an introduction with a famous or memorable quotation.

Are you putting yourself at risk? People who don't get enough exercise dramatically increase their risk of developing heart disease.

Use a shocking fact to make an impact.

New idea, new paragraph

All the sentences in a paragraph should be related to one another. A new point of discussion requires a new paragraph. Start the new paragraph by indenting the first few words of the text or by skipping a line.

Another way to start a new paragraph is to skip a line.

> ...Thus, regular exercise will not only improve your long-term health, but also make you feel happier and less stressed out.
>
> In addition to the health benefits, playing sports can improve your social life. It is an opportunity to see your friends on a regular basis and to meet new people by joining a team.

Once upon a time...

Fiction writers need to write good opening lines to draw readers into the story. For example, the author J.K. Rowling starts the first chapter of *Harry Potter and the Deathly Hallows* with these lines: "The two men appeared out of nowhere, a few yards apart in the narrow, moonlit lane."

— CHAPTER ONE —
The Dark Lord Ascending

Topic sentences

It can be effective to start a paragraph with a topic sentence. This is a statement that introduces the main idea in the paragraph. The rest of the paragraph needs to expand on the topic sentence or give evidence to back it up. This method can help keep a piece of writing focused.

The health benefits of regular exercise cannot be ignored.

This bold statement is a topic sentence. The rest of the paragraph will discuss the health benefits that it refers to.

Overall, there is no excuse. Getting regular exercise will reduce your chances of developing heart disease and other serious illnesses. In the short term, it will make you healthier, happier, and more energetic. Finally, it's an excellent way to meet new people, have fun, and perhaps discover a new talent.

A conclusion should make a decisive final statement.

Link a conclusion back to points in the introduction to give the piece cohesion.

- Referring **back** to points made in previous paragraphs makes a piece of writing more **connected** because it shows that the piece has been considered as a whole.
- Do not make **completely new** points in a conclusion.

A lasting impression

A conclusion should summarize the main points made in a piece of writing and make a decisive judgment about the topic. It should refer back to the original question and, ideally, any points made in the introduction. A sophisticated conclusion can end by referring to the wider implications of the question, and leave the reader with something to think about.

A conclusion should repeat the main points.

If you start now, perhaps you could be climbing the Olympic podium one day.

A final, memorable statement in a piece of writing is sometimes called a "clincher."

Seamless links

A good piece of writing should be cohesive. This means that the sentences, paragraphs, and ideas are all linked together in a flowing way. Sentences and paragraphs can be connected using linking words or phrases. However, use these sparingly.

**on the other hand
by contrast
however
nevertheless**

to contrast one idea with another

**therefore
thus
as a result of
accordingly**

to give logical reasons

**first
next
first of all
finally**

to order ideas in a sequence

**also
moreover
furthermore
in addition**

to develop an idea

Genre, purpose, and audience

ALL NONFICTION TEXTS HAVE A CLEAR GENRE, PURPOSE, AND AUDIENCE.

SEE ALSO

❮ **86–87** Colloquialisms and slang
❮ **180–181** Effective communication
❮ **182–183** Picking the right words
❮ **186–187** Planning and research
Reading and commenting on texts **192–193** ❯

Writers need to consider what type of text they are writing, as well as for whom they are writing and why. These factors influence the presentation style and language used.

Genre

A nonfiction text is one based on facts, rather than a story. The different types, or genres, of nonfiction text all have their own features and conventions. For example, a newspaper or magazine article will have a headline at the top and text written in columns, whereas a letter includes the sender's address at the top.

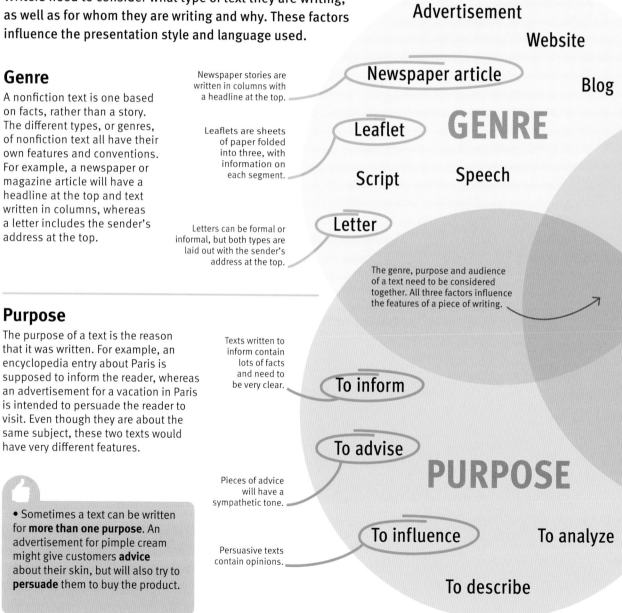

Newspaper stories are written in columns with a headline at the top.

Leaflets are sheets of paper folded into three, with information on each segment.

Letters can be formal or informal, but both types are laid out with the sender's address at the top.

The genre, purpose and audience of a text need to be considered together. All three factors influence the features of a piece of writing.

GENRE

Advertisement
Website
Newspaper article
Blog
Leaflet
Script
Speech
Letter

Purpose

The purpose of a text is the reason that it was written. For example, an encyclopedia entry about Paris is supposed to inform the reader, whereas an advertisement for a vacation in Paris is intended to persuade the reader to visit. Even though they are about the same subject, these two texts would have very different features.

Texts written to inform contain lots of facts and need to be very clear.

Pieces of advice will have a sympathetic tone.

Persuasive texts contain opinions.

PURPOSE

To inform
To advise
To influence
To analyze
To describe

• Sometimes a text can be written for **more than one purpose**. An advertisement for pimple cream might give customers **advice** about their skin, but will also try to **persuade** them to buy the product.

GLOSSARY

Adjective A describing word that tells the reader more about a noun.

Colloquialism A word or phrase used in informal speech.

Fact A statement that can be proved.

Jargon Specialized terms that are understood and used by a select, often professional, group of people.

Slang Words and phrases that are used in informal speech and often only understood by a select group of people.

REAL WORLD
Television audiences

Television advertising executives design advertisements to appeal to their target audience. For example, they might use actors who remind viewers of themselves. They will also aim to show the advertisements during television programs that are related to their product. Thus, advertisements for new food products might be shown during the break in a cooking show, because people who watch cooking shows are more likely to buy food products.

Teachers

A text written for a particular group of professionals can use terms that only they will understand.

Adults

Environmentalists

A piece written for a group of people who believe in something strongly can reinforce and flatter their opinions.

AUDIENCE

General public

Something written for a general audience should be simple enough to be understood by everyone. However, it should not be patronizing, because it needs to appeal to adults as well as children.

Teenagers

Young children

In some languages, such as French, speakers use **different words** depending on **who** they are talking to. For example, the French word for "you" is *tu* in an **informal** situation, but it is *vous* in a **formal** situation.

Audience

A nonfiction text always has a target audience. For example, it might be for adults, teenagers, or children. It could be for people with a particular interest or specialized knowledge, or it may be designed to appeal to a general audience. The key aspects of the text need to be tailored to attract this target audience.

Audience	Some common features
Adults	Sophisticated vocabulary, longer sentences, detailed subject matter, smaller font size, longer pieces of writing, formal tone and language
Young children	Simple vocabulary, short sentences, larger font size, simple subject matter, pictures and color to keep them interested
Teenagers	Slang, colloquial language, informal tone, humor, subject matter that seems relevant to them
Professionals	Jargon or specialized terms that are understood by them

Reading and commenting on texts

IT'S USEFUL TO BE ABLE TO INTERPRET AND WRITE ABOUT DIFFERENT PIECES OF WRITING.

SEE ALSO

❬ **88–89** Direct and indirect speech

❬ **102–103** Colons

❬ **108–109** Quotation marks

❬ **190–191** Genre, purpose, and audience

Layout and presentational features **194–195** ❭

Writing to influence **202–203** ❭

When answering a question about a text, a writer needs to understand the question, find the right information in the text, and use it to write a focused answer.

Understand the question

The first step is to read the question and understand what it is asking. Even a well-crafted answer will get no points if it does not answer the question. Underlining the key words in the question will make it easier to focus on what is being asked.

This question only asks about the opening paragraph, so don't make comments about the rest of the text.

What do you learn from the <u>opening paragraph</u> about...

What are the <u>four main reasons</u> that the writer gives...

How does the writer use <u>language</u> to <u>persuade the reader</u> that...

This question is asking specifically about language, so there is no need to write about presentation.

The right information

The next stage is to read the text and look for the relevant information or features. It is useful to underline the words, sentences, or passages that will help answer the question. Sometimes a question will refer to two texts.

- **Read** the whole text first. It is important to get an **overall idea** of what the text is about before analyzing the details.

- Refer to the text frequently, but be **selective—don't copy** out whole chunks of text.

- Become more **familiar** with different types of texts and the techniques they use by **reading** texts from **everyday life**, such as newspapers and even junk mail.

TEXT 1

<u>Are your parents always nagging you to eat breakfast?</u> Well, this time they're right. In the morning, your body needs <u>fuel</u>, just like a <u>car</u>. Once you've <u>filled up</u>, you'll be ready <u>to hit the road</u>.

compares the body to a car

Underline sections that will be useful when writing an answer.

Write observations and notes around the text.

This extract has the same subject matter as Text 1, but is written in complex, scientific language.

TEXT 2

Recent studies outline the many health benefits of eating a <u>nutritious</u> breakfast. In the morning, the body's glycogen stores start to <u>deplete</u>. Without breakfast, a person soon begins to feel <u>fatigued</u>.

Provide evidence

When writing about a text, every point made must be backed up with evidence. This can be made up of a quotation (the exact words from the text), or a reference (a description of the pictures, structure, or layout). If using a quotation, it must be surrounded by quotation marks to separate it from the answer.

The first extract was written to persuade young children to eat a healthy breakfast. It starts by asking the reader a question: "Are your parents always nagging you to eat breakfast?" The writer has also used phrases such as "fuel," "filled up," and "hit the road", to compare the process of eating breakfast to the process of filling a car up with fuel.

Long quotations need to be preceded by a colon. If it's longer than four lines, skip a line before the quotation.

Short quotations can be embedded in the text.

Explain why

After giving an example, it is essential to explain what it shows about the text. This will make the point clear.

This answer gives an example.

The writer has used words such as "fuel," "filled up," and "hit the road" to compare eating breakfast to filling a car up with fuel. This simple comparison makes the process easier for young children to understand. It also makes the text more fun, so it will hold a young audience's attention.

It then explains why this feature of the text is effective.

Fact or opinion?

Facts are pieces of information that can be proved. Opinions are what people believe or think. It is important to see the difference between fact and opinion when figuring out the purpose of a text. In general, informative texts use facts, whereas persuasive texts use personal opinions. Sometimes a text will use both.

This sentence states a fact.

Superflake cereal is made from wheat and oats.

Superflake cereal is delicious.

This statement is presented as a fact, but it is actually an opinion, because not everyone would agree with it.

Comparing texts

When comparing two texts, do not write about one text and then the other. Comparisons must be drawn between the two, which means picking out the similarities and differences. Some useful terms for making comparisons include *both texts, similarly, by contrast, on the other hand, whereas,* and *in comparison.*

These words help to compare and contrast the two texts.

***Both** texts are about the importance of a nutritious breakfast and both try to persuade the reader to eat more healthily. However, they use very **different** language techniques. **Whereas** the first text, for young children, uses simple language and basic explanations, the second text, for adults, goes into much **more** detail and uses scientific terms such as "glycogen stores"...*

Layout and presentational features

THE WAY THAT A TEXT IS PRESENTED ADDS TO ITS OVERALL IMPACT.

Layout refers to the way that a text is organized on a page. Presentational features are the individual elements, such as pictures, headlines, fonts, and color.

Headline

Headlines sit at the top of newspaper and magazine articles, leaflets, and sometimes advertisements. Headlines are usually in bold text and capital letters so that they stand out and attract the reader's attention.

Font

The font refers to the size, shape, and color of the text. Large fonts are often used for children, because they are easier to read. Colorful text and fun shapes are also used for a young audience, while serious pieces of writing are printed in a small standard font. Bold and italic fonts are used to draw attention to headings or certain words and phrases.

MYSTERIOUS INTRUDERS

This subheading could be printed in a fun font if the article were for children.

Bullet points

Bullet points are used to break up a dense block of text into a clear list of individual points. This makes the information easier to read and absorb.

SUPERNATURAL

Recently revealed statistics show a record number of supernatural sightings in the local area. The police have recorded 31 ghost sightings in the past five years, along with 25 reports of UFOs, 15 zombies, 10 vampires, and 8 witches.

MYSTERIOUS INTRUDERS

Often the calls appear to be serious incidents, such as intruders at a property, but then turn out to be something more mysterious. The police claim that the time spent answering the calls costs the force thousands of dollars every year.

More strange sights

- There have been 14 sightings of big cats in the past five years, as well as eight reported injuries blamed on big cats.
- Six people have claimed that they have seen a sea monster. Apparently, it resembles a huge alligator with purple scales.
- A ghost ship has been seen on four occasions on the harbor rocks. In 1876, a ship was wrecked on this exact spot.

REAL WORLD

Effective images

Charity advertisements often show images of the people or animals that they want to help. These are effective because they make the issue more real for the audience, and let them imagine the positive effect that their money would have for the cause.

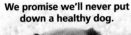

We promise we'll never put down a healthy dog.

Please promise to help us with a gift in your Will.

Every year, Dogs Trust cares for around 16,000 dogs in our 18 rehoming centres across the UK. We never put down a healthy dog. By leaving a gift in your Will, your love of dogs can live on and help us make the world a better place for them.

• When analyzing the layout of a piece, **don't just identify** the features—**explain why** they are **effective**.

Photographs and graphics

Images can be used for effect or to give more information. For example, an advertisement for a hair product might show a picture of a model with extremely glossy hair to persuade the audience to buy a new shampoo. A newspaper report about a terrible flood might show a photograph of the affected area to demonstrate exactly what has happened. Graphs and diagrams are used to make complicated topics or statistics clear.

SIGHTINGS SURGE

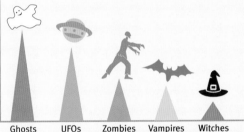

Ghosts   UFOs   Zombies   Vampires   Witches

The most common supernatural sightings are of ghosts.

Caption

Photographs and diagrams are usually accompanied by a short sentence that explains what the image is about. This is called a caption.

ZOMBIE WAS MOVIE EXTRA

Most of the sightings are easily and quickly explained. In 2011, a reported zombie sighting turned out to be a movie extra taking his lunch break. Another caller raised the alarm after seeing something suspicious floating in the air on a Saturday night: "I saw a big, orange, glowing sphere rising from the ground." The sighting turned out to be a Chinese lantern.

Subheading

Subheadings are used to break up a long text into shorter chunks, so that it's easier to read. They also summarize the content of the next paragraph, which helps the reader find the section they're interested in reading.

"I saw a big, orange, glowing sphere rising from the ground."

Pull quote

Newspaper and magazine articles often include quotes from eyewitnesses or experts. To draw attention to particularly interesting quotes, the words can be lifted out from the article and repeated elsewhere on the page, usually in bolder or larger type.

Writing to inform

THE MAIN PURPOSE OF SOME PIECES OF WRITING IS TO GIVE THE READER INFORMATION.

Informative texts, such as leaflets, encyclopedias, newspaper reports, and letters, give the reader information about a topic. Some texts also tell the reader how to do something, by giving instructions.

SEE ALSO

❮ **54–55** Voices and moods
❮ **116–117** Bullet points
❮ **194–195** Layout and presentational features
Newspaper articles **198–199** ❯
Letters and e-mails **200–201** ❯

Simple but detailed

Informative writing should give readers the details they need to know, clearly. It should include lots of facts, presented in short paragraphs and using simple vocabulary.

Sierra Nevada of California

3.7 million visitors

REAL WORLD

DIY dilemma

Sometimes people buy furniture in separate parts that need to be put together at home. The buyer needs to follow a set of instructions in order to assemble the item. Often, the instructions are not very clear, which can lead to a great deal of frustration.

A headline at the top of a leaflet tells the reader what it is about.

YOSEMITE
NATIONAL PARK

Yosemite National Park covers nearly 761,268 acres (3,081 sq km) of mountainous terrain in the Sierra Nevada of California. The park attracts more than 3.7 million visitors each year.

There are countless ways to explore and have fun in Yosemite National Park.

Pictures of the place show the reader what it looks like and make the leaflet look attractive.

Bite-sized chunks

It's effective to break down detailed text into short sections, so that the information is easy to find and absorb. Subheadings are useful for guiding readers through the text and leading them to important details. Bullet points divide up the information even further.

Please remember:
- Stay on the trails.
- Drink plenty of water.
- Do not litter.

Bullet points divide up the information.

- Avoid using unnecessarily **complicated** language that may **obscure** the information.
- Use **adverbs**, such as *carefully* or *quickly*, in **instructions** to give the reader more information on **how** to do something.

Here are some of the activities we have to offer:

Biking
More than 12 miles (19 km) of paved cycle paths are available in the park.

Birdwatching
Try to spot some of the 262 species of birds recorded in Yosemite.

Hiking
Get your hiking boots on and explore the park by foot.

Fishing
Following the regulations, see what you can catch in the lakes and rivers.

Horse riding
Saddle up and enjoy the park's majestic views on horseback.

Please remember:
- Stay on the trails.
- Drink plenty of water.
- Do not litter.

HOW TO GET HERE

Driving instructions
From San Francisco

1. Take the Bay Bridge (Interstate 80) east.
2. Take Interstate 580 east, following signs for Tracy/Stockton to Interstate 205.
3. Follow Interstate 205 to Highway 120.
4. Take Highway 120 into Yosemite National Park.

Numbered steps create an easy-to-follow sequence.

Not just a pretty picture

Adding images and color makes an informative text look more fun, but can also make the details clearer. Diagrams and maps show the reader something, rather than just telling them.

Easy instructions

Instructions are a type of informative text. They include travel directions, recipes, and product manuals. They are usually written in a numbered, step-by-step format. Commands are also used to give firm and clear instructions.

Commands tell the reader what to do.

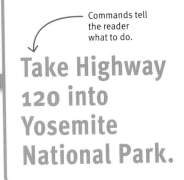

Take Highway 120 into Yosemite National Park.

Newspaper articles

NEWSPAPERS INFORM AND ENTERTAIN THE READER.

Journalists use certain techniques to inform and engage their readers. The specific content and language used in an article depend on the type of publication and the intended audience.

SEE ALSO

❮ **54–55** Voices and moods

❮ **190–191** Genre, purpose, and audience

❮ **192–193** Reading and commenting on texts

❮ **194–195** Layout and presentational features

❮ **196–197** Writing to inform

Which paper?

Some newspapers focus on serious, in-depth articles, while other papers run more sensational stories, such as political scandals or celebrity gossip. The scope of a paper also affects its content. National newspapers report on national or global events, but regional newspapers focus on local community finances, politics, and events, which are more relevant to local people.

MARKETS FALL AS ECONOMIC CRISIS CONTINUES

Some newspapers choose to run serious stories.

HOLLYWOOD COUPLE SPLITS

Other newspapers focus on celebrity stories.

SCHOOL TO CLOSE

Local newspapers report local news.

VILLAG **SUP**

A local grandmother was rescued from her burning home on Saturday by her pet dog. Shirley Williams, 65, was in bed with the flu when the blaze broke out at approximately 2:00 p.m., following an electrical fault.

Her golden retriever, Star, was in the backyard, but risked his life by bounding

Details, details, details

News articles need to explain what happened, where, why, and who was involved. All good journalists include as many details as possible in their stories, such as names, ages, and times.

Shirley Williams, 65, was in bed with the flu when the blaze broke out at approximately 2:00 p.m., following an electrical fault.

Drama

Newspapers often use exaggerated or dramatic language to catch the reader's attention and make an article more exciting to read.

blaze

The word *blaze* sounds more dramatic than *fire*.

GLOSSARY

Alliteration The repetition of certain letters or sounds for effect.

Headline The statement at the top of an article that tells the reader what it is about.

Pun The use of a word or phrase that has two meanings for comic effect.

Quote To repeat the words of a person. Quotations need to be surrounded by quotation marks.

Sales of **printed newspapers** have **declined** in recent years because many people read the news **online**.

ERALD VH

RDOG

AVES SICK

GRANNY

to the fire. He led her to safety through
e smoke and flames. Local firefighter Joe
tt, who later arrived at the scene, said,
Ve would have gotten there too late. That
g saved her life."
Shirley is recovering in the hospital. The
ayor has commended Star for his bravery.

Headlines

Headlines tell the reader what a story is about. They are short and dramatic and often use techniques such as alliteration or puns to grab attention and sell copies.

SUPERDOG SAVES SICK GRANNY

Using three words in a row beginning with the letter s creates a snappy headline.

Stay active

The news is usually written in the active rather than the passive voice. This is because sentences in the active voice are shorter, easier to read, and convey a sense of immediacy, which makes the news sound more exciting.

he led her

The active voice makes the story sound immediate.

she was led

The passive voice would make the story less engaging.

In their words

Journalists quote experts to give a news story authority. They also interview and quote the people who were involved. This makes the story seem more real for the reader.

"That dog saved her life."

Short and snappy

People often read newspapers in a rush, so journalists need to get the information across quickly and simply. Sentences and paragraphs should be short and clear.

Shirley is recovering in the hospital.

Letters and e-mails

LETTERS AND E-MAILS ARE FORMS OF CORRESPONDENCE
ADDRESSED TO A SPECIFIC PERSON OR GROUP.

Different types of correspondence are used in certain
situations, for different purposes. It is important to set
out each type correctly.

SEE ALSO

❮ 118–119 Numbers, dates, and time

❮ 188–189 Paragraphing

❮ 196–197 Writing to inform

Writing to influence   202–203 ❯

Writing to explain or advise   204–205 ❯

Writing from personal experience   210–211 ❯

Formal letters

Formal letters are written to someone the writer doesn't
know, or to someone in authority, such as a teacher or a
politician. Examples of formal letters include job application
letters and complaint letters. People send complaint letters
about faulty products or bad service in a hotel or restaurant.

The **first e-mail** was sent
in **1971**. Today, more
than **294 billion** e-mails
are sent every day.

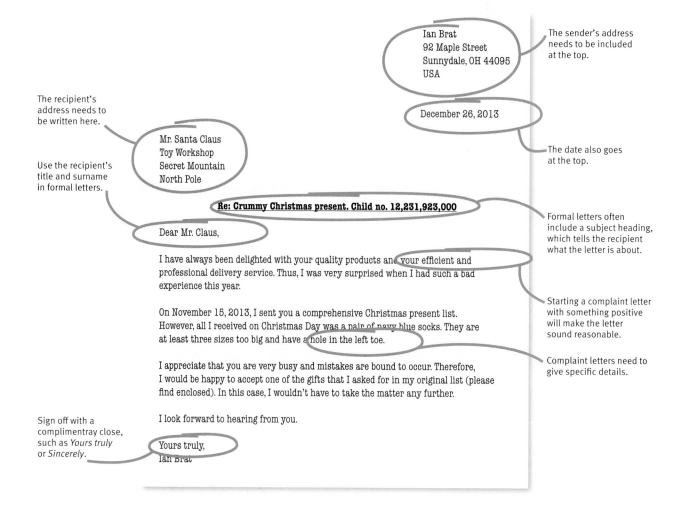

Ian Brat
92 Maple Street
Sunnydale, OH 44095
USA

The sender's address
needs to be included
at the top.

December 26, 2013

The date also goes
at the top.

The recipient's
address needs to
be written here.

Mr. Santa Claus
Toy Workshop
Secret Mountain
North Pole

Use the recipient's
title and surname
in formal letters.

Re: Crummy Christmas present. Child no. 12,231,923,000

Formal letters often
include a subject heading,
which tells the recipient
what the letter is about.

Dear Mr. Claus,

I have always been delighted with your quality products and your efficient and
professional delivery service. Thus, I was very surprised when I had such a bad
experience this year.

Starting a complaint letter
with something positive
will make the letter
sound reasonable.

On November 15, 2013, I sent you a comprehensive Christmas present list.
However, all I received on Christmas Day was a pair of navy blue socks. They are
at least three sizes too big and have a hole in the left toe.

Complaint letters need to
give specific details.

I appreciate that you are very busy and mistakes are bound to occur. Therefore,
I would be happy to accept one of the gifts that I asked for in my original list (please
find enclosed). In this case, I wouldn't have to take the matter any further.

I look forward to hearing from you.

Sign off with a
complimentray close,
such as *Yours truly*
or *Sincerely*.

Yours truly,
Ian Brat

Informal letters

Informal letters are used for someone the sender knows, such as a friend, a family member, or a person of the same age or younger. They might describe a place or experience, pass on news, or thank the recipient for something. Informal letters have a chattier tone, but still follow a set layout.

Informal letters include the sender's address at the top, but they do not need the recipient's address.

Santa Claus
Toy Workshop
Secret Mountain
North Pole

The date needs to be included at the top.

January 5, 2014

Informal letters can be addressed to the recipient's first name.

Dear Rudolf

I hope you are sticking to your New Year's resolutions! How is the diet going?

Informal letters can have a chattier tone and include some small talk.

Mrs. Claus and I wanted to thank you for hosting a fantastic New Year's Eve party. It was great fun for us all to celebrate together after a busy few weeks.

I hope that we can see you for dinner soon.

This phrase is friendlier than *Yours truly* or *Sincerely*.

Best wishes
Santa

• A **job application** letter gives an employer the **first impression** of a candidate, so it needs to be perfect.

• A complaint letter should be **firm but polite**. A **rude** letter will only **annoy** the recipient and reduce the chance of an apology or compensation.

E-mails

E-mails to friends or family don't have to follow any particular rules. However, e-mails to people the sender doesn't know should use appropriate language and have a clear structure. More and more correspondence is now sent via e-mail, so writing an e-mail isn't an excuse to be sloppy.

Send   **Save**   **Discard**

B *I* U T ▾ ᴛT ▾ A ▾ T ▾ ☺ ⊂⊃ ⅛≡ ⅛≡ ⊒ ⊒ " ≡ ≡ ≡ *I*ₓ

To   Joe@toycollege.com

Add Cc   Add Bcc

Subject   Junior Toymaker Vacancy

Attach a file

E-mails need to have an appropriate and descriptive subject heading.

Dear Joe,

Thank you very much for your recent application for the Junior Toymaker position.

An e-mail should have a focused structure and use clear paragraphs.

I have read your résumé and would be delighted to meet with you for an interview. Would 2:00 p.m. next Thursday be convenient?

Please let me know.

Professional e-mails should end with a complimentary close, just like letters.

Kind regards,
Santa Claus

Writing to influence

SOME TEXTS SEEK TO CHANGE AN AUDIENCE'S VIEWS OR BEHAVIOR.

SEE ALSO

❬ 186–187 Planning and research
❬ 188–189 Paragraphing
❬ 190–191 Genre, purpose, and audience
Writing to describe   208–209 ❭
Writing a speech   226–227 ❭

Pieces of writing that argue or persuade seek to influence the audience. However, there are subtle differences between arguing and persuading.

A strong argument

An argument tends to acknowledge the opposite opinion while providing well-reasoned arguments against it. For example, if someone were to argue that cats were better than dogs, that person would not simply list all the good things about cats. He or she would acknowledge why some people prefer dogs, then argue against those points.

Reasons why people prefer dogs to cats
- *Dogs are more intelligent than cats.* Cats are smart enough to hunt, wash, and fend for themselves.
- *Cats are unkind because they bring dead mice into the house.* This is their way of showing affection.
- *Cats are unsociable.* They are friendly but don't demand constant attention—an annoying characteristic of dogs.

To plan an argument, list the reasons why people take the opposite point of view.

Try to disprove each point with a counterargument.

Powers of persuasion

A persuasive piece is more one-sided and emotional than an argument. It often coaxes the audience to act: for example, to buy a product, join an organization, or donate money to charity.

- Persuasive writing should be firm but **not aggressive**.
- **Real-life stories** add emotion to a piece of writing.
- Use **confident language**, such as *you will* and *definitely*, rather than *you might* and *possibly*.

Persuasive writing does not accept the opposite opinion.

This type of writing coaxes the reader to act now.

WHY WOULD YOU EVER WANT A CAT?

DOGS ARE FANTASTIC.

GET ONE TODAY!

GLOSSARY

Exaggeration Representing something as larger or better than it actually is.

Hyperbole An extreme form of exaggeration that is not necessarily taken seriously, but grabs the reader's attention.

Rhetorical question A question that does not need an answer but is used for effect.

Superlative The form of an adjective or adverb that suggests the greatest or least of something.

Get your own way

Writers use particular methods to influence their audiences' opinions. These are called rhetorical devices. Writing that persuades uses more of these techniques than writing that argues.

Repetition rules

Sometimes a word, phrase, or structure is repeated to make an idea stick in the audience's mind, and convince them that it's true. Lists of three are a particularly common technique.

Dogs are loyal. Dogs are friendly. Dogs are the best!

Ask the experts

Writers use facts, statistics, and quotations from reliable and authoritative sources to back up their points and make them sound more convincing.

According to one recent study at Queen's University, Belfast, dog owners suffer from fewer medical problems than cat owners.

The **Ancient Greeks** called the art of using language to persuade "the art of rhetoric."

Tearjerkers

Some words and phrases make the reader feel an emotion, such as pain, sadness, guilt, or anger. Once the reader is feeling this way, they are often more susceptible to persuasion.

Cats bring comfort and friendship to the old, frail, and lonely.

Rhetorical questions

A rhetorical question is a question that does not require or expect an answer. However, it makes the reader reflect on points that he or she may not have considered.

Is a cat fun? Can you play fetch with a cat?

Getting personal

Addressing the audience directly with *you* will make them feel more involved. Using *we* can form a relationship between the writer and audience, and encourage the audience to trust and believe the writer.

We all know that you don't have to take cats for constant walks.

Simply the best

Exaggeration is used to emphasize a point and to grab an audience's attention. Exaggeration often includes superlatives, such as *the best*, *the worst*, and *the cheapest*. Extreme exaggeration is called hyperbole.

I couldn't live without my cat. My cat is my whole world.

REAL WORLD

I'm talking to you

This poster from 1914 was used to persuade men to join the British army in World War I. It shows Lord Kitchener, the British Secretary of State for War, telling the audience that their country needs them. By looking directly at the audience and addressing them with the word *YOU*, Lord Kitchener made a very effective appeal.

Writing to explain or advise

EXPLANATIONS AND PIECES OF ADVICE GIVE THE READER MORE THAN THE BASIC FACTS.

SEE ALSO

❰ **186–187** Planning and research
❰ **188–189** Paragraphing
❰ **190–191** Genre, purpose, and audience
❰ **192–193** Reading and commenting on texts
❰ **196–197** Writing to inform
❰ **202–203** Writing to influence

Writing to explain and writing to advise can be confused with writing to inform. However, explanations and pieces of advice include reasons, feelings, and suggestions, as well as information.

Extra explanation

An explanation gives reasons. For example, it can explain why or how an event has happened, or why someone feels a certain way.

Ask

Explaining experiences

People are sometimes asked to explain their views on a topic, or the reason an experience was important or difficult. These types of explanations should not only describe the topic or event, but also the feelings involved.

I've lost all my confidence

How and why

Explanations tell the reader how or why something happened, not just what happened. They use linking words and phrases to show cause and effect.

this is because
as a result of this
therefore

STOP THE STENCH!

Dear Annie,
I have a serious problem with smelly feet. It sounds silly, but it has an impact on my entire life. Not only does the smell irritate me, but other people have started to notice and make jokes. I've lost all my confidence and I can't even go to my friends' houses anymore because I'm too frightened to take off my shoes. What can I do?

Anonymous, 14

Dear Anonymous,

Don't worry—you're not alone! Stinky feet are a common problem. This is because there are more sweat glands in the feet than anywhere else in the body. When your feet release sweat, bacteria on the skin break it down. This process releases that cheesy smell.

Good advice

A piece of advice tells someone the best, easiest, or quickest way to do something, or suggests how to solve a problem.

• A good explanation must be **well structured** in order to deliver the information in a **clear** and **logical** way.

Sympathy

Advice needs to be authoritative but friendly. Using a sympathetic and positive tone will encourage the reader.

the good news is   **don't worry**

Annie

The good news is that there are lots of simple ways to stop the stench. First of all, you should wash your feet and change your socks every day. You could also try special foot deodorants, but I find that spraying normal deodorant on your feet works just as well. A guaranteed way to get rid of the smell is to wash your feet with an antibacterial soap. If you do this twice a day, you should banish smelly feet within a week.

Here are some other useful tips:

• Wear socks and shoes made from natural fibers because they let your feet breathe, unlike synthetic materials.

• Wear open-toed sandals in the summer and go barefoot at home in the evenings.

• See a doctor if these simple measures don't help.

Good luck.

Yours truly,

Annie

Personal pronouns

A writer can address the reader directly by using *you*, or refer to his or her personal opinion with *I*. This helps to build a relationship with the reader, who should then be more receptive to the advice.

you could   **I find**

Suggestions

Strong suggestions such as *you should* are effective because they encourage the reader to act. However, it's best to include a few gentler suggestions, such as *you could* or *you might*, to maintain a friendly tone.

you should wash your feet

Strong suggestions tell the reader what to do.

Guaranteed results

The text needs to show how the advice will help. It should emphasize what will happen if the advice is or is not followed.

If you do this twice a day, you should banish smelly feet within a week.

Bullet points

Advice leaflets or columns often break down the information into bullet points, so that the reader can read and follow the pieces of advice easily.

Writing to analyze or review

THESE TWO TYPES OF WRITING BREAK DOWN A TOPIC AND DISCUSS ITS KEY PARTS.

Both an analysis and a review discuss a subject in depth. However, while an analysis gives a balanced judgement, a review is usually opinionated and personal.

SEE ALSO

❬ **42–43** Simple tenses
❬ **186–187** Planning and research
❬ **188–189** Paragraphing
❬ **190–191** Genre, purpose, and audience

GLOSSARY

First person narrative When an author writes a piece from his or her point of view, using *I* and *my*.

Objective When a piece of writing is not influenced by personal opinions.

Subjective When a piece of writing is influenced by personal opinions.

Third person narrative When an author writes from a detached or outside point of view.

Balanced judgment

An analysis is an investigation of a topic. Unlike a persuasive piece of writing or a review, an analysis remains objective, which means that it is not influenced by personal feelings. It will look at the good and bad points of a subject, and come to a fair conclusion. A useful way to plan a balanced analysis is to use a table, listing arguments for and against.

Against reality television	For reality televison
Television producers make shows vulgar and offensive in order to boost ratings.	Reality television is popular and producers should give viewers what they want.
It encourages people to pursue celebrity status, rather than success through education and hard work.	If someone doesn't want to watch a show, they can change the channel or turn off the television.
The contestants are humiliated and treated poorly, which sets a bad example for viewers.	Some shows tackle important problems in society, such as unhealthy eating.
All the shows follow the same formula, and no creativity is involved in the making of a program.	Reality television tells us more about human nature, and how people behave in certain situations.

Distant and detached

To maintain the objectivity of an analysis, it's best to write in the third person and use an impersonal tone. For example, starting a sentence with the words *It is often argued* does not reveal the writer's personal opinion.

It is often argued...

It seems likely...

There is evidence to suggest...

Many people believe...

It is sometimes stated...

Rave reviews

A review is a piece of writing that provides a focused description and evaluation of an event or a publication, such as a book or a movie. It is much more subjective than an analysis, and is therefore written in the first person, with many personal opinions.

The travel website **TripAdvisor** contains more than **75 million** consumer **reviews** and opinions.

Sneak preview

The first part of a review should give a short summary of the movie, book, show, or other event without giving everything away. It should give the reader a general idea of what it is about.

Movie preview

TAKE
TO THE FLOOR 2

The rooftop tango scene is stunning and very moving.

Take to the Floor 2 is the latest in a series of teen dance dramas to spin into theaters. As usual, the story focuses on two young dancers from the opposite sides of town. When street kid Chad wins a scholarship to a prestigious dance school, he finds it hard to fit in. Then, one day, he catches the eye of ballet dancer Ellie, who is wowed by his moves.

Many of the dance scenes are spectacular, from a rooftop tango in the pouring rain to a shopping mall salsa extravaganza. The cast members are all highly trained movers; however, their acting skills were left at the stage door. Ellie and Chad fail to bring their sizzling dance-floor chemistry into the dialogue, which is disappointing.

Take to the Floor 2 is nothing new; the plot certainly doesn't offer any surprises. However, the film is saved by its show-stopping dance scenes and pumping soundtrack. Overall, it's incredibly fun to watch, even if you end up feeling like you've seen it all before.

The good and the bad

The middle part of a review should go into more detail about the strengths and weaknesses of the subject. It might discuss the acting in a play, the quality of writing in a book, or the use of special effects in a movie. It is important to back up any comments with examples.

The verdict

The final paragraph in a review should be a summarizing statement about the subject, and an overall recommendation—a final judgment on whether the subject is worth watching, seeing, or reading.

- An analysis should be **structured** clearly, using **paragraphs**. Discuss one point of view first, followed by the other. Finally, come to a **balanced conclusion**.
- When writing a review, think about the **audience** and what they will **want to know** about the subject being reviewed.

Writing to describe

DESCRIPTIVE WRITING TELLS THE READER WHAT SOMETHING OR SOMEONE IS LIKE.

Many types of writing use description, from stories to advertisements. Descriptive writing uses particular words to paint a vivid image of something in the reader's head.

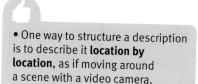

SEE ALSO

‹ 26–27 Adjectives	
‹ 40–41 Adverbs	
‹ 84–85 Idioms, analogies, and figures of speech	
‹ 182–183 Picking the right words	
‹ 184–185 Making sentences interesting	
Writing a narrative	**212–213 ›**

The senses

When writing to describe, it's important to appeal to the reader's senses. By describing what something looks, sounds, and feels like, a writer will allow the reader to imagine something in detail. Not all of the senses may be relevant, but try to think about as many as possible.

• One way to structure a description is to describe it **location by location,** as if moving around a scene with a video camera.

> Barbara walked into the kitchen and was confronted by a **rush of warm air** and the **smell of something sweet.** On the counter was a **triple-layer chocolate cake** with **fudge icing oozing** down the sides. She **eagerly cut** a slice and **stuffed** it into her mouth. The chocolate sponge was **rich** and **bitter** with a slight **nutty** flavor. The **sugar sprinkles crackled** in her mouth and **got stuck in her teeth.** Suddenly, the **doorbell rang.** Barbara jumped, and her **cake splattered** across the floor.

Describe what something looks, feels, smells, tastes, and sounds like.

Too good to miss

Advertising executives use description to create tempting pictures in an audience's mind to persuade them to buy something. For example, they might describe hair as *smooth*, *glossy,* and *rich* to sell a new shampoo or hair dye. Alternatively, an advertisement for a beach resort could include descriptions such as *azure blue*, *gently lapping waves,* and *golden sands.*

Descriptive details

Readers won't be able to imagine something unless they are given details. By selecting particular words, writers can add extra information and make a sentence more descriptive.

adverb   adjective

> She reached for a slice of cake and put it in her mouth.

> She reached **quickly** for a **big** slice of **sticky, delicious** cake and **eagerly** put it in her mouth.

△ **Lacking detail**
This sentence doesn't tell the reader very much about the scene.

Using this word is a more precise way to decribe the big slice.

△ **Adjectives and adverbs**
The addition of adjectives and adverbs instantly makes the sentence more evocative.

> She **grabbed** a **wedge** of **sticky, delicious chocolate** cake and **stuffed** it in her mouth.

> She **tentatively** reached for a **sliver** of **fattening** cake and **sneakily popped** it in her mouth.

△ **Precise vocabulary**
Sometimes it's better to use precise vocabulary that includes description within the words themselves.

△ **Different choices**
By using different descriptive words, a writer can give a sentence a totally different feel.

Figurative language

Figurative language is an exaggerated style of writing that draws comparisons between things to create a more vivid description.

Simile
A simile compares one thing to another by using the words *as* or *like*.

Her cheeks were pink **like** strawberries.

Metaphor
A metaphor is a word or phrase that describes something as if it were something else.

A **wave** of terror washed over him.

Personification
Personification is when human actions or feelings are given to objects or ideas.

The wind **screamed** and **howled.**

Onomatopoeia
Onomatopoeia is when a writer uses words that mimic the sound they stand for.

The leaves **crunched** underfoot.

Writing from personal experience

WHEN SOMEONE WRITES ABOUT THEIR LIFE OR PERSONAL EXPERIENCES, IT'S CALLED AUTOBIOGRAPHICAL WRITING.

Autobiography is a genre in itself, but it can also be used in other types of writing, such as a speech or an advice leaflet, to give a more personal touch.

SEE ALSO

❮ **34–35** Pronouns

❮ **184–185** Making sentences interesting

❮ **188–189** Paragraphing

❮ **204–205** Writing to explain or advise

❮ **208–209** Writing to describe

Writing a narrative   **212–213** ❯

Writing for the Web   **214–215** ❯

Writing a speech   **226–227** ❯

A life less ordinary

Everyday life may not seem very interesting, but readers find other people's lives fascinating. Earliest memories, embarrassing incidents, or particularly happy, sad, scary, or proud moments all make good topics. Readers also enjoy finding out about experiences that are very different from their own, such as celebrating certain festivals or living in different places.

This is my life

When writing a complete autobiography (from birth to the present day), it's important to work out the right order of events. One way to do this is to create a life map. This is a visual way of plotting events, and can be accompanied by pictures to suggest memories. Rather than listing every single memory, writers often give an autobiography a theme. For example, it might focus on a struggle from rags to riches or a love of sports.

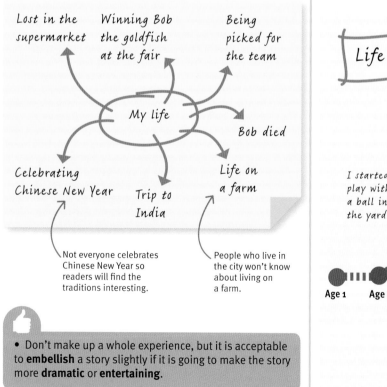

Not everyone celebrates Chinese New Year so readers will find the traditions interesting.

People who live in the city won't know about living on a farm.

• Don't make up a whole experience, but it is acceptable to **embellish** a story slightly if it is going to make the story more **dramatic** or **entertaining**.

Life map

I began to support the local team.

I started to play with a ball in the yard.

Age 6   Age 7

Age 3   Age 5

Age 4

Age 1   Age 2

Age

I got my first real ball.

My team lost in the final.

REAL WORLD

Travel writing

Travel writing is very different from the text found in travel guidebooks, which usually lists information. Pieces of travel writing recount the author's own travel experiences, including his or her feelings, opinions, and amusing anecdotes.

Edited highlights

Autobiographical writing is informative but also needs to be entertaining, so it shouldn't list boring details. For example, there's no need to give a minute-by-minute account of a game. It's much more interesting to tell the reader about feelings and reactions, such as fear, pride, or disappointment.

I felt sick and panicky all morning before the big game. We needed to win and I'd finally made the team. I had everything to prove.

Make it real

An autobiography tells stories, and the best stories include plenty of description. Describing sights, sounds, emotions, and tastes will allow the reader to picture the experience as vividly as the writer can remember it.

It was a hot night in the stadium. The noise of the supporters was deafening, and their chants boomed across the field like a roll of thunder in a storm.

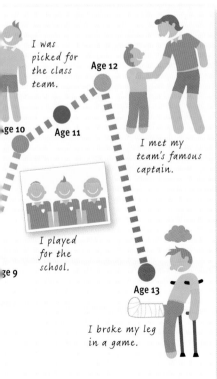

I was picked for the class team.

Age 12

Age 10   Age 11

I met my team's famous captain.

I played for the school.

Age 13

I broke my leg in a game.

Add character

Autobiographical writing needs to showcase the writer's unique personality. Therefore, it often includes his or her personal opinions, likes and dislikes, strange habits, and favorite vocabulary. Funny details add humor and give the piece character.

I was wearing my lucky socks. I had eaten my usual peanut butter sandwich and pet the cat three times. I was ready to play the game of my life!

You and me

An autobiography will naturally include the words *I* and *my*, but it can also be effective to address the reader using *you*. This is called direct address and helps to create a relationship with readers, making them feel more involved in the story.

I'm sure you've been on the losing side before, or watched your team miss that crucial shot. So you know what it feels like to be emotionally crushed by a loss.

Writing a narrative

A NARRATIVE IS A PIECE OF WRITING THAT TELLS A STORY.

A story is an account of events linked by cause and effect. All stories need a narrator, a plot, characters, and a setting. Some stories also include dialogue to show conversations between characters.

SEE ALSO
❰ **34–35** Pronouns
❰ **108–109** Quotation marks
❰ **182–183** Picking the right words
❰ **184–185** Making sentences interesting
❰ **208–209** Writing to describe

The word *my* shows that this story is in the first person.

> **My** master is the most fearsome pirate sailing the seven seas.

Whose view?

The narrator is the person telling the story. If the narrator is a character in the story recounting the events from his or her point of view, the narrative is in the first person. If the narrator is uninvolved in the story and always refers to characters as *he*, *she*, or *they*, then the story is written in the third person.

First person (main character)
Stories in the first person are often narrated by the main character, or protagonist, of the story.

> The scoundrels had deceived **me**, so **I** made them walk the plank!

First person (minor character)
Not all stories in the first person are told by the main character. Using a minor character as a narrator gives a different angle.

Third person
A narrative written in the third person tells the story from the author's or an outsider's point of view.

The word *his* shows that this story is in the third person.

> The ruthless captain made **his** crew walk the plank.

Don't lose the plot

The plot is what turns a list of events into a story. All the events happen for a reason and are caused by the actions and decisions of the characters. A good plot needs to have a clear beginning, middle (usually the main part of the action), and end.

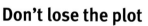

△ **Beginning**
The beginning introduces the main characters and the situation that they are in. One classic plotline starts with the main character facing a problem.

△ **Middle**
The middle of the plot often shows the character trying to overcome the problem. The main event or turning point in the plot usually happens in the middle of the story.

△ **End**
The end brings the story to a resolution. The main character may have solved his or her problem. Alternatively, a plot "twist" may introduce an unexpected ending.

Heroes and villains

A good story needs to have interesting characters that the reader cares about. Usually, there is a main character, or hero. There are also villains, who stop the hero from reaching his or her goals, and allies, who help the hero. Each character should be distinctive, with unique physical or personality traits.

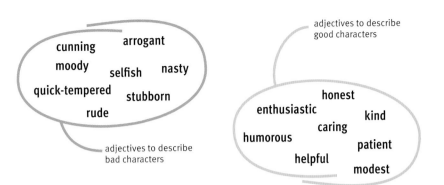

cunning arrogant moody selfish nasty quick-tempered stubborn rude

adjectives to describe bad characters

adjectives to describe good characters

honest enthusiastic kind caring humorous patient helpful modest

The perfect setting

The setting is the time, place, and situation where the action happens. The right setting will give the story mood and atmosphere. For example, a pirate story could be set on a deserted tropical island in the seventeenth century. Describing a setting in detail will enable the reader to imagine what it is like.

The island was **deserted**, except for the **multicolored** birds **circling** overhead. The **golden** sandy beach was **fringed** with **coconut** trees and **tropical** plants. A **ghostly** shipwreck in the distance was being **pounded** against the **craggy** rocks by **crashing** waves.

Words that contain description, such as sounds, paint a vivid picture of the scene.

Dramatic dialogue

Using dialogue in a story can reveal more about the characters and advance the plot. It should be concise and dramatic—overly long or pointless pieces of dialogue should be avoided. Choosing phrases such as *he grumbled*, *he screamed*, or *he gasped* instead of *he said* also adds more drama.

Pieces of dialogue need to go in quotation marks.

"Is that you, Captain?" shouted the first mate.
"Of course it is. Now, hurry up and lower a boat to fetch me," bellowed the captain.

A new speaker's dialogue needs to go on a new line.

Use more interesting words as an alternative to *said*.

- Use a mixture of **long** and **short** sentences to build up **tension** and **suspense**.
- **Figurative language** such as the simile *as fast as a cheetah* can **enrich** the description in a narrative. However, use it **sparingly**—too much description can **distract** the reader from the action.

Writing for the Web

WRITING FOR THE WEB IS VERY DIFFERENT FROM WRITING FOR PRINT.

Online readers are usually trying to find specific information and will move on if the website isn't clear or doesn't tell them what they need to know. Web writers use specific techniques to keep readers interested.

Business websites sometimes include company logos.

Easy on the eye

Reading words on a screen is harder than reading them on a printed page, so if online readers find something too difficult to read, they will click away. Therefore, online text should always be written in short and clear sentences and paragraphs.

Key words

The Web is huge and full of websites on the same topics. Web writers have to make their content easy to find by including the "key words" that users search for on search engines. This is called Search Engine Optimization (SEO). It means that headlines and subheadings should be obvious rather than obscure.

Go to kangaroo country

This title is fun but would not always be found in searches for "Australia."

Go to Australia

The word *Australia* will be picked up by search engines.

Go Travel

FLIGHTS | HOTELS | TOURS | INSURANCE | AROUND THE WORLD | BUS/TRAIN/C

Australasia travel guides

If you really want to get away from it all, you can't get much farther away than Australasia. Ride the waves on Australia's Gold Coast, hike through the mountains in New Zealand, or just relax on the beach in Fiji. Start planning your trip of a lifetime here.

Go to Australia

Australia has it all, from hip cities to idyllic islands to the remote outback. Scuba dive at the Great Barrier Reef, party in Sydney, or check out some fascinating wildlife.
Find out more...

Go to New Zealand

New Zealand is a thrill-seeker's paradise. Get your adrenaline rush from skydiving, white-water rafting, or bungee jumping. Or just take in the beautiful scenery.
Find out more...

Go to Fiji

If you want to relax on a stunning beach, Fiji won't disappoint. It has more than three hundred islands with crystal clear waters and beautiful coral reefs.
Find out more...

Attractive images make the website and the places look appealing.

Blogs

Blogs are a type of online journal written for an audience. They are usually written in an informal and personal style and should be entertaining to read. Bloggers often write in the style of casual speech (although the text should still be grammatically correct), so it's helpful to read a blog out loud to make sure that it has the right tone.

People read **online text** about **25 percent slower** than they can read printed material.

Tabs along the top of the page take the user to different sections of the site.

| ESSENTIALS | PLANNING | DESTINATIONS | VOLUNTEER | WORK

GLOSSARY

Blog An online journal containing the author's comments and reflections. It is updated regularly.

Hyperlink A word, phrase, or icon on the World Wide Web, which, if clicked, takes the user to a new document or website.

SEO Standing for "Search Engine Optimization," this is the process that increases the online visibility of a website so more Web users will visit it.

The Go Travel blog

Surfing at Bondi

I've finally made it Down Under!

It's early in the morning here, but I'm not on Aussie time yet so I thought I would update you all on my trip. Yesterday, I decided to cure my jet lag by throwing myself into the pounding surf at Bondi Beach!

Read more....

Blogs can include some slang. This is short for "Australian."

Give it some space

A clear layout also makes online text easier to read. It is often broken up into small paragraphs and bullet points and surrounded by plenty of white space. People often skim text when they are reading online, so clear and descriptive subheadings can help them find the information that they need.

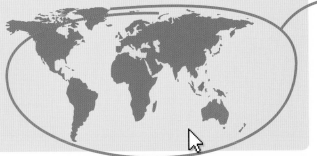

Click on our interactive destination map

Interactive graphics present information in a more entertaining way and keep readers interested.

Act now

All writing has a purpose, whether to give readers information, or to make them buy something. The Web, more than any other medium, can allow readers to act on what they have read right away. It is therefore important to include active hyperlinks that take readers to extra information or to the checkout page.

Get a quote by e-mail
Ask one of our team

Add to basket

Websites use links like this to encourage users to buy something.

Ask one of our team

Writing a script

VOICE-OVERS AND DRAMATIC SCRIPTS HAVE TO BE EFFECTIVE WHEN READ ALOUD.

The words in a script are spoken to an audience, so they have to be easy to understand. Scripts also need to be laid out in specific ways, and include instructions for the people involved.

Voice-overs

A voice-over is the audio commentary that accompanies a short video, such as a documentary, an advertisement, or a nonprofit campaign film. A useful way to lay out a voice-over script is to use a table with columns.

Easy listening

A voice-over needs to be written in simple language so that listeners will understand what is said immediately. They can't go back and read sections again. Using simple sentences and words will also make a script easy for narrators to read, so they won't stumble over their words.

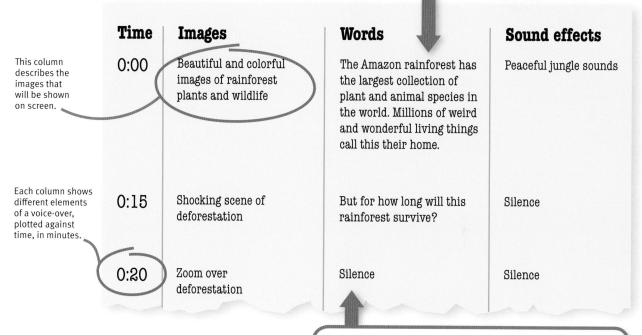

This column describes the images that will be shown on screen.

Each column shows different elements of a voice-over, plotted against time, in minutes.

Time	Images	Words	Sound effects
0:00	Beautiful and colorful images of rainforest plants and wildlife	The Amazon rainforest has the largest collection of plant and animal species in the world. Millions of weird and wonderful living things call this their home.	Peaceful jungle sounds
0:15	Shocking scene of deforestation	But for how long will this rainforest survive?	Silence
0:20	Zoom over deforestation	Silence	Silence

Words and pictures

In a voice-over script, the words need to relate to the images on screen, giving extra information about them. However, it is often effective to include occasional silences, so the audience can focus on and absorb what they see.

• The best way to test a voice-over is to read it **out loud**. If the narrator **runs out of breath**, or gets **confused**, the script needs to be **rewritten**.

On average, a narrator can read **180 words** out loud **per minute**.

Dramatic scripts

A dramatic script tells a story. However, unlike a written narrative, a script will be performed. Dramatic scripts can be for the theater, television, radio, or film. Each type has slightly different conventions, but they have some common features.

Directions

A script should include directions that tell everyone involved what to do. Directions indicate when actors should enter and exit, and in what tone they should perform a line. Other directions relate to lighting, sound effects, or camera shots, such as close-ups.

The title of the piece goes at the top.

PROTEST

Scene   A park that is going to be demolished to make way for a shopping center. There are protest chants.

The setting and the characters involved in the scene are listed at the top.

Characters
MEADOW An environmental activist
DETECTIVE STUBBS A police officer

Directions show when characters enter and exit the scene. They should be in parentheses.

(MEADOW starts to climb a tree.)
(Enter DETECTIVE STUBBS.)

DETECTIVE STUBBS:	What do you think you're doing?
MEADOW (angrily)	Saving our trees!
DETECTIVE STUBBS:	Get down immediately!

Directions also include adverbs that tell actors how to perform their lines.

(MEADOW laughs and scrambles to the top of the tree.)

DETECTIVE STUBBS: Hey you, come back!

Dialogue

The dialogue refers to the conversation between characters. In a play, the plot is controlled by the dialogue and action, so the words need to tell the audience what is happening. The speech also needs to be convincing, so it should reflect the age, nationality, personality, and mood of each character.

Re-creations

THE REWRITING OF A TEXT IN A DIFFERENT FORM IS CALLED
A RE-CREATION.

A piece of writing can be restyled in a variety of ways. For instance,
a text such as a story could be rewritten as an autobiography or
a newspaper article.

SEE ALSO

❮ **42–43** Simple tenses
❮ **190–191** Genre, purpose, and audience
❮ **194–195** Layout and presentational features
❮ **198–199** Newspaper articles
❮ **212–213** Writing a narrative

Transforming texts

A re-creation is turning one type of text
into another. This can be done by simply
changing the narrative viewpoint. For
example, a third-person narrative could be
turned into a first-person narrative. Similarly,
a story could be retold in a different tense.
A piece of writing can also be rewritten in a
completely different form—a poem could
inspire a story, or a play could become a
newspaper article.

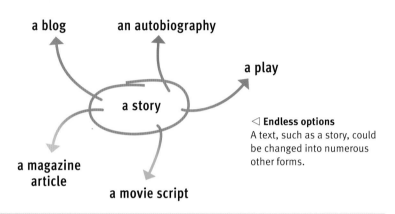

a blog   an autobiography

a play

a story

a magazine
article

a movie script

◁ **Endless options**
A text, such as a story, could
be changed into numerous
other forms.

REAL WORLD
Revised and updated

Sometimes writers rework classic
stories to appeal to modern
audiences. The action and
characters are often moved into
a modern setting. For example, the
musical *West Side Story* is loosely
based on William Shakespeare's
Romeo and Juliet, but it is set in
1950s New York City.

The original

The best way to start a re-creation is to read and understand
the original text. The rewritten form must include key details
from the original version, such as events in the plot and the
main characters. However, also think about minor details,
such as the mood and atmosphere of the piece.

Highlight the important plot
details in the original text.

extract from
Cinderella

The king's son, who was told that a great princess,
who nobody knew, had arrived, ran out to receive her. He
gave her his hand as she alighted from the coach, and led her
into the hall, among all the company. There was immediately
a profound silence. Everyone stopped dancing, and the violins
ceased to play, so entranced was everyone with the
singular beauties of the unknown newcomer.

Also look out for
smaller details.

The makeover

The next stage is to think of an original way to transform the text into something else. It is best to choose a form that will suit the main events and characters in the original text. The revised version should use the correct features and layout for the new form.

> • Be **creative** but stick to the important details. The new version should show an **understanding of the original text**.

Adding extra descriptive detail shows creativity.

Include details from the original text.

> *That night changed my life forever. I felt dizzy with excitement as I entered the ballroom. Women in multicolored dresses sashayed across the floor under sparkling chandeliers. The room was filled with the sound of guests chattering and violins playing. Then everything went silent. Everyone was looking at me.*

◁ **Cinderella's story**
The story *Cinderella* could be rewritten as her autobiography. In this case, it should be narrated in the first person and include her thoughts and feelings.

▷ **Royal scoop**
Cinderella could also inspire a scandalous newspaper article. In this case, the new text should be laid out with a headline and in columns, and the language should be short and snappy.

Front-page stories usually have an eye-catching headline.

Newspaper articles often include alliteration (the use of words beginning with the same letter or sound).

THE CASTLE

WHO IS SHE?

The secret stunner left the ball in a hurry just before midnight.

PARTY PRINCE SPOTTED WITH MYSTERY WOMAN

It was a sight that broke hundreds of hearts. Prince Charming, 24, was seen dancing the night away with a new woman on Saturday evening.

The prince, who has publicly announced his intention to wed this year, was apparently bewitched by the beautiful blonde. Dressed in a floor-length metallic gown and glitzy glass slippers, she was the center of attention at the prince's annual ball.

One attendee said, "Everyone went silent when she entered the room. We were all entranced by her beauty."

These details come from the original text.

There have been more than **400** feature-length film and television **adaptations** of **William Shakespeare's** plays.

Checking and editing

CHECKING AND EDITING WILL IMPROVE A PIECE OF WRITING.

All writers make mistakes or have better ideas. It's important to leave enough time after finishing a piece of work to check for errors and improve the quality of the writing.

The right answer

Even a perfect piece of writing will be poorly received if it answers the wrong question. When reviewing a piece of work, look at the question again, and make sure that the answer fulfills the brief.

The answer should discuss language and presentational features.

Discuss how the website uses language and presentational features to persuade readers to visit the theme park.

The answer should focus on how these features persuade the reader.

Tricky words

One of the most important things to do is to check for spelling mistakes. To correct a spelling in handwritten work, put the mistake in parentheses, draw a line through it, and write the correct version above. Do not rely on spell-checkers—it's better to identify mistakes and learn the correct versions.

particularly
It is (~~particulery~~) aimed

Discuss how the website uses language and presentational features to persuade readers to visit the theme park.

This website is designed to lure people to the Wild Waves Water Park. It is particulery aimed at young people who are on summer vacation. The range of images are persuasive. The selection shows groups of people who are obviously

Good grammar

Some grammatical mistakes to look out for include incomplete sentences, incorrect word order, and errors of verb agreement.

is
The range of images (~~are~~) persuasive.

The subject *range* is singular, so the verb needs to be singular too.

Strict structure

Structuring a piece of text using paragraphs is very important. A new point of discussion requires a new paragraph. If a paragraph break is missing in a piece of handwritten work, mark it with a paragraph symbol (¶).

reader's attention. ¶ The language used

Use this symbol to show that there should be a new paragraph.

Perfect punctuation

Punctuation marks may look small, but they need to be used correctly. It's easy to make mistakes when writing quickly, so look out for errors such as misused commas and apostrophes.

The colorful text is really eye-catching, and it immediately grabs the reader's attention.

The two clauses need to be joined with a conjunction or a semicolon, not just a comma.

enjoying themselves and the reader will want to join the fun. The colorful text is really eye-catching, it immediately grabs the reader's attention. The language used on the website is really persuasive. For example, the text is full of verbs suggest movement. The writer has challenged the reader with rhetorical questions, such as "Do you dare to ride the rapids?"

Varied vocabulary

A polished piece of writing should contain a good range of vocabulary. Repeatedly used words should be replaced with synonyms or similar appropriate words to add variety. Adverbs, such as *very* and *really*, should not be overused.

The language used on the website is convincing.

The word *persuasive* can be replaced with a synonym. The adverb *really* can be cut out.

Something missing?

If a word has been left out in handwritten work, insert a caret symbol (∧) where the words should go and write them neatly above. To insert a longer passage, put an asterisk (*) where the new text should start, put another asterisk at the bottom or side of the work, and write the extra text next to it.

*The text is full of verbs ∧ suggest
that
movement*.*

Use the asterisk for longer passages.

Use this mark to add single words.

*, such as "splash," "zoom," "race," and "spin."

REAL WORLD

George W. Bush

The former US president George W. Bush didn't always check his work. He is famous for making grammatical errors, such as "Rarely is the question asked: Is our children learning?" He also once said, "The goals of this country is to enhance prosperity and peace."

The spoken word

THE SPOKEN WORD IS DIFFERENT FROM WRITTEN LANGUAGE IN MANY KEY RESPECTS.

A person's speech is influenced by various factors, such as where he or she is from and to whom he or she is talking. It's important to consider these factors when writing or analyzing spoken language.

Standard English

Standard English is often considered the "correct" form of English, because it is grammatically correct and does not use any slang. It is usually spoken in a neutral accent without any regional pronunciation; this is called General American in North America, Received Pronunciation in the UK, and General Australian in Australia. Standard English is used in formal situations, by public officials, and traditionally by the media.

Good evening. Welcome to the nine o'clock news.

Standard English uses formal, unabbreviated vocabulary and correct grammar.

Dialect and accent

Varieties of spoken English have developed in different English-speaking countries across the world, and in the regions and communities within them. Each variety has its own colloquial vocabulary and grammatical constructions. These varieties are known as dialects. An accent is the way in which language is pronounced. People use dialectal words and constructions in informal situations.

REAL WORLD

Soap operas

The actors in television soap operas set in a particular location will use the accents from that place. For example, the actors in the show *Dallas* have Texas accents. This makes the dialogue seem more authentic. If the actors don't speak like this themselves, they have to learn the accent.

Hello, my friend. How are you?

This person is talking in Standard English, but it sounds odd in an informal situation.

G'day, mate. How ya goin'?

This is Australian slang for *hello*. It is a contraction of the greeting *good day*.

This is slang for *friend*.

The words *you* and *going* are spelled like this to show how they are pronounced in Australia.

Hey, dude. What's up?

This is another slang word for *friend*, more commonly used in North America.

Tone and pitch

Speakers adjust the tone and pitch of their voice according to what they are saying. For example, someone might sound sad and low-pitched if delivering bad news, but delighted and high-pitched if discussing good news.

Bao Bao, the world's oldest panda, has died at age 34.

In other news, the weather is going to be fantastic this weekend.

This sentence would probably be delivered in an upbeat tone.

Pauses and fillers

When people are thinking about what to say next, or lose their train of thought, they pause. Sometimes people fill the silence with a hesitation device, such as *er* or *huh,* or with a sigh.

Structure

People often leave out words and use incomplete sentences when they are having spoken conversations. Contractions such as *haven't* and *couldn't* are used more frequently in speech than in written text, because the words are easier to say and help make a conversation flow.

So...why did your team play so badly tonight?

Did you see the game last night?

An ellipsis stands for a pause when spoken language is written down.

Er...we...have no excuse.

Awesome, wasn't it?

This isn't a full sentence. The speaker is relying on what was said before for his or her words to make sense.

Yeah.

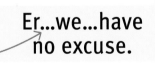

GLOSSARY

Accent The way in which a language is pronounced.

Colloquial A word used to describe the language that is used in informal, everyday speech.

Contraction A word that has been shortened by removing letters.

Dialect The informal vocabulary and grammar used by a particular social or geographic group of people.

Pitch The height of a sound.

Tone The feeling or mood projected by a voice—for example, happy, sad, angry, or excited.

Reckon we're going to the playoffs now.

The word *I* has been left out, and *we're* has been used instead of *we are*. The informal verb *reckon* is often used in colloquial speech.

Debates and role plays

DEBATES AND ROLE PLAYS ARE TYPES OF CONVERSATIONS THAT ARE PREPARED FOR IN ADVANCE.

A prepared conversation is very different from an informal chat with friends. Participants need to think about what they are going to say in advance, and consider how they should react to others.

• A **formal discussion** requires **formal language** so try to use Standard English.

The big debate

A debate is a formal discussion or argument about a topic. Participants need to express their own opinions confidently, and listen and respond to others.

I think Powerman is the best superhero because he has the most superhuman powers. He is **incredibly strong** and can **fly at supersonic speeds**.

Always back up an opinion with evidence.

Acknowledge the opposite point of view before disagreeing with it.

I understand your point. However, I think Birdman's lack of superpowers makes him more inspirational, **because** he has had to overcome challenges and learn his skills.

▷ **Prepare**
Participants need to convey their ideas and opinions. The best way to do this is to research the topic in detail, and consider the different points of view related to it. The most effective discussions will cover as many viewpoints as possible.

◁ **Listen and respond**
Listening is just as important as talking. Participants should show that they are listening to others by responding appropriately and asking relevant questions. They should either agree with someone and add to the point, or disagree and say why.

So, Melvin, **what do you think?** Maybe you prefer someone else, such as Tigerwoman?

Coax other participants to join in by asking questions.

Avoid hostile body language.

▷ **Involve others**
It's important to involve all the participants in a discussion and to act as a group. Everyone should be allowed to speak, without someone else talking over them. Quieter members of the group may need encouragement to join in.

◁ **Body language**
Body language helps participants interact with one another. Nodding in agreement is a simple way to do this. Making eye contact with everyone in the group, especially the speaker, is also effective. If someone folds their arms, it looks as if they don't want to be there.

Role plays

A role play is a made-up scenario in which participants each play a character. There isn't a script, so everyone needs to act spontaneously. The best way to prepare is to think about the character's personality, and how they would behave in the specific situation.

The first **American presidential debate** was between the candidates **John F. Kennedy** and **Richard Nixon** in 1960. It was one of the **most-watched** broadcasts in US television history.

Get inside their head

A good way to start is to imagine what the character would be thinking. Reflect on the person's story so far, and what they would think about the current situation. Consider their relationships with the other characters, and how they will behave around them.

Talk the talk

To make characters convincing, it's important to talk like them. An angry person might shout, a shy character might mutter his or her words, and an excited person might talk quickly. Use an appropriate accent if the person is from a particular country or region, and use the right vocabulary for the character's age group.

Not you again!

Walk the walk

The character's personality or mood should be reflected with appropriate body language. For example, a confident character would hold her head up high and her shoulders back and might walk with a swagger. A timid or uncomfortable character would look down at the ground, shuffle, slouch, and avoid eye contact.

In court

A criminal trial is a type of debate, because the lawyers argue about whether a defendant is guilty or not guilty. The prosecution and defense lawyers take turns making their points and giving evidence. A judge, and sometimes a jury, will then give a verdict. A lawyer's ability to persuade can make all the difference in a trial's outcome.

• Introduce some **controversial points of view** in a discussion. Even if no one agrees with them, unusual ideas can get a debate going.

• Do not **shout**. Even if there is a disagreement, it's important to remain **polite**.

Writing a speech

A SPEECH IS A TALK ON A SUBJECT GIVEN TO AN AUDIENCE.

People make speeches for many different reasons, but they are often for work or social occasions. The techniques used for writing a speech are similar to those used in written work, but a speech must be effective when read aloud.

SEE ALSO
❮ 34–35 Pronouns
❮ 182–183 Picking the right words
❮ 188–189 Paragraphing
❮ 202–203 Writing to influence
❮ 222–223 The spoken word
Presentation skills 228–229 ❯

Talking point

Every speech needs to have a clear and passionate message for its audience. For example, a politician makes speeches to persuade people to vote for him or her, or to support his or her policies. Activists speak to raise awareness about an issue, such as animal rights.

• Informal speeches can include some **slang**, but it's best to use **Standard English** so that the audience will **understand** what is **being said**.

GLOSSARY

Alliteration The repetition of certain letters or sounds for effect.

Pronoun A word that takes the place of a noun, such as *I, me,* or *she.*

Rhetorical question A question that does not require an answer but is used for effect.

Slogan A short but memorable statement that sums up a message.

Standard English The form of English that uses formal vocabulary and grammar.

Ideas for my speech:

- *Save the Brussels sprout!*
- *When I met my favorite sports hero.*
- *Mullet hairstyles are a fashion disaster.*
- *Why I should be the next James Bond.*
- *Cell phones should not be banned in school.*

Structure

Like any piece of writing, a speech needs to have a focused structure, with a clear beginning, middle, and end.

I have a shocking secret. I like Brussels sprouts!

Brussels sprouts are incredibly good for you. There is more vitamin C in a sprout than an orange.

So next time you eat dinner, give the little green things a chance.

△ **Beginning**
The opening lines should capture the audience's attention, with a joke, a surprising statistic, or an inspirational quote.

△ **Middle**
The middle part of the speech should deliver the main points, one by one. Each point should be backed up with evidence.

△ **End**
The last section needs to sum up the message of the speech and ideally end with something memorable.

Smooth talker

Speechwriters use particular techniques to create interesting speeches that will engage an audience. Most importantly, they consider what the words will sound like when they are spoken out loud.

Rhetorical questions

Sometimes, a speaker will ask the audience a question, often without expecting an answer. Posing questions makes listeners feel involved and encourages them to think about something in depth.

> You say that you hate Brussels sprouts, but have you ever given them a chance?

Repetition and lists

Repeating words and phrases gives a speech a good rhythm and emphasizes important words and ideas. Patterns of three are particularly common in speech writing. Listing subjects, places, or names can reinforce how many there are of something.

> Sprouts are bursting with goodness. They are packed with **vitamin C, vitamin A, potassium, calcium, iron, and protein.**

REAL WORLD

I would also like to thank...

Actors often give speeches when they win prizes at awards ceremonies. The Academy Awards have become famous for having overly long and emotional speeches. The record for the longest speech is still held by Greer Garson, who rambled on for seven minutes in 1942. Since then, ceremony organizers have imposed a 45-second rule, so speeches longer than 45 seconds are cut off by the orchestra.

Emotive and sensational language

A speech isn't just a list of events or a logical argument. It needs to appeal to the audience. Speechwriters use emotive language to evoke a response in the audience, such as sympathy, guilt, or excitement.

> Every year, thousands and thousands of untouched Brussels sprouts are **thoughtlessly dumped** in the trash.

Pronouns

Using the pronouns *I, you,* or *we* in a speech can make it more personal. Speakers also use friendly terms of address, such as *friends* or *comrades*, to relate to the audience.

> I changed my mind about Brussels sprouts. **You** can, too. **Together we** can make this vegetable popular again.

Slogans

Speeches often contain memorable statements called slogans, which sum up an argument. They are usually short and powerful, and sound good when spoken out loud, often because they use alliteration.

> **Bring back the Brussels!**

The best speeches are often **short**. Abraham Lincoln's Gettysburg Address, one of the most famous speeches in history, lasted for less than **three minutes**.

Presentation skills

THE BEST PUBLIC SPEAKERS ARE CLEAR AND ENGAGING.

Even a well-written speech will be dull if it is badly presented. It's important to speak clearly and to engage an audience with the right tone of voice, body language, and even props.

SEE ALSO

‹ 116–117 Bullet points
‹ 202–203 Writing to influence
‹ 222–223 The spoken word
‹ 224–225 Debates and role plays
‹ 226–227 Writing a speech

Flash cards

It's tempting to read out a speech word by word, but a spontaneous delivery is more entertaining for an audience. It's best to learn as much of a speech as possible, and prepare small cards with the important points, quotations, and statistics to use as prompts.

Write the important points on a flash card. These can be written in note form.

Include statistics because they are easy to forget.

Why I love Brussels sprouts
- *I have a secret. I love Brussels sprouts!*
- *The day I changed my mind.*
- *They have a bad reputation but don't deserve it.*
- *Largest producer is the Netherlands, with 82,000 tons a year.*

Speak up

A speaker should never shout, but should project his or her voice so that it can be heard around the room. It's also important not to speak too quickly, as the audience may find it difficult to keep up. In fact, pausing occasionally can be very effective because it gives an audience time to think about what is being said. Finally, there is no need to hide an accent, but the pronunciation should be clear.

Some nutritional facts about Brussels sprouts
- *Brussels sprouts contain more vitamin C than oranges. (pause)*
- *There is almost no fat in Brussels sprouts. (pause)*
- *Unlike most vegetables, Brussels sprouts are high in protein. (pause)*

Include pauses on a flash card to show when to break for a few seconds.

Intonation

When people talk, their voices go up and down and get louder and quieter. This natural variation is called intonation. If a person's voice stays the same, it will sound robotic and put the audience to sleep. Stressing important words or phrases helps to create a good rhythm, and will emphasize those points.

Underline or highlight important words or phrases that need to be stressed.

History of Brussels sprouts
- *Forerunners to the Brussels sprout were cultivated in Ancient Rome.*
- *American Founding Father Thomas Jefferson grew Brussels sprouts.*
- *Today, production is huge. Approximately 32,000 tons are produced in the United States every year.*

Gestures and movement

Gestures can make a presenter seem more enthusiastic and engaging. Speakers often wave their hands around to emphasize certain points and catch an audience's attention. Walking around a room makes a delivery more personal because the speaker moves closer to certain individuals. Making eye contact with individuals in an audience is also important.

- A speaker must sound **enthusiastic**. If he or she sounds bored, the audience will be, too.
- It can be useful to **practice** a speech in front of a **mirror**.

Maintain eye contact to engage the audience.

△ **Enthusiasm**
Enthusiastic gestures, such as punching the air or waving, can make a speaker seem more passionate.

△ **Big ideas**
Some actions—for example, spreading out the arms—can emphasize the size of an issue.

△ **Distraction**
It's important not to move around too much. Awkward movements can distract an audience from what the speaker is saying.

Visual aids

Sometimes speakers use visual aids to engage their audiences. These include images, graphs, and diagrams that explain complicated information or make it more interesting. Summarizing key points on a projector slide or handout will also emphasize the most important details, and help the audience to remember them.

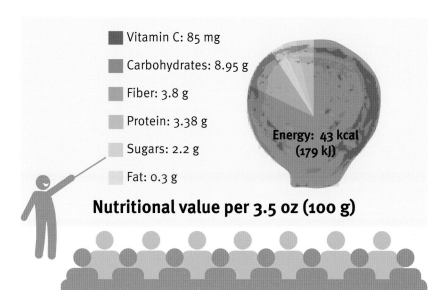

Vitamin C: 85 mg
Carbohydrates: 8.95 g
Fiber: 3.8 g
Protein: 3.38 g
Sugars: 2.2 g
Fat: 0.3 g

Energy: 43 kcal (179 kJ)

Nutritional value per 3.5 oz (100 g)

Dressing down

Public speakers even think about the way they dress when speaking to an audience. Some politicians or business professionals decide not to wear a suit and tie when making a speech to the public. By wearing more casual clothes, they hope that they will look more relaxed and approachable, so the audience will relate to them.

Reference

Grammar reference

Parts of speech

The different types of words that make up sentences are called parts of speech. Only nouns and verbs are essential elements of a sentence, but other parts of speech—such as adjectives and adverbs—can make a sentence more descriptive.

Part of speech	Meaning	Examples
noun	A name	cat, Evie, girl, house, water
adjective	Describes a noun or pronoun	big, funny, light, red, young
verb	Shows action or a state of being	be, go, read, speak, swim, walk
adverb	Describes verbs, adjectives and other adverbs, giving information on where, when and how much	briskly, easily, happily, here, loudly, quite, rather, soon, together, very
pronoun	Takes the place of a noun	he, she, you, we, them, it
preposition	Relates a noun or pronoun to another word in the sentence	about, above, from, in
conjunction	A joining word, used to link words and phrases	and, because, but, while, yet
interjection	An exclamation or remark	ah, hey, hi, hmm, wow, yes
article	Used with a noun to specify whether the noun is a particular person or thing, or something general	a, an, the
determiner	Precedes a noun and puts the noun in context	all, her, my, their, your

Negative and positive words and phrases

Some words have negative meanings—for example, *no*, *none*, *not*, *insult*, and *deny*. Other words can be made negative by adding a negative prefix, such as anti-, dis-, or un-, or suffix, such as -less. These words can then be used to make a sentence structure positive, which helps to simplify the sentence and make it easier to understand.

Negative structure	Positive structure
was not typical	was atypical
is not social	is antisocial
have no defenses	is defenseless
was not hydrated	was dehydrated
does not approve	disapproves
was not legal	was illegal
is not balanced	is imbalanced
was not direct	was indirect
was not spelled correctly	was misspelled
does not exist	is nonexistent
was not happy	was unhappy

Irregular verbs

Not all verbs follow the rules: Regular verbs follow a specific spelling pattern when they are converted into the past tense, but irregular verbs do not. Here are some of the irregular verbs and their past-tense and past-participle spellings.

Infinitive form	Simple past tense	Past participle
awake	awoke	awoken
bear	bore	born
beat	beat	beaten
bend	bent	bent
bind	bound	bound
bite	bit	bitten
burn	burned/burnt	burned/burnt
deal	dealt	dealt
dig	dug	dug
dream	dreamed/dreamt	dreamed/dreamt
feed	fed	fed
fight	fought	fought
forbid	forbade	forbidden
forget	forgot	forgotten
forgive	forgave	forgiven
forsake	forsook	forsaken
grind	ground	ground
hide	hid	hidden
hit	hit	hit
hurt	hurt	hurt
kneel	knelt	knelt
leap	leaped/leapt	leaped/leapt
light	lit	lit
overdo	overdid	overdone
prove	proved	proved/proven
read	read	read
ring	rang	rung
seek	sought	sought
shine	shone	shone
slay	slew	slain
stink	stank	stunk
tread	trod	trodden
wake	woke	woken
weave	wove	woven

Pronouns

Pronouns are used to represent nouns, so that sentences do not become repetitive. Singular nouns should be replaced by singular pronouns, and plural nouns should be replaced by plural pronouns. Some pronouns can be singular or plural.

Type	Singular	Plural
personal pronouns	I you he she it me him her	we you they us them
possessive pronouns	mine yours his hers its	ours yours theirs
relative pronouns	that what which who whom whose	that what which whose
reflexive pronouns	myself yourself himself herself	ourselves themselves
demonstrative pronouns	this that	these those
interrogative pronouns	who whom what which whose	what which
indefinite pronouns	all another any anyone anything each more most neither nobody none no one nothing other some somebody	all any both few many most none others several some

Common grammatical errors

Dangling participles

The introductory phrases in the first two sentences below set the sentence up for a noun that doesn't follow. This is called a "dangling participle" because the first part of the sentence is left dangling, with nothing to support or explain it. The noun that starts the second part of the sentence must be the noun that relates to the first part.

✘ **Smiling** from ear to ear, **the school** confirmed Jo's position on the debate team.

✘ **Smiling** from ear to ear, **Jo's position** on the school debate team was confirmed.

✓ **Smiling** from ear to ear, **Jo** learned that her position on the school debate team was confirmed.

Double negatives

Two negatives make a positive in math, and the same is true in language—two negative words in a sentence cancel each other out to upset the intended meaning.

✘ Charlie **couldn't** have **none** of the sweets.

✓ Charlie **could** have **none** of the sweets.

✓ Charlie **couldn't** have **any** of the sweets.

Incomplete sentences

A complete sentence must make sense, and to do this it must contain a subject and a verb. Even though the second sentence below is made up of only two words, it is complete because it has a subject and a verb. The first sentence is incomplete because it doesn't have a subject.

✘ Where is.

✓ I slept.

Misuse of *me*, *myself*, and *I*

If the following sentence is split into smaller parts, the sentence "Me traveled by train" is wrong.

✘ Luke and **me** traveled by train.

✓ Luke and **I** traveled by train.

Likewise, if this sentence is split into smaller parts, the sentence "It was a long journey for I" is wrong.

✘ It was a long journey for Luke and **I**.

✓ It was a long journey for Luke and **me**.

Myself always needs to have a subject to refer back to. There is no *I* or *me* in the first of the following sentences, so the use of *myself* in this instance is wrong.

✘ Luke wondered about **myself** in the same situation.

✓ I wondered about **myself** in the same situation.

Misplaced modifiers

A modifier needs to be close to the word that it is modifying; otherwise, confusion can occur. In the following sentence, the modifier *hot* should refer to the warmth of the porridge that Becky eats every morning, and not the heat of the bowl.

✘ Becky ate a **hot** bowl of porridge every morning.

✓ Becky ate a bowl of **hot** porridge every morning.

Misusing gender-neutral pronouns

Some pronouns, such as *they*, don't specify a gender. *They* is a plural pronoun and is sometimes misused in sentences where a singular pronoun is needed. In the following sentence, *they* is wrong because it is plural while the subject *someone* is singular. *They* should be replaced with *he or she,* or the sentence should be rewritten.

✘ If **someone** did that, then **they were** wrong.

✓ If **someone** did that, then **he or she was** wrong.

Split infinitives

An infinitive is the simplest form of a verb, such as *to run* or *to have*. It is preferable to keep the word *to* with the infinitive verb in a sentence. In the first sentence below, the adverb *secretly* has separated *to* from the verb *like*. This is a split infinitive and should be avoided.

✘ She used **to** secretly **like** football.

✓ She secretly used **to like** football.

Subject-verb disagreement

In the example below, the subject has been misidentified as *presents*—a plural noun—so the plural form of the verb (*were*) has been used. The subject of the sentence is actually the singular noun *sack*, so the singular form of the verb (*was*) should be used instead.

✘ The **sack** of presents **were** delivered late.

✓ The **sack** of presents **was** delivered late.

Non sequiturs

Literally translated, *non sequitur* means "it does not follow" and is an instance where one statement or conclusion doesn't logically follow from what was previously said or argued. Here are some examples:

You have a big nose. Therefore, your face looks young.

I will win the game. I have a hat.

Commonly misused words and expressions

Using *bored of* instead of *bored by* or *bored with*

✗ She was bored **of** studying.

✗ He was bored **of** the classes.

✓ She was bored **with** studying.

✓ He was bored **by** the classes.

Confusing *compared to* and *compared with*

Compared to should be used when asserting that two things are alike. In this sentence, Jess was like the best in the class.

✓ The teacher compared Jess **to** the best in the class.

Compared with should be used when comparing the similarities and differences between two things. In the sentence below, the teacher was considering how similar Jess was to the best in the class.

✓ The teacher compared Jess **with** the best in the class.

Using *different than* instead of *different from*

✗ The left side is different **than** the right side.

✓ The left side is different **from** the right side.

Using *like* as a conjunction instead of *as if* or *as though*

Like is correctly used as a preposition in the final example sentence; it should not be used as a conjunction.

✗ He acted **like** he didn't care.

✓ He acted **as though** he didn't care.

✓ It looks **like** a turtle.

Using *or* with *neither*

Either and *or* go together, and *neither* and *nor* go together.

✗ Use **neither** the left one **or** the right one.

✓ Use **either** the left one **or** the right one.

✓ Use **neither** the left one **nor** the right one.

Using *should of*, *would of*, and *could of* instead of *should have*, *would have*, and *should have*

Of is often wrongly used to mean *have* in spoken English.

✗ Steve **should of** stood up for himself.

✓ Steve **should have** stood up for himself.

✓ Steve **should've** stood up for himself.

Using *try and* and *go and* instead of *try to* and *go to*

The conjunction *and* is often wrongly used instead of the preposition *to* with the verbs *try* and *go*.

✗ We should **try and** change our flights.

✓ We should **try to** change our flights.

✗ I'll **go and** see the show.

✓ I'll **go to** see the show.

Using nouns as verbs

In spoken English, especially jargon, it is common for nouns to be used as verbs. This practice is best avoided.

✗ The fire will **impact** the environment.

✓ The fire will have **an impact** on the environment.

Rules for forming sentences

• A sentence must always contain a subject and a verb, start with a capital letter, and end with a period, question mark, or exclamation point. A sentence may also contain an object.

• The basic structure for a sentence to follow is subject–verb–object.

• Never join two main clauses using only a comma. Either separate the clauses into two separate sentences by using a period or a semicolon, or add a joining word such as *and* or *but* after the comma.

• Ensure that a sentence makes sense. If it doesn't make sense, one of the essential ingredients is probably missing, so the sentence is incomplete. For example, a subordinate clause does not make a complete sentence on its own; the main clause is also needed.

• Make sure that the subject and verb match. If the subject is singular, then the verb should be singular; if the subject is plural, then the verb should be plural.

• Use the active voice instead of the passive voice. The active voice is simpler, so the meaning is conveyed more clearly.

• Use positive sentence structure instead of negative sentence structure whenever possible in order to simplify sentences and make them easier to understand.

• Sentences should have a parallel structure. This means that the same patterns of words should be used to show that different parts of the sentence have equal importance.

✗ Darcy likes swimming, running, and to ride her bike.

✓ Darcy likes to swim, run, and ride her bike.

Punctuation reference

Punctuation mark	Name	How to use
.	period	• marks the end of a complete statement • marks the end of an abbreviated word
...	ellipsis	• marks where text has been omitted or an unfinished sentence
,	comma	• follows an introductory word, phrase, or clause • can be used as parentheses, to separate a nonessential part of a sentence • can be used with a conjunction to join two main clauses • separates words or phrases in a list • represents omitted words to avoid repetition in a sentence • can be used between an introduction to speech and the direct speech
;	semicolon	• separates two main clauses that are closely related • precedes adverbs such as *however*, *therefore*, *consequently*, and *nevertheless* to connect clauses • separates items in a complex list
:	colon	• connects a main clause to a clause, phrase, or word that is an explanation of the main clause or that emphasizes a point in the main clause • introduces a list after a complete statement • introduces quoted text
'	apostrophe	• marks a missing letter • indicates possession • creates plural forms if just adding an *s* is confusing
-	hyphen	• links two words in compound modifiers • can be used in fractions and in numbers from twenty-one to ninety-nine • joins certain prefixes to other words
" "	quotation marks	• can be used before and after direct speech and quoted text • separates a word or phrase in a sentence • can be used around titles of short works
?	question mark	• marks the end of a sentence that is a question
!	exclamation point	• marks the end of a sentence that expresses strong emotion • can be used at the end of an interruption to add emphasis
( )	parentheses	• can be used around nonessential information in a sentence • can be used around information that provides clarification
—	dash	• can be used in pairs around interruptions • marks a range of numbers (5–6 hours) • indicates direction of travel (Trys–Qysto route)
•	bullet point	• indicates a key point in a list
/	slash	• can be used to show an alternative instead of using the word *and* or *or*

Contractions

	be	will	would	have	had
I	I am I'm	I will I'll	I would I'd	I have I've	I had I'd
you	you are you're	you will you'll	you would you'd	you have you've	you had you'd
he	he is he's	he will he'll	he would he'd	he has he's	he had he'd
she	she is she's	she will she'll	she would she'd	she has she's	she had she'd
it	it is it's	it will it'll	it would it'd	it has it's	it had it'd
we	we are we're	we will we'll	we would we'd	we have we've	we had we'd
they	they are they're	they will they'll	they would they'd	they have they've	they had they'd
that	that is that's	that will that'll	that would that'd	that has that's	that had that'd
who	who is who's	who will who'll	who would who'd	who has who's	who had who'd

Verbs and *not*	Contraction
is not	isn't
are not	aren't
was not	wasn't
were not	weren't
have not	haven't
has not	hasn't
had not	hadn't
will not	won't
would not	wouldn't
do not	don't
does not	doesn't
did not	didn't
cannot	can't
could not	couldn't
should not	shouldn't
might not	mightn't
must not	mustn't

Auxiliary verbs and *have*	would have	should have	could have	might have	must have
Contraction	would've	should've	could've	might've	must've

Common punctuation errors

Comma splice

A comma between two clauses creates a "comma splice" if it is used without a conjunction. The comma needs to be replaced with either a semicolon or a period, or the text can be rewritten to use a comma and a conjunction.

✗ You cook**,** I'll do the dishes.

✓ You cook**, and** I'll do the dishes.

Greengrocer's apostrophe

An unnecessary apostrophe incorrectly placed before the plural s is called a "greengrocer's apostrophe."

✗ carrot**'**s ✗ apple**'**s

✓ carrots ✓ apples

Hyphen in a compound modifier

Using a hyphen in a compound modifier that includes an adverb ending in -ly is incorrect. These compound modifiers are never hyphenated.

✗ cleverly-planned meeting

✓ cleverly planned meeting

Misuse of *your* and *you're*

Confusion between *your* and *you're* can be avoided by remembering that *you're* is a contraction made up of two separate words: *you* and *are*.

✗ It's in **you're** bag. ✗ **Your** mistaken.

✓ It's in **your** bag. ✓ **You're** mistaken.

Spelling reference

Commonly misspelled words

There are many difficult words in the English language that people struggle to spell correctly. Here are some of the most commonly misspelled words, with handy tips on how to spell them correctly.

Correct spelling	Spelling tips	Common misspelling
accommodation	there are two *c*'s and two *m*'s	accomodation
apparently	*ent* in the middle, not *ant*	apparantly
appearance	ends with **-ance**, not **-ence**	appearence
basically	ends with **-cally**, not **-cly**	basicly
beginning	double *n* in the middle	begining
believe	remember the "*i* before *e* except after *c*" rule	beleive or belive
business	starts with **busi-**	buisness
calendar	ends with **-ar**, not **-er**	calender
cemetery	ends with **-ery**, not **-ary**	cemetary
coming	there is only one *m*	comming
committee	double *m*, double *t*, and double *e*	commitee
completely	remember the last **e**; ends with **-tely**, not **-tly**	completly
conscious	remember the *s* before the *c* in the middle	concious
definitely	*ite* in the middle, not *ate*	definately
disappoint	there is one *s* and two *p*'s	dissapoint
embarrass	there are two *r*'s and two *s*'s	embarass
environment	remember the *n* before the *m*	enviroment
existence	ends with **-ence**, not **-ance**	existance
familiar	ends with **-iar**	familar
finally	there are two *l*'s	finaly
friend	remember the "*i* before *e* except after *c*" rule	freind
government	remember the *n* before the *m*	goverment
interrupt	there are two *r*'s in the middle	interupt
knowledge	remember the *d* before the *g*	knowlege
necessary	one *c* and two *s*'s	neccessary
separate	*par* in the middle, not *per*	seperate
successful	two *c*'s and two *s*'s	succesful
truly	there is no *e*	truely
unfortunately	ends with **-tely**, not **-tly**	unfortunatly
which	begins with **wh**	wich

Two words or one?

Some words in the English language are often used together, so it's easy to mistake them for a single word. Here are some phrases that many people fall into the trap of writing as one word instead of two.

a lot	full time	ice cream	real time
bath time	hard copy	life cycle	seat belt
blood sugar	high chair	never mind	side effect
cash flow	hip bone	post office	time frame
first aid	home page	race car	time sheet

Commonly confused words

The English language is full of similar-sounding words that have different meanings. It is essential, therefore, to spell the words correctly to achieve the correct meaning in a sentence. Here are some of the most commonly confused words that sound alike, with examples of their correct usage.

accept and **except**
I **accept** your apology.
Everyone was on the list **except** for me.

adverse and **averse**
She was feeling unwell due to the **adverse** effects of her medication.
He was lazy and **averse** to playing sports.

aisle and **isle**
The bride walked down the **aisle**.
They visited an **isle** near the coast of Scotland.

aloud and **allowed**
She read the book **aloud**.
He was **allowed** to choose which book to read.

amoral and **immoral**
Her **amoral** attitude meant that she didn't care if her actions were wrong.
He was fired from the company for **immoral** conduct.

appraise and **apprise**
The manager needed to **appraise** the employee's skills.
The lawyer arrived to **apprise** the defendant of his rights.

assent and **ascent**
He nodded his **assent**.
They watched the **ascent** of the balloon.

aural and **oral**
The **aural** test required her to listen.
The dentist performed an **oral** examination.

bare and **bear**
She went outside with **bare** feet.
The large **bear** roamed the woods.

break and **brake**
The chocolate was easy to **break** apart.
The car didn't **brake** fast enough.

broach and **brooch**
He decided to **broach** the subject for discussion.
She wore a pretty **brooch**.

capital and **capitol**
Richmond is the **capital** of Virginia.
The state **capitol** is an impressive building.

cereal and **serial**
He ate a bowl of **cereal** for breakfast.
She found the **serial** number on her computer.

complement and **compliment**
The colors **complement** each other well.
He paid her a **compliment** by telling her she was pretty.

cue and **queue**
The actor waited for his **cue** before walking on stage.
There are three jobs left in the printer **queue**.

desert and **dessert**
The **desert** is extremely hot and dry.
She decided to have cake for **dessert**.

pore and **pour**
He had a blocked **pore** on his nose.
She helped **pour** the drinks at the party.

principle and **principal**
The man was guided by strong **principles**.
He was given the role of the **principal** character.

stationary and **stationery**
The aircraft landed and remained **stationary**.
She looked in the **stationery** cabinet for a pen.

Tricky capitalized words

Certain words sometimes begin with a capital letter and other times they don't. It's important to know when to use a capital letter, so that written sentences make sense.

In some cases, capital letters are the only distinguishing factor between two words that are spelled the same way, but mean very different things.

Confused words	Lowercase meaning	Capitalized meaning
alpine and Alpine	relating to mountainous areas	relating to the Alps
august and August	majestic	the eighth month of the year
cancer and Cancer	a disease	a constellation and astrological sign
china and China	porcelain	a country in eastern Asia
earth and Earth	soil, dry land	the planet we live on
jack and Jack	a device for lifting heavy items	a male name
italic and Italic	a sloping typeface	relating to Italy
lent and Lent	the past tense of the verb *lend*	in Christianity, the period preceding Easter
march and March	to walk briskly and rhythmically	the third month of the year
marine and Marine	relating to the ocean	a member of the Marine Corps
mercury and Mercury	a chemical element	the closest planet to the Sun
nice and Nice	pleasant	a city in the south of France
pole and Pole	a long cylindrical object	a person from Poland
turkey and Turkey	a bird	a country in the Middle East

Common Latin and Greek roots

Latin root	Meaning	Examples
act	do	**act**ion, en**act**
ang	bend	**ang**le, tri**ang**le
cap	head	**cap**ital, de**cap**itate
dic	speak	**dic**tate, pre**dict**
imag	likeness	**imag**e, **imag**ination
just	law	**just**ice, **just**ify
ques	ask, seek	**ques**tion, re**ques**t
sci	know	con**sci**ence, **sci**ence

Greek root	Meaning	Examples
arch	chief	**arch**bishop, mon**arch**
auto	self	**auto**biography, **auto**matic
cosm	universe	**cosm**opolitan, **cosm**os
gen	birth, race	**gen**eration, **gen**ocide
log	word	apo**log**y, dia**log**ue
lys	break down	ana**lys**is, cata**lys**t
morph	shape	meta**morph**osis, **morph**ology
phon	sound	sym**phon**y, tele**phon**e

Prefixes and suffixes

Prefixes	Meanings	Examples
aero-	air	aerodynamic, aerosol
agri-	of earth (relating to soil)	agribusiness, agriculturalist
ambi-	both	ambiguous, ambivalent
astro-	star	astrology, astronaut
bio-	life, living things	biodiversity, biofuel
contra-	against, opposite	contraband, contradict
deca-	ten	decade, decahedron
di-, du-, duo-	two	dioxide, duet, duotone
electro-	relating to electricity	electrolysis, electromagnet
geo-	relating to Earth	geography, geology
hydro-	relating to water	hydroelectricity, hydropower
infra-	below, beneath	infrared, infrastucture
kilo-	one thousand	kilogram, kilometer
mal-	bad	malaise, malnourished
maxi-	large	maximize, maximum
multi-	many	multicultural, multiply
nano-	one-billionth, extremely small	nanosecond, nanotechnology
ped-	foot	pedestrian, pedometer
proto-	first	protocol, prototype
sy-, syl-, sym-, syn-	together, with	system, syllable, symbol, synthesis
tele-	distant	telephone, telescope

Suffixes	Meaning	Examples
-ade	action	blockade, masquerade
-an	person, belonging to	guardian, historian
-ancy, -ency	state	vacancy, agency
-ar, -ary	resembling	linear, exemplary
-ard, -art	characterize	wizard, braggart
-ence, -ency	state	dependence, emergency
-ess	female	lioness, waitress
-fy	to make into	beautify, simplify
-iatry	healing, medical care	podiatry, psychiatry
-ile	having the qualities of	projectile, senile
-or, -our	condition	humor, glamour
-ory	having the function of	compulsory, contributory
-phobia	fear of	agoraphobia, arachnophobia
-ure	action	exposure, measure
-wise	in the manner of	clockwise, likewise

Homonyms

Homonyms are words that have the same spelling and pronunciation, but different meanings.

Homonym	Meaning 1	Meaning 2	Meaning 3	Meaning 4
back	a person's back, from shoulders to hips	the back part of an object, opposite to the front	to go backward	in return
board	a thin, flat piece of wood	a decision-making body	regular meals	to get on to a ship or train
bore	to make a hole	a hollow part of a tube	a dull person or activity	to make someone weary
cast	to throw forcefully in a specific direction	to cause light or shadow to appear on a surface	to register a vote	actors in a drama
clear	easy to interpret or understand	having or feeling no doubt or confusion	transparent	free of obstacles
course	a route or direction	a dish forming one of the parts of a meal	the way in which something develops	a series of lessons on a particular subject
dock	an enclosed area of water in a port	the place in a court where defendants stand	to deduct, usually money	to cut short, for example, an animal's tail
fair	treating people equally or appropriately	light hair color or complexion	fine and dry weather	an event with exhibitions and amusements
tie	fabric worn around neck	to fasten with string or cord	the same score in a game	a bond that unites people

Homophones

Homophones are words with identical pronunciations, but different spellings and meanings.

Spelling 1	Meaning 1	Spelling 2	Meaning 2	Spelling 3	Meaning 3
aisle	a passage	isle	a small island	I'll	Contracted form of *I will*
buy	to purchase	by	through the agency of	bye	short for *goodbye*
cent	a monetary unit	scent	an odor	sent	past tense of the verb *send*
cite	to mention	sight	vision	site	a place
for	in support of	fore	situated in front	four	the number (4)
meat	animal flesh as food	meet	to get together	mete	to dispense a punishment
rain	precipitation from the sky	rein	a strip attached to a horse for guidance	reign	the period of rule by a monarch
raise	to lift something	rays	beams of light	raze	to completely destroy or demolish
vain	conceited	vane	a device for showing wind direction	vein	a blood vessel

Useful spelling rules

• The **"ee"** sound at the end of a word is almost always spelled with a **y**, as in *emergency* and *dependency*. There are exceptions to this rule, such as *fee* and *coffee*.

• When *all* and *well* are followed by another syllable, they only have one *l*, as in *already* and *welcome*.

• When *full* and *till* are joined to a root syllable, the final *l* should be dropped, as in *useful* and *until*.

• When **two vowels** go walking, **the first one** does the talking. This means that when there are two vowels next to each other in a word, the first one represents the sound made when spoken, while the second vowel is silent, as in *approach* and *leather*. There are some exceptions to this rule, including *great* and *build*.

• When words end in a **silent -e**, drop the **silent -e** when adding endings that begin with a vowel: for example, when adding **-ing** to *give* to form *giving*. Keep the **silent -e** when adding endings that begin with a consonant: for example, when adding **-s** to *give* to form *gives*.

• If a word ends with an **"ick"** sound, spell it using *ick* if it has one syllable, as in *click* and *brick*. If the word has two or more syllables, spell it using *ic*, as in *electronic* and *catastrophic*. Some exceptions to this rule include *homesick* and *limerick*.

• The letter *q* is usually followed by a *u*, as in *quiet* and *sequence*.

Mnemonics and fun spelling tips

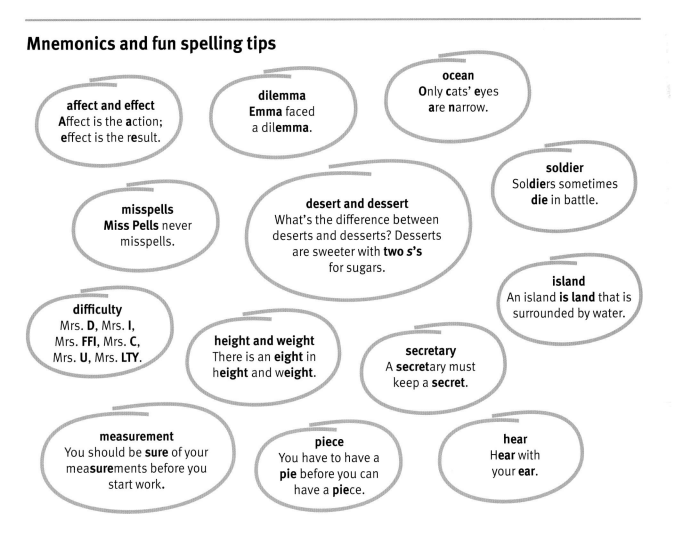

affect and effect
Affect is the **a**ction;
effect is the **re**sult.

dilemma
Emma faced
a dil**emma**.

ocean
Only **c**ats' **e**yes
are **n**arrow.

soldier
Sol**die**rs sometimes
die in battle.

misspells
Miss Pells never
misspells.

desert and dessert
What's the difference between
deserts and desserts? Desserts
are sweeter with **two s's**
for sugars.

island
An island **is land** that is
surrounded by water.

difficulty
Mrs. **D**, Mrs. **I**,
Mrs. **FFI**, Mrs. **C**,
Mrs. **U**, Mrs. **LTY**.

height and weight
There is an **eight** in
h**eight** and w**eight**.

secretary
A **secret**ary must
keep a **secret**.

measurement
You should be **sure** of your
mea**sure**ments before you
start work.

piece
You have to have a
pie before you can
have a **pie**ce.

hear
H**ear** with
your **ear**.

Communication skills reference

Synonyms

Good writers use a wide range of vocabulary. Rather than using the same word repeatedly, try to use different words that mean the same thing. These are known as synonyms. Some alternatives may give more information than the original choice: For example, *she whispered* tells the reader much more than *she said*.

dramatic **thrilling** **sensational** — exciting

cried **muttered** **whispered** **remarked** **demanded** **yelled** **gasped** **exclaimed** — said

gorgeous **attractive** **elegant** **exquisite** **stunning** **graceful** — beautiful

clearly **categorically** **positively** **surely** **inescapably** — unquestionably — definitely

dull **monotonous** **tedious** **tiresome** **mundane** — boring

remarkable **overwhelming** **astonishing** **impressive** **spectacular** — amazing

absorbing **appealing** **arresting** **fascinating** **captivating** **inspiring** — interesting

gigantic **huge** **immense** **monstrous** **vast** **enormous** **tremendous** **massive** — big

browse **gawk** **gape** **glimpse** **observe** **stare** **peep** **watch** — look

demanding **trying** **challenging** **arduous** **exacting** **grueling** — difficult

march **amble** **lumber** **wander** **prance** **plod** **swagger** **waddle** — walk

livid **annoyed** **furious** **irate** **incensed** — angry

Adjectives to describe characters

The best stories include unique characters. Use unusual adjectives to describe a character's mood and personality.

absentminded
argumentative
bossy
charismatic
considerate
eccentric

flamboyant
generous
glamorous
gregarious
intelligent
intuitive

materialistic
morose
optimistic
responsible
ruthless
witty

Tautologies

Some phrases say the same thing twice. These are called tautologies and should be avoided because they are unnecessary.

Tautology	Reason to avoid
tiny little baby	*Tiny* and *little* mean the same thing.
a round circle	Circles are always round.
an old antique	An antique has to be old.
an unexpected surprise	All surprises are unexpected.
yellow in color	Something can't be yellow in anything other than color.
month of May	May is always a month.
new innovation	An innovation has to be new.

Clichés

A cliché is a colloquial expression that has been overused. Clichés should be avoided because they make a piece of writing unoriginal, and because they are informal and often ambiguous.

face the music
as light as a feather
up in the air
at the end of the day
at all costs
in a nutshell
on a roll
cost an arm and a leg

Emotive language

Writers use emotive language to have a greater emotional impact on their audience. This technique is useful when trying to persuade or entertain an audience. It's important to be aware of the effect this language can have in order to analyze and write emotive texts.

Normal version	Dramatic version
she cried	she wailed
a good result	a staggering result
disturbance in town square	riot in town square
school fire	school blaze
brave person	heroic citizen
unhappy workers	furious workers
animals killed	animals slaughtered
house prices fall	house prices plummet
problems in schools	chaos in schools

Less wordy

Using more words than necessary can obscure the meaning of a phrase. Concise writing is both clearer and more stylish.

Wordy version	Concise version
a considerable number of	many
are of the same opinion	agree
as a means of	to
at the present time	currently, now, today
at this point in time	now
give an indication of	show
has a requirement for	requires, needs
has the ability to	can
in close proximity to	near
in the absence of	without
in the course of	during
in the majority of instances	usually
in the very near future	soon
is aware of the fact	knows

Cover letters

A cover letter is a formal letter written to accompany a résumé for a job application. It should be laid out like any formal letter, and include certain details that will promote the application. A good cover letter should be concise and no more than one page long.

The applicant's details go at the top right.

Joe Elf
Hollow Tree
Snowy Forest
North Pole

September 15, 2013

The date needs to be included under the applicant's address.

The employer's details go at the top left.

Mr. Santa Claus
Toy Workshop
Secret Mountain
North Pole

The first paragraph should state which role the applicant is applying for, and where he or she saw the vacancy.

Dear Mr. Claus,

I would like to apply for the position of Junior Toymaker advertised in the *North Pole Chronicle*. As requested, I have enclosed my résumé and two references.

The role would be an excellent opportunity for me to start my career in toy manufacturing. I believe that my internship experience and degree from the Toy College would make me an asset to the company.

The middle of the letter needs to explain why the applicant wants the job, and what skills and experience he or she has.

I can be contacted at the address and phone number on my résumé. I am available for interview next week.

Ending with a positive phrase will show enthusiasm.

I look forward to discussing this role with you soon.

Yours truly,

Joe Elf

Joe Elf

Citations

In academic work, writers have to cite their sources. This is to prove that they have not copied another scholar's writing, taken credit for someone else's ideas, or made up information. A citation needs to be added if another writer's direct words have been quoted, or his or her original ideas or findings are described. Statistics also need to be cited. There are several citation systems to choose from; however, the same system must be used throughout a piece of writing.

▷ **Numbering system**
In a numbering system, a small number is placed after each fact or quotation that needs to be cited. This corresponds to a numbered source placed at the bottom of the page, called a footnote. The details are repeated in the bibliography at the end of the work.

> Pizza purists argue that pizzas should only be topped with tomatoes, herbs, and sometimes mozzarella. According to a prominent Italian food writer, "There are only two types of pizza—Marinara and Margherita. That is all I serve." [1]
>
> 1. Gennaro Rossi, *The Perfect Pizza* (London: Pizza Press, 2010), 9.

The title of the book is written in italics.

The location and name of the publisher appear in parentheses, separated by a colon. A publisher's name is followed by a comma and the publication date.

The specific page reference(s) should also be included. There is no need to include abbreviations such as *p.* or *pp.*

▷ **Parenthetical system**
In a parenthetical system, citations appear in parentheses within the text. In North America, the two most common parenthetical systems are MLA style (shown here) and APA style, named after the Modern Language Association and the American Psychological Association, respectively.

> Pizza purists argue that pizzas should only be topped with tomatoes, herbs, and sometimes mozzarella. According to a prominent Italian food writer, "There are only two types of pizza—Marinara and Margherita. That is all I serve" (Rossi 9).

The last name of the author is included because it is not mentioned in the surrounding text. If the author's name is mentioned in the text, there is no need to include it in the citation.

The exact page reference is always included.

The period is placed outside the quotation marks, after the parentheses.

▷ **"Works Cited" list**
When using a parenthetical system, the rest of the information about the sources needs to be included in a "Works Cited" list at the end of the assignment. Unlike a bibliography, this list only includes the sources that have been quoted or paraphrased; it does not list books used for background research.

> Romano, Silvio. *The History of Italian Cooking*. New York: Food Books, 1982. Print.
>
> Rossi, Gennaro. *The Perfect Pizza*. London: Pizza Press, 2010. Print.

The sources should be listed alphabetically by the author's last name.

The title is italicized.

The publisher's details are separated by a colon.

End each entry with the medium of publication.

Glossary

abbreviation

A shortened form of a word, often with one or more periods to represent missing letters.

abstract noun

The name given to something that cannot be touched, such as a concept or a sensation.

accent

The way in which a language is pronounced, which varies across geographic areas.

acronym

An abbreviation made up of the initial letters of the main words in a phrase. These letters are pronounced as a word (rather than as separate letters), which represents the meaning of the original phrase.

active voice

When the subject of a sentence is performing the action of the verb, and the object is receiving it.

adjective

A word that describes a noun.

adjective phrase

A group of words that describe a noun or pronoun.

adjective prepositional phrase

A prepositional phrase that describes a noun.

adverb

A word that modifies the meaning of an adjective, verb, or other adverb.

adverb prepositional phrase

A prepositional phrase that describes a verb.

adverbial phrase

A group of words that behave in the same way as an adverb and answer questions such as: How? When? Why? Where? How often?

alliteration

The repetition of certain letters or sounds for effect.

Arabic numerals

Everyday numerals such as 1, 2, and 3.

attributive position

When an adjective is placed directly in front of the noun or pronoun that it is modifying.

auxiliary verb

A "helping" verb such as *be* or *have* that joins the main verb in a sentence to the subject. Auxiliary verbs are also used with other words to form contractions and negative sentences.

bibliography

A list of all the sources used in a piece of academic work.

blog

An online journal that contains the writer's comments and reflections. It is updated regularly.

cardinal number

A counting number such as *one*, *two*, *ten*, or *twenty-one*.

clause

A grammatical unit that contains a subject and a verb. Sentences are made up of one or more clauses.

collective noun

The name given to a collection of individuals—people or things.

colloquial language

The language that is used in everyday speech.

colloquialism

A word or phrase used only in informal speech.

command

A sentence that gives an instruction.

common noun

The name given to everyday objects, places, people, and ideas.

concrete noun

The name given to an ordinary, physical thing, such as an object or animal.

conjunction
A word or phrase used to connect words, phrases, and clauses.

consonant
A letter of the alphabet that is not a vowel.

contraction
A shortened form of a word or words, in which letters are omitted from the middle and replaced with an apostrophe.

coordinating conjunction
A word that connects words, phrases, and clauses of equal importance.

dangling participle
When a modifying phrase or clause that starts with a participle is put in the wrong place in a sentence, and has no subject to hold on to.

dialect
The informal vocabulary and grammar used by a particular social or geographic group.

direct object
The person or thing directly affected by the action of the verb.

direct speech
Text that represents spoken words and is written in quotation marks.

exaggeration
When something is represented as larger or better than it actually is.

exclamation
A sentence that expresses a strong emotion, such as surprise, or a raised voice, and ends in an exclamation point.

fact
A statement that can be proved.

first person narrative
When an author writes a piece from his or her point of view, using *I* and *my*.

gerund
The name given to the present participle when it is used as a noun.

headline
The statement at the top of an article that tells the reader what the article is about.

hyperbole
An extreme form of exaggeration that may not be taken seriously, but grabs the reader's attention.

hyperlink
A word, phrase, or icon on the World Wide Web, which, if clicked, takes the user to a new document or website.

indefinite pronoun
A pronoun such as *everyone* that refers to nobody or nothing specific.

indirect object
The person or thing indirectly affected by the action of the verb.

indirect question
A sentence that reports a question that has been asked, without expecting an answer, and ends in a period.

infinitive
The simplest form of a verb: the form that is used in dictionaries.

interjection
A word or phrase that occurs alone and expresses emotion.

intonation
The variation of pitch and loudness in a person's voice.

intransitive verb
A verb that does not require an object.

italics
A style of type in which the letters are printed at an angle to resemble handwriting.

jargon
A type of slang that includes specialized terms that are used and understood by a select, often professional, group of people.

linking verb
A verb, such as *be*, that joins the subject of a sentence to a word or phrase—often an adjective—that describes the subject.

main clause
A group of words that contains a subject and a verb and makes complete sense on its own.

metaphor

A word or phrase that is used to describe something as if it were something else.

misplaced modifier

A modifier that has been placed so far from the person or thing it is intended to modify that it appears to modify a different person or thing.

modal auxiliary verb

An auxiliary verb such as *could* that is used with an action verb to express a command, an obligation, or a possibility.

morpheme

The smallest meaningful part of a word.

noun

A part of speech that refers to a person, place, or thing.

noun phrase

Several words that, when grouped together, perform the same function as a noun.

number

The term used to identify a noun or pronoun as singular or plural.

object

The person or thing (a noun or pronoun) that is receiving the action of the verb.

objective

When a piece of writing is not influenced by the writer's personal opinions.

onomatopoeia

The use of words that mimic the sounds they represent.

opinion

A statement based on someone's personal view.

ordinal number

The form of a number that includes *first*, *second*, *tenth*, and *twenty-first*.

participle

The form of a verb that ends in -ing (present participle) or -ed or -en (past participle).

passive voice

When the subject in a sentence is receiving the action of the verb, and the object is performing it. It is formed using the auxiliary verb *be* and the past participle.

past participle

The form of a verb that usually ends in -ed or -en. It is used with the auxiliary verbs *have* and *will* to form the perfect tenses, and with the auxiliary verb *be* to form the passive voice.

personal pronoun

A pronoun such as *she* that takes the place of a noun and represents people, places or things.

personification

When human actions or feelings are given to objects or ideas.

pitch

The height of a sound.

plural noun

When more than one person or thing is being described.

possessive determiner

A word that is used before a noun to show ownership.

predicate position

When an adjective follows a linking verb at the end of a sentence.

prefix

A group of letters attached to the start of a word that can change the original word's meaning.

prepositional phrasal verb

A verb followed by a preposition, which together act as a single unit to describe an action.

prepositional phrase

A preposition followed by a noun, pronoun, or noun phrase that together act as an adjective (describing a noun) or an adverb (describing a verb) in a sentence.

present participle

The form of a verb that ends in -ing. It is used with the auxiliary verb *be* to form the continuous tenses.

pronoun

A word, such as *I*, *some*, or *who* that takes the place of a noun.

proper noun

The name given to a particular person, place, or thing, which always starts with a capital letter.

pun

The use of a word or phrase that has two or more meanings for comic effect.

question

A sentence that asks for information.

quotation

Text that reproduces another author's exact words, and is written in quotation marks.

quote

To repeat the words of a person.

relative pronoun

A pronoun such as *which* that links one part of a sentence to another by introducing a relative clause, which describes an earlier noun or pronoun.

rhetorical question

A question that does not require an answer but is used for effect.

Roman numerals

Numbers represented by certain letters of the alphabet, such as *i* (one), *v* (five), and *x* (ten).

root

A whole word or part of a word that can attach to a suffix or prefix.

SEO

Standing for "Search Engine Optimization," this is the process that increases the online visibility of a website, so more Web users will visit it.

simile

A phrase that compares one thing to another using *as* or *like*.

slang

Words and phrases that occur in informal speech and are often only used by a select group of people.

slogan

A short but memorable statement that sums up a message.

Standard English

The form of English that uses formal vocabulary and grammar.

statement

A sentence that conveys a fact or piece of information.

subject

The person or thing that is performing the action of the verb.

subjective

When a piece of text is influenced by the writer's personal opinions.

subordinate clause

A group of words that contains a subject and a verb but depends on a main clause for its meaning.

subordinator

A conjunction used to connect words, phrases, and clauses of unequal importance.

suffix

An ending made up of one or more letters that is added to a word to change its form or its meaning.

superlative

The form of an adjective or adverb that suggests the greatest or least of something.

syllable

A unit of pronunciation that has one vowel sound.

synonyms

Words that have the same or similar meanings.

tautology

Saying the same thing more than once using different words.

tense

The form of a verb that indicates the timing of an action.

third person narrative

When an author writes from a detached or outside point of view, using *he/his* or *she/her*.

tone

The feeling or mood projected by a voice: for example, happy, sad, angry, or excited.

transitive verb

A verb that must be used with an object.

verb

A part of speech that describes the action of a noun or pronoun, or a state of being.

vowel

One of the five letters *a*, *e*, *i*, *o*, or *u*.

Index

Acknowledgments

DORLING KINDERSLEY would like to thank David Ball and Mik Gates for design assistance, Mike Foster and Steve Capsey at Maltings Partnership for the illustrations, Helen Abramson for editorial assistance, Jenny Sich for proofreading, and Carron Brown for the index.

The publisher would like to thank the following for their kind permission to reproduce their photographs:

(Key: a-above; b-below/bottom; c-center; f-far; l-left; r-right; t-top)

29 Alamy Images: Niday Picture Library. **39** Alamy Images: Moviestore Collection Ltd. **45** Alamy Images: Kumar Sriskandan. Alamy Images: Kumar Sriskandan. **45** Alamy Images: Kumar Sriskandan. Alamy Images: Kumar Sriskandan. **54** Fotolia: (c) Stephen Finn. **63** Corbis: Bettmann. **69** Corbis: Susana Vera / Reuters. **75** Alamy Images: Vicki Beaver. **80** Corbis: Michael Ochs Archives. **84** Alamy Images: Stephen Finn. **86** Alamy Images: Jon Challicom. **98** Alamy Images: Papilio. **101** Corbis: Ken Welsh / * / Design Pics. **104** Alamy Images: Jamie Carstairs. **109** Getty Images: NBC. **111** Alamy Images: Eddie Gerald. **112** Alamy Images: flab. **121** Alamy Images: incamarastock. **134** Alamy Images: Phillip Augustavo. **138** Corbis: National Archives / Handout / Reuters. **143** Alamy Images: David Page. **156** Corbis: Franck Guiziou / Hemis. **158** Alamy Images: Martin Shields. **163** Dreamstime.com: Urosr. **166** Corbis: Darren Greenwood / Design Pics. **172** Corbis: Richard T Nowitz. **175** Getty Images. **177** Corbis: Bettmann. **182** Alamy Images: Paul David Drabble. **185** Dreamstime.com: Shariffc. **191** Corbis: JGI / Jamie Grill / Blend Images. **195** Used with kind permission of Dogs Trust, the UK's largest dog welfare charity with 18 rehoming centres nationwide and they never put down a healthy dog. **196** Alamy Images: Alistair Scott. **203** Alamy Images: Mary Evans Picture Library. **208** Corbis: Frank Lukasseck. **211** Alamy Images: Nancy G Photography / Nancy Greifenhagen. **214** Getty Images: Darryl Leniuk (b); Nicholas Pitt (t); Jochen Schlenker (c). **218** Corbis: John Springer Collection. **221** Alamy Images: Kristoffer Tripplaar. **222** The Kobal Collection: Warner Horizon TV. **225** Corbis: Heide Benser. **227** Corbis: GARY HERSHORN / Xoo129 / Reuters. **229** Corbis: Joshua Bickel

All other images © Dorling Kindersley
For further information see: **www.dkimages.com**